DAILY LIFE IN THE VIENNA
OF MOZART AND SCHUBERT

Daily Life in the

VIENNA

of Mozart and Schubert

Marcel Brion

translated from the French by Jean Stewart

NEW YORK

THE MACMILLAN COMPANY

A DIVISION OF THE CROWELL-COLLIER PUBLISHING COMPANY

1962

Printed in Great Britain

CONTENTS

LIST OF ILLUSTRATIONS

CHAPTER ONE

VIENNA, THE FORTUNATE CITY

Vienna and the Romans—A Cosmopolitan City—A Harmonious City—An International City—Political Quietism—Good Living—A Beggars' Wedding—Maria Theresa and Joseph II—Freemasonry and the Church—Enlightened Despotism—Lampoons and Broadsheets—The Pope in Vienna—An Emperor's Shyness—The Wonders of Vienna—Palaces and Castles—Fashion and Elegance—Etiquette and Simplicity

The destiny of a city and the character of its inhabitants are predetermined by its geographical situation, by the pattern of the surrounding landscape, and by the extent to which that city welcomes or resists external influences; while the strength and persistence of these influences depends, in turn, upon the ease with which the city's natural barriers can be penetrated, upon the degree to which its citizens' mentality is accessible to things from outside, and upon the character of its political régime, whether favourable or hostile to cosmopolitanism.

A city is like a living creature; consisting of a body and a soul which act and react positively on one another, it follows the common rule of all living creatures; it has its periods of growth and decline; but all the vicissitudes which it may undergo, for better or worse, are determined by the geographical factor; like any biological organism, it has to take advantage of the 'trumps' allotted it by chance, or rather by the will and intuition of its founders when they first established it. And the various 'ages' through which this city will pass in the course of its natural expansion, while attaining inward maturity and enduring the buffets of external events, only emphasize the more clearly that one constant factor, its enduring character.

Vienna and the Romans

When the Romans – primarily preoccupied with the complex strategic requirements of an expanding empire which needs to provide secure bases for its armies, to provision the legions sent out on distant expeditions into barbarian lands, to maintain a free passage for messengers, for troops in wartime and for traders when peace is restored – when the Romans chose, for their city of Vindobona, a particularly favourable site on the bank of the Danube, in a fertile valley surrounded by mountains of moderate height – scarcely more than hills – and established there a junction of roads ensuring easy connection between West and East, North and South, they settled for hundreds and even thousands of years to come the fate of that town which was to become Vienna.

Vienna owes much to the Romans; if it does not possess the spectacular monuments to be found elsewhere, at Arles or at Trier, its subsoil bears perpetual witness to the ample scale of Roman construction. Vienna is built on the remains of houses, temples and palaces, and like Rome it has its catacombs. Perhaps the generals who founded it foresaw that it was itself to become the capital of an Empire, when from a simple fortress set up to bar the way against the savage hordes of Quades and Marcomans they made a great political and economic centre, an emporium into which flowed the products of a supremely fertile region, predestined thereby to rapid transformation into a settlement of great importance.

The plain in which Vienna, escaping from its Roman cradle, grew and expanded was remarkably fertile. Cereals grew there in great abundance, and the vines that ripened on the sunny hillsides provided a light, clear, lively wine, conducive to carefree and lighthearted gaiety. The wooded heights were thick with game, and although none rose above three thousand feet (the Kahlenberg is 1570 feet high, the Hermannskogel 1764, the Leopoldberg 1407) they were 'mountainlike' enough to afford the inhabitants their favourite pleasure-ground, where they could feel far away from the noise and bustle of the great city.

The Danube, which flows through this plain, has always been a navigable water-way, easy for traffic and widening out towards distant horizons that set stay-at-home fancies roaming. Contact with the Black Sea and the Mediterranean brought into the Viennese plain that atmosphere of exoticism which has always been one of the city's charms, and a powerful influx of cultural elements from widely differing sources; Vienna owes to its river that ceaselessly shifting tide of ideas, forms, customs, picturesque expressions and even fashions which were to make of the Austrian capital the cosmopolitan city *par excellence*.

A Cosmopolitan City

Let us be clear about the meaning of the word 'cosmopolitan'. Elsewhere it implies a sort of caravanserai where foreigners foregather for amusement or business, but take no root in a soil with which they have no biological affinity, chance passers-by, here today and gone tomorrow, unaltered by the city which they themselves have not altered. All the great capitals of ancient or modern times have known such aliens (the Greeks called them *metics*), who may live in a city for several generations, from father to son, and yet remain quite foreign to it, such as the dwellers in the European concessions of Shanghai or Hong Kong for instance.

Owing to the character of the town, its countryside, its inhabitants, there have never been such alien groups in Vienna; the foreigners who settled there have been immediately assimilated. They did not on that account lose their racial or national peculiarities; on the contrary they infused and integrated them into that aggregate of nationalities which has, during the course of centuries, become the population of Vienna, in a blend which is harmonious without being uniform. From being, thus, a turntable susceptible to movements from North and South, East and West, Vienna has become a crucible where the most diverse races meet and mix. They might have remained distinct and isolated, but the liveliness of the Viennese landscape, the mildness and clarity of the air, the charm of the climate and perhaps also the secret magic which is the city's prerogative, have wonderfully achieved this fusion.

Historical events worked in the same direction and combined to blend the most varied elements into a relatively homogeneous whole. Vienna under the Romans was a great

3

centre for military ventures towards the East, and a perpetual fair where traders from all lands foregathered; during the course of the Middle Ages she consolidated this truly imperial destiny of hers. The Hapsburg Empire provided the final form (final, that is to say, until war and the surge of conflicting nationalisms shattered this harmony with the destruction of the two-headed Empire at the end of the first world war), giving official consecration and political unity to this mixture of populations, who had instinctively chosen Vienna as their dwelling and had felt so much at home there that they had fused freely, smoothly and unconstrainedly into an 'Austrian' whole.

A Harmonious City

In the delightful book in which he surveys the European capitals that he has loved, *Europäische Haupstädte*,[1] Wilhelm Hausenstein has justly stressed that characteristic quality which makes Vienna unique among cities, its faculty of acclimatizing all those who come to live on Viennese soil without depriving them of their individuality, by the sheer elementary force of its atmosphere and its landscape.

Even the architectural formation of the town, as he points out, reveals this elementary force, like that involved in the growth of a plant. Vienna has never endured the tyranny of forcible collective organization, and it is only of recent years that town-planning has been deliberately imposed. Until then (that is to say until the middle of the nineteenth century, when the fortifications were pulled down to give place to circular boulevards – the rings, or The Ring itself – according to plans analagous to those of Baron Haussmann in Paris) the town grew haphazard, the layers of the past superimposed on one another, interpenetrating and combining in the most natural and harmonious fashion.

In Vienna the words 'natural' and 'harmonious' spring constantly to mind, for the peculiar harmony of this city is derived precisely from that concord with nature, that organic flexibility with which the collective being has grown and developed. This old city, so full of history and of stories, retains the good-humoured simplicity of old people.

4

It is no museum-city. Antiquity is here bound up with a living present, and it, too, is still alive, thanks to this close contact with today. A street bearing the name of the great emperor-philosopher reminds us that Marcus Aurelius came here and lived here, that he conquered the Marcomans, who had come down from the mountains of Bohemia, in the plain of Marchfeld between the left bank of the Danube and the right bank of the March – that plain where the Hungarians under Bela IV were crushed in 1260 by Ottakar II, King of Bohemia, who himself was defeated and slain there eighteen years later by Rudolf of Hapsburg: the same plain where Napoleon's troops fought the famous battle of Essling on May 21, 1809.

When Hausenstein tells us that Vienna stands on a Roman base he is referring not only to the foundations of St. Stephen's Cathedral or to the catacombs, but more especially to that imperial destiny which was Vienna's from the very beginning of her existence, and which was given concrete form under the Hapsburg dynasty until its collapse in 1918 summed up and symbolized, or prefigured, the destruction of old Europe.

And the outward aspect of Vienna took shape in the same fashion, until the time when town-planning took the place of individual growth with free choice of forms and materials; styles intermingled as races had done, dwelling together like good neighbours. Even after the ferocious destruction of two world wars Vienna today reveals the natural unity of present and past, a whole freely formed and felicitously assembled, composite and yet unified, like a symphony in which the timbres of the various instruments contribute to the essential unity of the whole.

An International City

During the period which we are to examine here, from about 1789 to 1850 – these dates not being strict limits but chosen only to define the 'field of operations' as far as possible – of what was the population of Vienna composed? Certain dates may be stressed as of capital importance in the history of the private life of the Viennese people: the accession to power of Joseph II is our starting point, and the revolution of 1848

5

our terminal point. Until the death of Maria Theresa the empire was still subject to a rigid and somewhat formal autocracy, almost medieval in character and in appearance; with the revolution a cleavage was made, deep and ever widening, between the different categories of the population; the dawn of class war, at the same time, marks the decline of this friendly co-existence between aristocracy, bourgeoisie and proletariat which reached its summit in the period of time of which we shall speak.

There was no question of 'nationalities' amongst the inhabitants of Vienna at the end of the eighteenth and the beginning of the nineteenth century, diverse as were their origins. They all rubbed shoulders good-humouredly with one another, and if jokes were sometimes made in songs, comedies and operettas about Magyar characteristics or Czech accents, this did not affect the basic unity of the population any more than the traditional raillery about the speech of Marseillais or Auvergnats does in France. And yet if ever a State offered a complete sample-sheet of all European races, it was the Hapsburg empire! Germans, Italians, Poles, Hungarians, Bohemians, Slovaks and Slovenes, Serbs and Croats, that is to say all the various shades of Germanic, Latin and Slav races, and a considerable number of Jews who poured in from East and West, North and South, and took solid root thanks to their intelligence, their skill and shrewdness. They were not confined to ghettoes as in so many other towns, and if they foregathered from preference in the Leopoldstadt quarter, situated on an island between the Danube canal and the principal arm of the river, it was because since 1622 Jews had lived there and had their stores and their synagogues there.

Consider the names of the great Viennese nobles: Lobkowitz, Pallavicini, Kinsky, Harrach, Czernin, Esterhazy, Schwarzenberg; these, for a start, suggest the most diverse origins. And next, leaving the aristocracy for commerce, let us study the names of tradesmen on their shop fronts; here are some that Wilhelm Hausenstein noted during a brief tram-ride: Demetriades, Apfelgrün, Trnka, Schwarzbrod, Benvenisti, Srp, Zuckerkandl, Vytlacil, Vertery von Vertesalja ...

6

that is to say, Hungary, Czechoslovakia, Italy, Germany and the East. And the general effect of all this, as he says, constitutes an essentially local, Viennese style.

There is nothing haphazard about the way these various peoples have combined. States have their destiny like towns, and the destiny of the Austrian State was to be cosmopolitan; Vienna has remained so, even after the political reduction of Austria to a tiny republic, very different from the former two-headed monarchy of Maria Theresa and Francis Joseph. If Austria today, following countless disasters, is no longer what it was, Vienna, with its face altered but its soul unchanged, remains the prodigious cosmopolitan crucible of two hundred years ago.

Political Quietism

If we were to analyze the Viennese character we might perhaps end by assigning to the various races living in Vienna the elements of which it is composed, but these have been so perfectly fused, so homogeneously amalgamated, that only the epithet 'Viennese' seems apt. Obviously, the political life of the country played its part in shaping this character; monarchical absolutism as practised by Maria Theresa, a great Empress conscious of her duties and responsibilities, favoured the development among the Viennese (at any rate during the period we are discussing) of that sort of political absenteeism, indifference and passivity, which was moreover justified by the security and wellbeing enjoyed by the subjects of the Empire. The Viennese were not a politically-minded people, in the sense that they did not insist on taking part in the discussion and solution of problems concerning the life of the Empire.

By and large their ideological position was somewhat as follows: God in His gracious providence has given us rulers on whom He has bestowed all the qualities necessary to govern well. We ought therefore to respect them as children do their parents, obey them and accept their decisions as being those most conducive to the good of the country. While the Catholicism almost universally practised by the Viennese led to a sort of quietism that cancelled spiritual anxiety, the monarchy was based on a sort of political quietism. The citizen of Vienna, little inclined to insist on his theoretical and abstract rights and primarily anxious to enjoy life in peace and comfort, seldom if ever showed himself a rebel. He was quite ready to conform, and his social philosophy was limited to 'live well and let live', unconcerned with argument about political systems.

The social question did not arise; the 'idea of 1789' which had such violent repercussions in Germany did not disturb Austria, for the simple reason that no pretext existed there on which a revolutionary movement could be based. The richness of the country allowed everyone to enjoy abundance. The fertility of the soil ensured an ample supply of substantial, tasty and varied foodstuffs; the diversity of the population contributed to the excellence of Viennese cooking, and the various territories of the Empire produced all that was necessary and more than was necessary. Consequently living was very cheap, and the humble artisan earned enough to enjoy a feast when he felt like it. This he often did, and religious festivals, family anniversaries, great court occasions, pilgrimages and excursions into the country provided frequent pretexts.

Good Living

The Viennese have always been greedy; they love good fare, especially those sweets and pastries of theirs which are still world famous. Certain foreign visitors, whether from natural cantankerousness or that tendency common to so many travellers to criticize and condemn whatever they find abroad, have blamed the Viennese for their greedy delight not only in their native concoctions of flour, sugar and particularly cream, of which vast quantities have always been consumed both in cafés and private houses, but also in dishes from every province of the Empire. Austrian gastronomy has thus come to include specialities from many nations – Slav, Magyar, Italian, German and Czech – for the greater delight of the gourmet.

The Berlin bookseller Christopher Nicolai, who visited Vienna in 1781, complained unceasingly of everything that he saw – and heard – there (for, being an amateur musician, he fancied himself as a judge of opera and concert, and even Gluck's *Orfeo* did not find favour with him). This Nicolai expressed himself in the crudest terms about what he called Viennese gluttony, for which (like a loyal subject of Frederick II of Prussia) he blamed Catholicism and the Austrian monarchy. The former seemed to him a religion 'all in show, lacking high culture and preoccupied with sordid material matters' (his own words) 'with results that are worse than the paganism of old.' Priests and rulers encourage the popular tendency to care about nothing but good living and good eating. The traveller notes, with sour rancour, the number of plump cheerful faces he sees in the streets and comments with secret satisfaction on the number of young people burdened with precocious stoutness, whose high colour foretells that a large proportion of them are doomed to die of apoplexy.

It was easy in those days to indulge one's greed, since for an extremely modest sum, 31 kreutzers for instance, one could enjoy, in 1786, a meal consisting of two meat dishes, soup, vegetables, unlimited bread and a quarter-litre of wine. Such a meal was practically within everybody's means; not only did nobody suffer from hunger in that fortunate city, but all, except for a few inveterate idlers or impenitent wastrels, could, at little cost, satisfy their appetite amply and pleasantly.

If extreme poverty was practically non-existent in Vienna, why were beggars so numerous there? Perhaps because, as Nicolai acidly remarks, 'the Viennese are not fond of hard work'. Whether out of need or out of laziness, there were beggars in Vienna as elsewhere, but their vocation proved profitable, for people were generous, and even industrious citizens accepted the fact that some individuals might prefer begging to working. This was clearly seen when at the beginning of the nineteenth century the Emperor set up a commission to assist the needy. War and a disastrous succession of bad harvests had brought about a sharp rise in the cost of living: the commission therefore decided to set up popular soup kitchens of the sort advocated by the American Rumford, at that time considered to be the leading specialist in such palliatives for poverty.

Rumford had been summoned to Austria and invited to construct workhouses for the aged and the indigent. He had also invented a set of rules to control mendicancy, but his principal effort lay in the distribution of food and the profitable use to be made of foodstuffs hitherto neglected; roots, tree-barks, weeds and even bones were judged by the ingenious American to be rich in nutritive value. He was so efficient that in 1792 he was granted the title of Count.

Soup kitchens had given excellent results in less greedy cities, in Switzerland and in Germany for instance, but they could never be really popular in Vienna. When one of these charitable institutions was set up in the Wipplingerstrasse, providing the needy with a plateful of food for one kreutzer – practically gratis – people flocked to it at first out of curiosity, or perhaps attracted by the bargain. Unfortunately Rumford soup, as it was called, had no attraction for people used to more succulent fare. You could barely fish a minute scrap of smoked meat out of a thin skilly of cabbage, beans and turnip. A shrewd and witty commentator of those days, Karoline Pichler, relates in her journal that while a few paupers got their Rumford soup from the popular restaurant in the Wipplingerstrasse, the restaurants and cafés in the suburbs and outlying districts of Vienna – Hietzing, Grinzing, Lerchenfeld – and those that stood in that part of the Prater called Wurstelprater, were crammed as usual with working-class people in their Sunday clothes, eating their fill without bothering about the cost of living.

A Beggars' Wedding

Bauerle, too, in his Journal, tells an amusing story dating back to his childhood, which clearly illustrates the social situation of the different layers of the population of Vienna. He had gone one day with his father to the restaurant at Penzing, and both of them were struck by the lively bustle that filled the place, the bright lights in the dining-room and the noise of a band playing there. Bauerle's father enquired of the landlord what important personages were feasting in his establishment, and was told that a beggars' wedding was being celebrated. The bride's parents were well known in the town, the father having his recognized post at the Stone Bridge; he was known as Duckerl; his wife begged for alms at the Burgtor, and their trade was so profitable that they lived easily on it and could even set aside several hundred florins every year; thus they had been able to provide their daughter with a dowry of several thousand florins, and to celebrate the wedding in fine style.

They had come to the Penzing beerhouse, the host added, because they were too well known in the city to be able to enjoy themselves there freely without surprising and possibly shocking people, although the Viennese were not easily shocked by anything. In the suburbs, on the other hand, and the inns in the Vienna woods, where they drove in a barouche, nobody knew them or recognized them and they could carouse at will like gentlefolk, with musicians and singers.

Bauerle's father then enquired into the social status of the young couple; did they too belong to the honourable brotherhood of beggars? Not exactly, said the host; the bride rummages in the rubbish thrown on to the streets, and quite often discovers some precious object discarded by mistake, a gold coin, a silver spoon, even a jewel sometimes, and easily makes a living by this activity. As for the bridegroom, he trades in bones which he picks out from kitchen rubbish and then sells to button manufacturers. One shouldn't despise anybody's trade. . . .

This is no exaggeration. The comic writer Schildbach wrote a play about well-to-do beggars; it was called *The Millionaire*, and it ran for a hundred nights in the theatre run by Schikaneder, Mozart's collaborator in *The Magic Flute* and one of the most original and interesting theatrical figures of Vienna at that time. The chief attraction of the play was the wedding of the beggars in a suburban restaurant, realistically represented, just as Bauerle had seen it with his father.

Reichsl,[2] moreover, in whose book this story can be read, has set out a curious classification of Viennese beggars and their hierarchy in the field of mendicancy; obviously Duckerl and his wife belonged to the higher category of those who had a regular beat, recognized and respected by everyone; the lowest category of poor folk appealed to the pity of passers-by in the streets by means of all kinds of real or artificial wounds, ostentatiously displayed. Some of them had discovered how to squat on the ground with their legs buried in a cleverly concealed hole; beside these apparently legless cripples, uttering their pitiful lamentations, there was a little boy who joined his voice to theirs and ran up to the doors of coaches and carriages, worrying the travellers until he had got what he wanted from them.

Actually Vienna was an industrial city, even if its inhabitants allowed idleness its place in their lives as well as work, and quite naturally, as is only human, preferred idleness. The presence of the court and the nobility chiefly encouraged luxury trades such as tailoring, embroidery, braidmaking, jewellery and leather work. The sumptuary laws laid down by Joseph II were not as wise as they seemed at first, for they hit a number of flourishing small-scale family industries on which depended the livelihood of an important section of the working population. Vienna has always been a leading centre for rare, exquisite objects of precious material and fine workmanship, and the luxury of the nobility, far from exciting envy and jealousy, appeared a legitimate source of profits for all.

Maria Theresa and Joseph II

During the forty years of her reign, Maria Theresa had maintained an autocratic régime in the Spanish tradition, rigorous and exacting. No doubt this was necessary, for the Empire was by no means solidly united. The upsurge of various nationalisms was a constant danger, the Turks still threatened, and the war with Prussia had exhausted the country's finances.

The Empress was fully conscious of the duties and responsibilities of her 'kingly' vocation; she never failed in them.

She had moreover a virtue often found in truly great men; she knew how to choose her associates. Her confidential adviser was Chancellor Kaunitz, who had his faults, no doubt, but was intelligent enough to understand the Empress's personal policy and devoted himself to it wholeheartedly. In spite of the series of wars in which Austria was frequently defeated, Vienna remained a prosperous city, and its population rose during the reign of Maria Theresa from 88,000 to 175,000 inhabitants; this factor, indeed, complicated the housing problem, particularly acute in a town surrounded by fortifications out of which it was continually forced to overflow into suburbs to house the surplus population.

This state of overcrowding in a city of moderate dimensions is moreover, as we shall see later, one of the causes of that love of nature, that longing for the green countryside which has been one of the most constant features of the Viennese character ever since the eighteenth century. The daughter of Charles VI, in spite of all opposition, succeeded in turning to good account the dangerous circumstances which so often threatened her, for she acted with great courage and intelligence, and her sound common sense counterbalanced natural audacity and dauntless determination, qualities highly necessary to a woman inheriting the Imperial throne by right of the Pragmatic Sanction, Charles VI having left no male heir.

Despite her absolutism and her severity, despite that unremitting grandeur with which she insisted on surrounding her throne, particularly in the presence of foreign rulers and their ambassadors – for her private life at the Hofburg and at Schönbrunn was marked by an extreme simplicity (which Marie-Antoinette was so often to regret amidst the tortuous mazes of life at Versailles, full of pitfalls laid by her enemies) – despite her majestic and authoritarian manner, or perhaps even on account of all these, Maria Theresa was immensely popular among the Viennese, far more so than her son Joseph II, for all his somewhat Utopian projects.

We cannot attempt here to sketch the political history of the house of Hapsburg, yet we must note with interest its repercussions on the private lives of the citizens of Vienna. The reforms of Joseph II, whether soundly based or fantastic, inevitably brought about great changes in the habits and behaviour of his people; we must therefore take them into consideration and see how far they altered the appearance and the way of life of Vienna.

Joseph II, readily accessible to new ideas and conscious that an absolute monarchy stubbornly defending its illusory and outdated privileges was an anachronism in the age of Enlightenment, was anxious to be a 'modern' ruler. Greatly struck by the achievements of Peter the Great in Russia, he aspired to imitation of the latter's 'realism', and foreseeing the inevitability of revolution, he felt that it would only be effective and salutary if imposed from above. This idea was widely current in Freemasonry in those days, and accounts for the presence in the Lodges of so many eminent men devoted to the well-being of society, so many artists – Goethe and Mozart for instance – so many great noblemen and even sovereigns who expected the movement to bring about a renovation of society, an authentic revolution but an orderly one, with no violent upheaval, directed by the élite of intellectual Europe.

The ideal of the Enlightened Despot was to surround himself with distinguished men chosen, according to intelligently democratic principles, from every walk of life, all sincerely devoted to the new theories and, above all, disinterested. The recruitment of the 'best men' of every rank, with the aid of 'tests' like those symbolically described in *The Magic Flute*, was expected to lead to a progressive revolution under the control of that frankly cosmopolitan European élite that was Freemasonry.

Maria Theresa was too deeply rooted in old autocratic Europe to share in these ideas, and she had banned Masonic Lodges throughout her empire; which did not, of course, prevent them from secretly proliferating and attracting ever more numerous adherents. The lodges of Vienna included such eminent men as Ignaz von Born, who had so powerful an influence on Mozart's thought. This learned geologist was a keen proselytizer, but he was obliged to exercise the greatest discretion, for his audacious opinions on nature and the properties of metals had won him the reputation of a heretic; he had written a pamphlet against the monastic orders entitled *Monachologia*, and he was known to be in close contact with the Illuminati of Adam Weishaupt, towards whom the Church was openly hostile.

Freemasonry and the Church

Although the bulk of the Viennese population at the end of the eighteenth century was sincerely and fervently attached to Catholicism, to the authority of the Church and to its religious practices, Freemasonry had none the less made immense progress despite the interdictions promulgated by the Empress. As regards the piety of the Viennese, certain foreign visitors dismissed it as vulgar superstition; such was the opinion, as we have seen, of the Prussian bookseller Nicolai, but in view of his resolute hostility to all things Viennese his violence may appear somewhat suspect. Others have maintained that the great number of religious festivals celebrated in Vienna was merely a pretext for multiplying the opportunities for idleness and dissipation; such was the view of Count Fekete of Galanta, who denounced the excessive love of pleasure he met with in all classes of society.

Given the lively and cheerful character of the Viennese, one would hardly expect their pilgrimages to urban or rural shrines to be marked by ascetic solemnity. A sombre and morose religion would scarcely have been popular, and the devotion they displayed during these pilgrimages for the Virgin and the saints resembles the ingenuous, somewhat puerile, but deeply sincere and touching trust of a child for its parents. This familiar, almost homely aspect of Austrian religious feeling lies at the base of the spiritual life of the people; it must not be forgotten that Catholicism according to the Council of Trent, of whose artistic manifestations Emile Mâle has made so learned a study, encouraged this gracious piety, this intimate relation between man and the deity. It is hard to imagine a Puritan or a Jansenist Austria; nothing could be more unnatural.

Adherence to freemasonry was by no means incompatible with an attachment to the practices and faith of the Catholic church; witness the example of Mozart, who never failed to go on pilgrimages and who showed an intense and sincere piety in all his actions; this did not prevent him from belonging to two Masonic lodges. As Alfred Einstein the musicologist has put it, for Mozart Catholicism and Freemasonry were two concentric spheres. In the eighteenth century freemasonry does not appear as an anti-Christian movement. If the Church looked askance at the spread of illuminist sects, whose growing power might some day interfere with its own authority, yet monarchs, in general, showed themselves more tolerant. The most clearsighted and prudent among them, during the decades preceding the French Revolution, had realized that the only way to avoid the disasters of general revolution, which some of them probably judged inevitable, was not to counter the revolutionary movement with an anachronistic autocracy but on the contrary to put themselves at its head in order to direct and control it and lead it towards useful and moderate achievements.

It was for this reason that Francis of Lorraine, husband of Maria Theresa, had been admitted to the Order at The Hague in 1731, through Lord Chesterfield, the English ambassador; and he refused to implement, throughout his Empire, the Bull against freemasonry issued by Pope Clement XII in 1738. Only after his death did the Empress, more docile to the injunctions of the Church and dreading on principle anything that seemed to threaten the absolute power of her throne, hasten to obey the supreme pontiff and to hunt down freemasons, who were forced to resort to the greatest secrecy in order to carry on their activities. But she could not prevent her own son, the future Joseph II, from becoming an initiate in the proscribed society, towards which, once on the throne, he was to show the generous goodwill befitting a member of the Brotherhood.

Enlightened Despotism

The social reforms which Vienna enjoyed under the reign of this enlightened despot belonged to the programme of Masonic idealism at that time. These reforms were quite contrary to the traditions of his predecessors, firm upholders of the strictest monarchical and aristocratic principles, and they went far beyond those undertaken at that time in other European states. Whether they were always opportune or practicable was a question which Joseph II, in his zeal for progress, did not ask himself. Undaunted by the hostility of those whom his reforms might injure or inconvenience, he pursued his task with that singlemindedness and tenacity which, after his death, called forth these words from the Prince de Ligne, in a letter announcing the news to Catherine II: 'He is no more, madame; he is dead, that prince who brought honour to the name of man, that man who brought honour to the name of prince.'

Everybody, unfortunately, did not share this opinion, and the brief funeral oration pronounced by Chancellor Kaunitz expressed the mistrust, apprehension and irritation felt by the nobility of the Empire towards the ruler who had struck so harsh a blow at its privileges. As for what Joseph himself thought of his achievement, his last words reveal it in a touching fashion: 'I have no regrets at leaving my throne; the only thing that grieves me is to have made so few men happy, in spite of all my efforts.' No doubt he foresaw, too, to his sorrow, that after his death his work would not be carried on. The future was to prove him right; Leopold II and Francis I, his successors, were to set about actively undoing what he had done. But during his lifetime he worked for the happiness and well-being of the Viennese far more than any other Emperor before or since.

If his daring and impatient reforms too often irritated the easy-going Austrians, the proud and touchy Hungarians who were openly hostile to him, and the susceptible Bohemians always on the verge of rebellion, it was because his longing to do good led him to go too fast and too far. He was a sad and lonely man, surrounded by courtiers who mocked at his simplicity of dress and manners and accused him of currying favour with the mob. Actually his political ideas were lofty, generous and progressive, but to impose them he had to fight hard and without respite against his mother, Chancellor Kaunitz, the nobility, the clergy; the Austrian people in whose interest he acted were too much lacking in political maturity and too indifferent to affairs of State to appreciate them as they deserved.

The Viennese were grateful to him chiefly for the immediate advantages he procured them; in 1775, for instance, he opened the imperial garden, the Augarten, to the public, and when he turned his former hunting ground, the Prater, into a public park, he did not merely hand it over to the Viennese, but had it laid out in pleasing and harmonious fashion; he even planted it with full-grown trees, so that people walking there could immediately enjoy their shade and the beauty of their foliage. He himself delighted to walk there; but lest he should embarrass plebeian strollers by his presence, he gave orders that nobody should bow to him; his greatest wish was to pass unnoticed.

In fact, there was nothing imperial about his dress and behaviour when he mingled with the townsfolk of his city; one could easily have jostled unawares such a shabby individual. Again, during official ceremonies he would have no one kneel to him nor kiss his hand, according to the ancient ritual of princely courts. But the simplicity of his dress did not, as he imagined, win the approval of the people, who have always enjoyed admiring royal pomp and splendour. They accused him of meanness and avarice, instead of recognizing how admirable and how touching was his desire to react against the excesses of luxury.

A Hungarian writer, Francis Kasinszy, who saw him one day at table, describes him thus: 'I beheld to my amazement that the Emperor's green coat, with its red collar and yellow buttons, was patched at the elbows. His waistcoat and breeches were lemon yellow, and he wore white linen gaiters . . . He detested waste and luxury; he wanted to give an example of simplicity by wearing a patched coat.' He had had a most unbecoming cap made for himself covered with oil-cloth, and he wore this singularly unregal headgear for preference, even at the theatre.

He was genuinely democratic; there was nothing of the demagogue about him. His social beliefs are clearly summed up in the inscription he had placed over the entrance to the park of his favourite castle, La Favorita, which he presented to the people of Vienna on April 30 1775, and which has become the Augarten: 'These pleasure grounds are offered to all men, by one who respects them.' For he respected men, which is more important and sometimes more difficult than loving them. Every one of his actions reflects that 'respect', and if he still upheld the custom of punishing prostitutes caught soliciting by making them clean the streets, it was because Vienna was a serious town, though not a prudish one, and discipline must be maintained. On the other hand he abolished torture, which was still in use during his mother's reign, so much so that during Maria Theresa's lifetime an official illustrated handbook was published about the use and degree of different methods of torture.

Lampoons and Broadsheets

Liberal measures of a general character, such as the abolition of the death penalty and of serfdom, were approved by all the Viennese, but when the Emperor tried to make rules for the internal administration of the guilds, the artisans felt that he was meddling with something that did not concern him. Conservative-minded people were disturbed by the way in which authors of lampoons and broadsheets took advantage of the freedom of thought and of the press. Vienna was swamped with pamphlets on every kind of subject, and particularly on those that might be expected to excite public curiosity and amuse public malice.

Goethe was no doubt being duly cautious when he wrote in the Tierfurter Journal: 'The latest news received from the capital of our homeland gives us unanimous assurance that the dawn of the brightest day is beginning to break there, and although we are far from those regions we are disposed to believe it. May that bright day dawn for them, for the present time reminds us of those early hours when the mist rising from valleys and rivers heralds the rising sun.' The following list of titles, quoted by Kralik,[3] illustrates the point: 'For ten kreutzers you could get information on any topic, high or low: *Ladies' Maids; Bourgeois Young Ladies; Ladies of the Court; Young Girls of Vienna; The Nobility of Vienna; Doctors, Surgeons and Pharmacists; Viennese Tradesmen; Gentlemen of Fashion; Tailors; Bakers; Wigmakers; Hairdressers; A Confidential Word in the ear of Householders; To Herr Sonnenfels, Master of the Lodge of Strollers along the Graben; Meals at Schönbrunn; On the abuse of the words 'von' and 'Your Grace'; Congratulations; A Word about the Ladies of Vienna who dress their hair high; Is Antichrist Blue or Green? Miracle-Working Relics and Images . . .'*

In 1782 the following pamphlets appeared, among many others: *What is the Emperor?* by Fessler; *Is the Emperor Right? Monks and the Devil; A Trip into Hell; What is the Church? Letters from Nuns; The Degradation of the Lay Clergy; What are indulgences? Defence of the Pope, by a Protestant; The End of Celibacy; Can the Emperor introduce Tolerance?* In 1783 there appeared: *What is a Canon? Remarks about the Devil of Seefeld, in the Tyrol; The Travels of the Popes; A Priest exhorts the Emperor; Reflections upon Tolerance; The Capuchin Monk who Dabbles in Politics, or the Forthcoming Advent of Antichrist; Silver Angels talking at Mariazell; On Purgatory, etc.; Mamma wants to send me to a Convent.* In 1784 there appeared: *Mysteries of the Clergy; On Oral Confession; On the Worship of the Virgin Mary and the Saints; On Miracles and Relics.* And in 1785; *Should one read aloud? An Impious little Handbook for Good Princes; In Which it is proved that Joseph II is a Protestant; The Face of a Roman Nun and the Raptures of a German Hermit; Does the Sixth Commandment still concern Christians?* . . .

The list of pamphlets published during these years and sold publicly would fill a volume in itself; it is instructive, in that it shows that as soon as the Viennese were granted the right of free criticism they made full use of it to attack the Government and the Church.

The Pope in Vienna

Joseph himself set the example of hostility to the church by his openly anti-Roman policy, which appalled a great many of his subjects. Although he laid his ban on heretics, Illuminists and those whom he called 'deists', his orthodoxy was in doubt. Note that the chastisement allotted to deists – twenty-four blows on the backside – was intended as a punishment not for wrong beliefs but for ignorance, and lest this measure should provoke a dangerous witch-hunt the Emperor decreed that 'the deist must be treated thus not because he is a deist but because he claims to be one without knowing what deism is; and similarly, ten blows shall be inflicted on anyone who denounces a deist in his parish.'[4] The adversaries of the Enlightened Despot pointed out that the liberalism he affected with regard to the circulation of anticlerical libels did not hold good with regard to religious publications, since he forbade the revision of the Lives of the Saints in the *Acta Sanctorum* of the Bollandists, on the pretext that they were merely 'fictions about canonized individuals' in an 'obscure and idiotic work'. This anticlericalism in the Hofburg itself was most disturbing to the Pope, who, dreading lest Austria, that eminently Catholic country, should lapse into impiety following her ruler's footsteps, came in person to Vienna, to the delight and edification of the Viennese, who naturally followed with the keenest interest the doings of the illustrious visitor.

Vienna became for a short while another Rome, a suddenly-discovered holy place. Joseph did not keep the Pope in seclusion; as he wrote to his sister Maria Christina, 'During these last days there has been an extraordinary crowd in front of his windows. It was a wonderful sight, such as I have never seen before and never expect to see again. It is impossible to say how many people there were.' Bourgoing, a Protestant, wrote: 'The presence of the Pope has had an amazing effect. I am not a Catholic and I am not easily moved, but I must confess that the sight touched me deeply.' More than fifty thousand people, he said, were assembled in the public square; they had but a single thought; their faces betrayed solemn rapture and enthusiasm; they were packed so tight they could not breathe, but this mattered little to them. Then the Pope appeared; 'bowing forward as if in prayer, he raised his hands to heaven like one deeply convinced of presenting to God the entreaties of a whole nation and expressing, with his looks, an ardent longing for their fulfilment.' And when the crowd fell on its knees to receive his blessing, the author adds: 'This scene made an unforgettable impression on me.'[5]

The Holy Father had celebrated the services of Holy Week amidst an unprecedented crowd of deeply reverent worshippers; he had washed the feet of twelve beggars representing the apostles, and it was said in jest (for the irony of the Viennese was unfailing even under such circumstances) that he was going to do the same to the twelve apostles of Austrian politics, in which Kaunitz represented St Peter, Sonnefels, Doubting Thomas and Eybl, Judas Iscariot. I fancy that the people of Vienna, in their heart of hearts, during that time when the Pope was dwelling amongst them, secretly took his side against their Emperor.

An Emperor's Shyness

Joseph II displayed that excessive daring which is a frequent characteristic of shy people. He was shy with women, and probably also with his subjects, in spite of his constant wish to act for the public good in every sphere. During his stay in Paris he made a point of visiting the Abbé de l'Epée in the Institute where deaf-mutes were received and cared for, so great was his desire to organize something on the same lines in Vienna. He took care that the children of peasants showing aptitude for study should enjoy the same schooling as the sons of nobles and bourgeois. And since he could not bring about equality of wealth, as he had once dreamed of doing, he strove in every way to reduce class distinctions, to bring the various social classes closer together. And yet he was not beloved as much as he should have been by the very people in whose interest he worked, because his shyness made him ill at ease, and made others ill at ease too.

He had himself drawn up the epitaph he wanted, a few days before his death: 'Here lies a prince who had the best of intentions and whose plans were all doomed to failure.' It was quite true. Herder was right when he wrote in his *Letters on Mankind*:

'Without having known the Emperor, without ever receiving any benefit from him, I could have wept when I learnt the details of the end of his life. Nine years ago, when he came to the throne, he was worshipped like a tutelary deity, and the greatest things were expected of him, the most useful, wellnigh impossible things; and now they have laid him in the grave like a victim of time. Was there ever an Emperor, was there ever a mortal I should say, who had nobler projects, who took greater trouble, who made more strenuous efforts, who worked with greater zeal? And what a fate was that monarch's, who, confronted with death, was forced not only to renounce the aim he had set himself during his noblest years, but also to disavow, formally, the whole of his life's work, to annul it solemnly, and then to die!'

The Wonders of Vienna

Thanks to the reforms of Joseph II or possibly in spite of them, Vienna had attained, during the last decades of the eighteenth century, a splendour and brilliance she had never had before; and yet ever since the Middle Ages her beauty had often been celebrated by poets and travellers such as Walther von der Vogelweide, the Minnesinger, and, possibly even earlier, in the folk song which said: 'In Austria there stands a town brightly bedecked with pretty blue flowerets; its walls are of marble; there is a green forest round it and a green forest in the midst of it, where a nightingale sings of our love.' As early as 1485 the Italian Antonio Bonfini, official historian to Matthias Corvino, King of Hungary, had rhapsodized on the rare merits of this uniquely lovely city; he was especially impressed, familar though he was with all the glories of his native land, by the majesty and grace of the dwellings. Until the middle of the nineteenth century there were still to be found in Vienna some of those medieval and Renaissance houses which in their brilliant newness had so delighted the visitor that he described them thus:

'The city proper seems like a royal palace amidst the surrounding suburbs; and yet several of these vie with it for beauty and grandeur. Entering the city you might fancy yourself walking amongst the buildings of a huge royal castle, so perfect is the disposition of all the houses. Everything delights the eye of the observer; each house seems to stand more proudly than its neighbours. You have to pause constantly to enjoy so many beauties. The houses of the great, in particular, look like palaces. Almost every house has, in addition to its front portion, a rear building with vast peristyles covered or uncovered, offering protection from the cold winds that blow from the surrounding heights. The dining-rooms are often splendidly panelled with pine and heated with great stoves. The windows are all glazed; some of them are beautifully painted and protected with an iron trellis. The houses have bathrooms and kitchen offices, and bedrooms which can be

C

23

rented. All of them are provided with cellars to store wine and provisions. The luxury of the windows and mirrors is almost equal to the splendour of olden days. So many birds sing in their cages that you fancy you are walking through a sylvan glade.'

Vienna was densely populated, perhaps too densely for its area; in appearance, it was a maze of little lanes of close-packed houses, streets that twisted to avoid the bitter winds – a feature neglected by modern town-planners, who build cities on the grid system. The fortified walls protected Vienna with a rigid circle, and every time the Turks and Hungarians had threatened its safety the value of these solid ramparts was fully appreciated by the inhabitants. Until the terrible devastation of the Austrian capital during the last war, which caused such irreparable ravages, it was still possible, in spite of the 'rings' laid out in the middle of the nineteenth century by an imitator of Baron Haussmann, to find parts of the town that had remained unchanged since the patina of centuries had first begun to settle on them, and countless historic memories clung to dwellings made memorable by fame or by some exceptional, picturesque circumstance: the 'Elephant's House', for instance, on which the sculptor had carved a lifelike portrait of the amazing pachyderm offered by the Grand Turk to the Emperor Maximilian in 1552, and not far from there the famous *Stock im Eisen*, a warning to the imprudent of the dangers incurred when dealing with the devil.*

---

* It was still to be seen, at any rate, in the eighteenth century; it was an old tree trunk with two branches, 'a vestige of the virgin forest which once surrounded Vienna' (Kralik, *op. cit.* p. 202) encircled with an iron ring to which hung a lock. The legend ran that this lock had been forged and set there, in olden times, by a master locksmith so proud of his skill and cunning that he had defied all the other locksmiths of Vienna and of foreign lands to open this unpickable masterpiece. The master, unfortunately, had a proud and ambitious apprentice who dared to take up his challenge. This youth forged every conceivable sort of key, but not one of them opened the lock. Enraged and mortified, in a fit of anger he offered his soul to the Devil, who in exchange promised to help him make the key; on one condition, however, said the cunning Devil – namely that if while opening the lock he let fall the key the Evil One would have complete power over him. As you can imagine, this was exactly what befell him; as he was pushing the key into the lock he let it fall, and the

The first important transformation was the expansion of the baroque city, on that great wave of patriotic enthusiasm and civic euphoria which followed the departure of the Turks in 1683. The town had suffered severely from their assaults, and had been cruelly bombarded between July and September; the suburbs had been razed to the ground, the bastions had in part crumbled under the enemy's fire, and tunnels had been pushed forward right under the town itself. Peace could provide the opportunity for a renewal and embellishment of the imperial capital, and the princes vied with the Emperor in luxury and magnificence as the new city arose within the heart of the old.

Fortunately there were at that time great architects who understood the spirit of their age and built according to the most up-to-date ideas. Fischer von Erlach, Hildebrandt, Gabrielli de Rovereto, Montinelli willingly complied with the fever for building that possessed the aristocracy. All the nobles, even those who lived in distant provinces of the Empire, wanted to have their palaces in Vienna itself, betokening their power, their wealth and their prestige.

Palaces and Castles

To Fischer von Erlach we owe, besides the Karlskirche, the palaces of Schönbrunn, whose admirable entrance hall is a perfect example of the baroque-rococo style prevalent at the beginning of the eighteenth century; the Chancellery of Bohemian affairs, dating from 1714; the Brenner palace,

---

Devil carried him away immediately. Since that time nobody had dared touch the lock of the *Stock im Eisen*, which stood there as a salutary warning to those who count on the help of the Evil One to succeed in their undertakings. This anecdote is found in the work of the poet Jakob Sturm, who tells us moreover that the name of Vienna is derived from that of Fabianus, a Roman general said to have lived in those parts and built a castle which, later, the Huns razed to the ground. 'Vienna is the queen of cities, the seat of Emperors; the city of Tiberius pales before its brilliance.' These rhapsodic utterances are frequently heard from those who adore Vienna, and we may also quote that of the German minstrel Wolfgang Schmelzl, who in 1548 composed a song in praise of the *Famous City of Vienna in Austria*, exclaiming: 'He who has not seen Vienna has wasted his whole life.'

25

whose baroque façade was built in 1730; the Schwarzenberg palace on the Rennweg, whose gardens were said to equal those of the Belvedere. The latter castle, Hildebrandt's masterpiece, with its grace and classic elegance, was begun in 1713, and the garden in the French style lying between the two buildings is rightly considered a model of the Viennese baroque style, free from any pomp or heaviness, picturesque and piquant and full of surprising effects.

The baroque and rococo palaces of Vienna reflect that fondness for display which was common to all social classes, and in accordance with which rich men and nobles laid out their homes like stage sets for everybody to enjoy and admire, from the outside at any rate. There was no spirit of ostentation in that predilection for magnificence; there was a lingering memory of old-time grandeur, but also a kindly wish to please the people by a display of splendid buildings. And so, not only were the vestibules and halls and staircases laid out in a spacious and harmonious manner befitting the pomp of society life, but the façades, too, were conceived by their architects as things of beauty, freely offered to the sight of all and capable of being, to all, a joy for ever. The democratic side of baroque and rococo decorative art was a very real thing and corresponded perfectly to the native kindliness of the Viennese character, that simplicity of manner which is not incompatible with, nor hostile to luxury, but on the contrary can readily combine with it.

The Baroque, was, indeed, the golden age of Austria. Castles like Schönbrunn, Ebersdorf, monasteries such as Melk, Göttweih, St Florian, Klosterneuburg displayed ever fresh beauties in that grandiose style, dramatic or picturesque, or more often both at once. The Emperor Charles VI had sought to make of Klosterneuburg, which is not far from Vienna, something like an Escurial. He had embarked on the construction of a monumental and splendid edifice in 1730 and, shortly before his death, he retired there to meditate on the latter end of man and prepare himself to leave this world. Some may see profanity in this adaptation to religious buildings of a somewhat theatrical magnificence, such as the baroque style often displays, but the style corresponds exactly to Austrian religious feeling, which delights to see liturgical ceremonies take place amidst a splendour equal to that of the Hofburg receptions.

The old Hofburg, built in 1221 by Duke Leopold VI of Babenberg, had itself undergone a dazzling metamorphosis under the reign of Charles VI, in the purest eighteenth-century spirit, thanks to Fischer von Erlach, whose cosmopolitan genius aimed at associating German majesty, Italian grace and French classicism in a happily eclectic fashion. The Academy of Sciences, built between 1753 and 1755 on plans laid out by a Frenchman, Jadot de Ville-Issy, has an admirable banqueting-hall in which this composite character of Viennese baroque is especially evident. For the Winter Palace of Prince Eugene of Savoy, Fischer von Erlach and Hildebrandt had worked together, uniting their architectural conceptions, tastes and talents; and they had succeeded in making of this marvellous building, situated in the Himmelfortgasse, a perfect synthesis of all the beauties of that Baroque style which had become a national art – particularly in the broad and graceful staircase with its fantastic twists and turns.

To enumerate the Viennese palaces built during the eighteenth century would be to catalogue all the great families of the Austrian, Hungarian and Bohemian aristocracy: the Zichy family, who claimed Turkish origin; the Lobkowitzes, who owned an almost royal castle near Prague; the Schwarzenbergs, who had come from Franconia many centuries before; the Colloredos, who originally came from Italy; the Kollowraths, of ancient Czech lineage; the family of Windischgrätz, Bohemian too, as was also the house of Harrach, ennobled in the eleventh century (whereas the ancestors of the Lobkowitzes were illustrious in the ninth); the Kinsky family, for whom Hildebrandt built a palace with a superb façade on the Herrengasse; the houses of Czernin, Palfy, Lichnowsky; as for the Russian ambassador, Razumovsky, who was to play so important a part in the life of Beethoven, he had built himself a princely home where might be heard the greatest musicians of that century so rich in masterpieces and in virtuosi.

Fashion and Elegance

The fashions vied in richness, beauty and taste with the new architecture. Karoline Pichler, whose novels and memoirs so well reflect the Vienna of her day, has described the ladies of the nobility going off to church wrapped in great black capes trimmed with Polish fur, edged with red satin and blue fox and spangled with tufts of gold. The men wore black velvet coats lined with rose-coloured satin, over embroidered waistcoats of cloth-of-gold; they had periwigs, white silk stockings and red-heeled shoes with diamond buckles.

These aristocrats, living in their theatrical palaces, drove about in those luxurious carriages for which Vienna became famous. They were preceded by bodyguards in Hungarian costume and couriers carrying messages in the gold pommel of the long stick with which they cleared their way through the crowd, and wearing Turkish dress, according to the fashionable Orientalism of the day, with scarves and aigrettes and boots with curled-up tips. All this gave the town a festive air, for just as the palaces often rose amidst a jumble of middle-class houses and even quite poor homes, so did these nobles, so proud of their long lineage and their power, walk freely amidst the common people wherever they foregathered in everyday life.

Etiquette and Simplicity

This did not prevent them, however, from being scrupulously observant of precedence at Court and in their own salons, with an almost superstitious regard for etiquette which was probably part of the Spanish tradition. On the other hand, when they walked about the streets and gardens, the most distinguished personalities liked to pass unnoticed and mingle with the crowd as though they belonged to it. The Comte de Sainte-Aulaire, who was Ambassador in Vienna in the first third of the nineteenth century, has described this admirably in his *Memoirs*, edited by Marcel Thiébaut.[6] The French diplomat had accompanied the Archduke Charles and the Duke of Orleans on an excursion into the country.

'At the close of day,' (he writes) 'we came back into town; in the middle of the public gardens we found a choice repast served under a tent which was open on all sides. People were thronging all round it. There was not a single soldier or police officer to guard the entrances; cases full of silver, plates laden with fruit were freely at the disposal of these worthy citizens. When we arrived the crowd parted silently to make way for us. Instead of the noisy shouts of Paris we were met by friendly looks and respectful familiarity. Strauss and his orchestra were playing national airs. The air was mild, the sky serene; nothing was lacking to the delights of the evening, which we enjoyed until ten o'clock.'

The Imperial family itself dropped rigorous protocol when they took part in popular festivities, and one is struck by the delicacy shown by either side, the discreet mutual avoidance of embarrassment. The people's attachment for their rulers was shown not by explosions of delight on their appearance but rather by a sort of deferential friendliness, as if it were perfectly natural and a matter of course that the sovereign should move amidst his subjects in familiar fashion. For the Comte de Sainte-Aulaire, accustomed to French crowds, it was 'a curious sight' to see the Emperor taking his ease in the Prater or in the Augarten, practically unescorted; without police supervision, in any case, since a father has nothing to fear in the midst of his children, not even impertinence. The word 'friendly' recurs each time the Ambassador describes the relations between the sovereign and the people of Vienna; there did in fact exist a real and deep-seated mutual affection between rulers and ruled.

Joseph II, as we have said, wanted his presence to be 'ignored', as if he had been invisible; it was exceedingly embarrassing. Ferdinand I, the Magnanimous, had no such object; his familiarity was simpler and perhaps even more natural, for he was less shy than Joseph, and thus suffered and caused less embarrassment. He allowed people to take notice of him and bow to him, but only as they would have done to any other passer-by.

Sainte-Aulaire, noting this in his Memoirs, comments on the characteristic way in which the Viennese never allow familiarity to degenerate into disrespect.

'Bows were exchanged, with a friendly smile and with every appearance of equality. The number of individuals whom the

Emperor knew by name was prodigious; he often addressed a few kindly words to them, which were always welcomed with affectionate respect, and never called forth an indiscreet reply. If he happened to stop in some crowded walk, people would move away to form a circle round him at some distance, although nobody had set the limit beyond which they might not pass. On such occasions all the distinctions of rank, elsewhere so clearly defined, were obliterated. The first lady of Vienna would not have dared to jostle a burgher's wife in order to come closer to her sovereign. He himself, in the presence of his people, delighted in setting an example of this respect for equality, and would submit to personal inconvenience rather than infringe any of the meticulous police regulations to which private citizens are subjected.'[7]

The happiness of the Viennese, in spite of such public calamities as war, pestilence and floods, and the private sufferings from which the Austrians have never been more exempt than any other nation, was based on that 'art of living' which had developed spontaneously, organically; in favourable material circumstances, it must be admitted, but also, and chiefly, by virtue of a natural disposition towards happiness which is a highly important characteristic, and without which these worthy folk would probably have considered themselves oppressed by their rulers and would have resented the familiarity and goodwill of the latter, for all their affectionate simplicity, as an insidious form of paternalism aimed at destroying their natural liberties.

Nations, like individuals, display a greater or less capacity for making their own happiness from the elements which fate has set at their disposal; nobody would deny that external events play their part in the allocation of earthly goods on which happiness is in part dependent; but the dazzling splendour that Vienna put on after her sufferings under the Turkish siege, the energy and courage with which she rebuilt her city after the disasters of the 1939–1945 war, reveal with striking clarity that gift bestowed on her by the fates of knowing how to smile equally at good and evil fortune.

CHAPTER TWO

THE VIENNESE

The People of Vienna as depicted by Joseph Richter, Grillparzer and Adalbert Stifter—Lovers of Nature—Viennese Religion— St Bridget's Day—City Pleasures—Country Walks—Music

---

It is hard enough to portray a city, but it is harder still to portray that city's typical inhabitant. Particularly when one is dealing, as here, with a cosmopolitan centre where all the races of Europe have intermingled for centuries. Obviously there is no such person as the typical Viennese; one's portrait, physical or moral, is likely to be wholly arbitrary. In this city whose population grew incessantly and with extreme rapidity during the period we are considering, into which all the States of the Empire poured their most outstanding citizens, who can properly be called a Viennese? How long must one have been settled in the city, how many generations of strictly Viennese ancestors or how many quarters of civic nobility must one boast, in order to have the right to that title? And if we choose a citizen at random we may happen upon a recent immigrant or an atypical outsider.

There is one relatively safe method, namely to consider only illustrious Viennese who are at the same time authentically Viennese: Schubert, Grillparzer or Stifter for instance. But how dare one extend to all the inhabitants of a city the characteristics of a few exceptional beings? No doubt, with the generalizing tendency which is so common today, one might make some sort of mechanical portrait, superimposing a large number of images and retaining only the features they have in common; but what would such a process produce? Everybody's portrait, hence nobody's portrait . . . And yet there is such a person as a Viennese, there is a collection of individuals whom we call 'the Viennese'; people have been doing so for centuries, and there is probably something to be said for the custom. Moreover, the best way to get to know a person is to watch him living; his actions, his behaviour, his reactions, his likes and dislikes will provide evidence of his character. We can rely on that admirable novelist Adalbert Stifter, and refer to his book on Vienna and the Viennese,[1] to become acquainted with his compatriots.

The People of Vienna as depicted by Joseph Richter, Grillparzer and Adalbert Stifter

From the top of that strange tower-shaped house in the Adlergasse, which had once been the Viennese home of Paracelsus, and from the tall house in the Seitenstettergasse where he settled later, Adalbert Stifter enjoyed a wide panorama over the town and its surroundings. This writer, who was also one of the best painters of the Romantic school, could contemplate at will the landscape of plain and forest and, at the same time, observe the actions of his neighbours, the attitudes and gait of the people in the streets. Like Grillparzer, Stifter loved Vienna passionately – one can hardly help doing so – but this did not blind him to her minor faults. As we read his novels, which describe his compatriots' way of life, we are made more specially aware of the aspect of the town as it was in the early nineteenth century (Stifter was born in 1805), but we recognize also those constant factors by which a nation remains broadly the same through the course of centuries. Thus the comical characteristics reported by Joseph Richter's 'Eipeldauer' before 1800 were still valid during the whole of the nineteenth century, and a good many of them are still recognizable today.

Stifter's novels are quite as 'documentary' in their way as the letters of the fictitious Eipeldauer, Bauerle's Journal and the memoirs of Karoline Pichler; we can consult them with just as much confidence and profit, not only for what they tell us of their subject but also for what the authors teach us about themselves. The same is true in the next century of the novels of Arthur Schnitzler, which recreate so faithfully, with tender irony, the Vienna of the early years of the twentieth century.

The letters of the 'Eipeldauer' have certain unusual characteristics; they are hard to understand for anyone unfamiliar with the Viennese dialect, but this rendering of the popular speech with its raciness, its humour, its fantasy, its shrewd good nature, its common sense, is in itself infinitely fascinating and adds an air of authenticity to Joseph Richter's ingenious pastiche. They were written between 1785 and 1794, and they provide an almost inexhaustible mine of information about fashions, political ideas, theatrical programmes and public entertainments at the end of the eighteenth century.

Joseph Richter mischievously supposes these letters to have been sent to a provincial cousin by a peasant from the neighbourhood of Vienna who has come to settle in the capital, and who beholds all its strange sights with a bewildered eye, while retaining the wariness and sound sense of the countryman. He is 'the man from Eipeldauer', the yokel fresh from his village which, during the course of centuries, has also been known as Eupoltau, Elpeltau and even Alpiltowe. At the end of the eighteenth century, Eipeldau consisted of 133 houses, with 871 inhabitants. Popular humour represented the 'man from Eipeldau' as dazed and ungainly, oddly attired, carrying a sucking-pig under one arm and a goose under the other, and wandering terrified through the streets, confused by the noise, jostled by couriers, half crushed by the carriages with their galloping horses driven in the best tradition of Viennese coachmen, the most daring in the world and the most skilful.

This typical figure, who was to be met with any day in public squares and market places, and whom Joseph Richter immortalized, was bound to appear also on the comic stage. He was brought into opera for the first time in 1805, when the actor Thaddai appeared as 'the man from Eipeldau' in Joseph Ellmenreich's *Kappellmeister*, with music by Domenico Cimarosa. The Eipeldauer was seen again in 1809 on the stage of the Leopoldstadter Theater, in *Hans in Wien*, a comedy by Keingsteiner. He even had the honour of taking part in a ballet by Schubert, *The Seasons of Love*, in 1814. There was, too, a whole series of farces making this comic personage the hero of the most varied adventures, and even going so far as to bring him to court in Ferdinand Eberl's farce, *The Eipeldauer at the Hofburg*.

The clumsiness with which the yokel uses and distorts the foreign names and French terms then in fashion is extremely entertaining, and the *Eipeldauerbriefe* can be read with great enjoyment today, because of the natural verve they display and the first-hand information they provide about the life of different classes of society and their fashions and opinions in late eighteenth-century Vienna.[2]

If the Viennese had ever wished to cast their eyes on a *memento mori* which would counteract their favourite motto, *memento vivere*, they would merely have had to walk among the catacombs that underlie part of the inner city, and which probably date from Roman Vindobona; there they would have beheld that tragic sight which has been so impressively described by Adalbert Stifter in one of the most curious and striking chapters of *Wien und die Wiener*. Thousands of corpses are collected there, preserved from total decomposition by some chemical process, some of them piled up in terrifying mounds, others carefully lined up along the walls, with their backs to the sides of the winding passages. The torchlight dances in sinister fashion on these grinning faces, these bodies still clad in tattered garments, quickening them into a sort of illusory Dance of Death.

Unlike the ancient Romans, who at the end of banquets used to circulate pictures of dead bodies and jerking skeletons so as to stimulate, by this solemn warning, the enjoyment of living and of tasting all earthly delights, the citizen of Vienna needs no such reminder of his latter end; it would spoil his joy, rather than impel him to savour the passing moment; it would cast a gloom over that innocent, naïve and almost childlike satisfaction which the Viennese feel at being alive and at enjoying, without excess, the pleasures which life continually offers them. Dürer's melancholia, which calls all things in question, including the value and meaning of life itself, is foreign to their character. Viennese melancholy, as we shall sometimes meet it in Mozart, in Schnitzler, is fleeting and light; a cloud's shadow rather than a cloud. The individual is never crushed by it nor driven by it to discouragement or to despair.

The description given by Franz Grillparzer of his birthplace, of his family, of the conditions in which he spent his childhood, provides an excellent analysis of the Viennese character. He was born on January 15th 1791, in a noble and gloomy house in the Bauernmarkt, full of endless vestibules leading nowhere and huge rooms almost empty of furniture, for his parents lived in a constant state of financial anxiety. In his autobiography, he has drawn a striking picture of this old house, neglected, almost falling into decay, whose former splendour was gradually fading in deplorable decrepitude.

'During the longest summer days,' (he writes) 'it was only towards midday that a few sparse sunbeams reached my father's study, and we children gazed with delight at this meagre trail of light on the floor. The very layout of the rooms was fantastic. Beside the kitchen was the woodshed, so large that it could have contained a whole house; you could only find your way about it with a lantern, the light of which could scarcely reach the walls. Nothing prevented us from imagining these regions inhabited by brigands, gipsies, or even ghosts. To these imaginary terrors was added a very real one, namely the prodigious number of rats that swarmed there and sometimes found their way right into the kitchen.'

The princely façade which could be admired from the street gave no hint of all the gloom, discomfort and anxiety in the home of the lawyer Wenzel Grillparzer, who tried to display a wealth and luxury which his family was far from enjoying in fact. Living beyond one's means, sacrificing a great deal to appearances, not so much for love of vain ostentation as from a naïve ambition to cut a fine figure and thus participate from afar in the *grandezza* of the Court and its princes, might have been considered a fault in the Viennese had they not shown so much courage, elegance, gaiety and even dandyism in refusing to admit their poverty.

Grillparzer's picture of family life in that splendid house in the Bauernmarkt is very characteristic of the social code of the Viennese at that time. There was a popular tendency to consider everything belonging to the upper classes as 'noble'. The word had been borrowed from the French, it was pronounced *nobel*, and it recurs constantly in the writings of this period: in the letters of the man from Eipeldau for instance. It implies everything that conforms to a popular standard of majesty, distinction, opulence, good manners, elegance in dress: a blend of Maria Theresa's *grandezza*, which was paramount in the eighteenth century, and of Germanic informality. It implies, too, not merely the outward aspect of nobility, but an inward nobility chiefly marked by sensuous refinement, delicacy of feeling, rarefied tastes, politeness and discreet charm of manner.

A man of *nobel* appearance might have the title of Count or Excellency ascribed to him even if he had no right to it, and a *von* added to his name in defiance of all the rules of heraldry, by such people as waiters, coachmen and hairdressers. At the time when Grillparzer was spending his early childhood in the gloomy dilapidated palace of his parents, that is to say during the last years of the eighteenth century, a ruined gentleman had no reason to try and pass for a rich one, unless he were an adventurer; it was at the beginning of the following century, and particularly during the 'Biedermeier' period, that this flaunting of wealth began to take a place in the concept of 'nobility'.

To live up to one's rank, to cut a figure even if one had to perform miracles of ingenuity to pay one's most pressing debts, seemed an imperative necessity to Grillparzer's parents, who belonged to a class that was probably quite a large one. Their household included a cook, a kitchen maid, a butler, a lackey who carried the missal when Madame went to church, and a music master. They owned a country property at Enzersdorf, where they gave parties in summer, rural balls of exquisite refinement. Withal, not a penny to pay their debts. The father was indolent and listless; the mother, a good musician and incapable of coping with the slightest practical task; the children grew up as best they could and read everything they came across in their parents' rich library.

The poet's biographers have interpreted the conditions that surrounded his childhood as a symbol of the Vienna of that period, the 'twilight of the monarchy' against which Metternich was to struggle so desperately; but the blend of fantasy and resignation, of 'keeping cheerful in spite of it all' and real poverty, of indifference to material conditions while organizing theatrical entertainments and concerts, displayed by Grillparzer's parents, is merely an exaggerated manifestation of a genuinely Viennese characteristic, and that is why we call attention to it.

The palace in the Bauernmarkt, where the writer's imagination blossomed in the gloom of huge empty drawing-rooms, amidst fairy tales and stories of ghosts or brigands, was no exception in that old city, despite its teeming population. In a handful of decades the number of inhabitants had grown from some 80,000 to over 190,000. All these people lodged where they could, and the result of this overcrowding was that one had to go ever further in search of the groves and meadows, blossoming bushes and bird-song, which had grown ever rarer, and which the Viennese could not do without. Contact with nature was vital to these people who like to take their pleasures freely in the fresh air and in open spaces.

Lovers of Nature

Every window had its flowerpots, its climbing plants, its caged songbirds, but still this was not Nature; and from the attic windows overlooking rooftops, longing glances were cast towards the wooded heights of the Viennese forest, that forest sung by poets and musicians from Walther von der Vogelweide to Schubert and Strauss. The city was fortunate indeed to have at so short a distance from its gates a real forest, with scattered hamlets buried among the trees, a forest where one could walk without meeting a creature save the timid, graceful fawns that fled at the approach of man.

In Vienna, love of nature was not, as it might be elsewhere, the sign of a misanthropic temperament. The ramblers in the Vienna woods did not shun the company of their fellows; they foregathered gladly with them, after the excursion, in

37

some suburban tavern, or some pleasure garden within the forest itself; often, indeed, a whole party went walking together, the more the merrier. The Viennese asked nothing better than to pile up into a carriage with baskets of food and drive off for a woodland picnic, and they seized every opportunity of spending the day in the country.

Official religious holidays were readily supplemented by days sacred to intercessory or local saints, to miraculous images or supernatural apparitions, all of which furnished pretexts for pious pilgrimages.

To these were added the anniversaries and feast-days of the Emperor and members of the imperial family, which demanded dutiful and joyous celebration, and all the traditional holidays not prescribed by law but sanctioned by long custom. 'Blue Monday', for instance, was a very old and much cherished Viennese custom. A psychological necessity in this city more than elsewhere, given the Viennese character, its function was to prolong Sunday and above all to prevent that end-of-holiday gloom that darkens Sunday evenings with the mere thought that one will have to work again next day.

The thought that next day was to be a holiday too left Sunday its full share of unclouded joy, its absolute freedom, and the expectation of Blue Monday's delights enhanced Sunday's still further. In fact, when, at a later date, the Government rashly attempted to suppress Blue Monday in order to increase industrial productivity, the workers rose up in angry protest.

Viennese Religion

The mental attitude of the Viennese to religious matters was not very different from their political opinions. The Reformation had had little or no effect on their solid, traditional Catholicism. Just as their sovereign had been chosen by God to watch over the safety and well-being of the nation, like an earthly Providence whose decrees must be accepted and respected because they were made in their subjects' interest, so a heavenly Providence kept watch over the physical and moral well-being of Christendom. Moreover this Providence had delegated a large number of saints to assist men in their struggle against evil. The Fourteen Intercessors, to whom so many churches were dedicated in Austria and Germany, lived in a familiar relationship with town and village, protecting them against fire and flood, cattle diseases, thunderbolts and the innumerable ills that threaten mankind. Each of them had his own function, which popular piety and trust had attributed to him long centuries ago, and which he exercised scrupulously, on condition, of course, of receiving his just tribute of prayers and offerings.

If the majesty of God was awe-inspiring and deterred those petitioners who were afraid to address Him directly, they could always invoke the Intercessors who had been men like ourselves and therefore were well acquainted with the needs of men and the dangers that lie in wait for them. Baroque painters and sculptors excelled, just as medieval artists had done, in the representation of these intercessors, each with his respective attributes, and their images looked down on the kneeling petitioner with a kindly gesture and a smile. The natural consequence of the cult of intercessory saints was that on their feast days, ceremonies and pilgrimages attracted pious crowds. These religious rites were celebrated in each parish with joyful excitement as well as with pious fervour, and when a suburban or village church happened to house a particularly venerable sanctuary, this provided the opportunity for family outings that combined gaiety with reverence, and also the excuse for rustic merrymaking which in no way detracted from the saint's popularity.

Above the Intercessors, sitting by the side of God himself, was the Virgin, the Holy Mother to whom no one ever prayed in vain. The most incongruous complaints were addressed to her, for popular piety was convinced of her infinite indulgence towards human weakness. Owing to the natural sentimentality of the Viennese the cult of the Virgin, in the seventeenth and eighteenth centuries, developed on a more impressive scale in Austria than in Italy itself, and even recently there have been touching illustrations of this.

Before the 1939 war there was a church in Vienna (I do not

know whether it is still standing, for Vienna suffered appalling destruction) which housed a particularly sacred statue of the Virgin. The walls of the chapel in which it stood were scribbled all over with humble and naïve supplications: most of them prayers from wives begging Mary to bring back their unfaithful husbands, but also an occasional tender and disarming plea from a woman wanting to keep her lover, or a girl imploring the Madonna to help her awaken the interest of some handsome youth: all of which was infinitely touching and highly instructive as to the sentimental psychology of the Viennese. These *graffiti*, which one could scarcely read without tears in one's eyes, comprised only women's prayers; I read none written by a man, not that these lacked faith in the Virgin, but either they relied more on themselves and on their own powers of attraction, or else they went to pray and write their messages in some other chapel with which I am not acquainted.

I cannot guarantee the absolute authenticity of a story that was being told in Vienna, and which bears close relation to this tradition of pious *graffiti*. It happened one day that a girl who felt that her lover, or her betrothed, was drifting away from her, went to pray in this church, but – consciously or unconsciously – instead of kneeling in the Virgin's chapel she went to prostrate herself at the foot of the Cross. An old woman, ripe in years and experience, hearing her sobs, asked the cause of her despair; the girl having told her everything, the old woman raised her from the ground and led her to the Virgin's chapel, then left her with the whispered words: 'Pray to her, my child; men always help one another.'

Vienna, that feminine city, was naturally bound to venerate above all other supernatural powers the Holy Virgin who had always defended her during the long centuries of her uncertain, peril-fraught existence. The rout of the Turks was due as much to the Virgin as to Prince Eugene; she it was who in 1715 rid the city of the plague which had already claimed so many victims; she, again, who allayed the furies of the cholera. The *Mariensäule* expressed the gratitude of the people of Vienna towards their chief auxiliary, to whom no prayers were uttered in vain, whether for the defeat of an invading enemy or the restoration of an erring husband. And so pilgrimages to those churches dedicated to the Virgin were the most popular and enthusiastic, and the number of sanctuaries in town and country entitled *Mariahilfe* (Mary Our Helper) shows the immense devotion borne by the people of Vienna towards the Mother whom each loved as his own.

Besides those pilgrimages attended by all and sundry, in family groups, in bands of friends or workmates, there were the great solemn processions which were a constant source of delight and wonder to the Viennese; on those days, the clergy came forth in great pomp, swinging fragrant censers, raising many-coloured banners and gilded crosses, each religious order in its robes of brown, black or white. The choirs sang, the bishop's vestments glittered under his purple *baldacchino*. Sometimes, too, the orders of chivalry took part; then one might behold in full ceremonial costume, adorned with plumes, chains and swords, the Knights of Malta, Knights Templar and Knights Hospitaller, Knights of Santiago and of Calatrava. But the finest of all these processions was undoubtedly that of the Corpus Domini, for custom required that all the dignitaries of the Court, the Imperial family and the Emperor himself should follow the Holy Sacrament. This occasion brought forth all the most glittering uniforms and the precious bejewelled pelisses of Magyar princes, and each national costume worn by some high-ranking nobleman symbolized, in this pious parade, the infinite external diversity of this empire and its single soul.

The natural piety of the Viennese, their authentic and zealous Catholicism, ensured the essentially religious character of these festivals, but love of pageantry also played its part therein. Nothing could be more elaborately organized, more sumptuously produced, than these processions which gave the citizens the pleasure of admiring their rulers and the Imperial nobility at close quarters and at leisure, for the march past was slow and stately; each spectator felt that he shared the same intimate faith with the masters of his earthly destiny.

41

In the devotion offered by Vienna to its own saints, there was a very old inherited tradition of customs and beliefs whose origin was lost in the night of time. Why were some of these more popular than others? Only hagiographers and students of religious psychology can decide. As is customary, each district owed special reverence to its parish saint, and tradition demanded that the patron saints of the Imperial family should be celebrated with particular pomp. But popular zeal, led by instinct and still inspired by ancient traditions of which the origin and often the very meaning has been lost, had chosen two saints whose feast-days every year provided occasions for prodigious rejoicing: St Anne and St Bridget.

St Anne's day in Vienna was as famous as St Valentine's in England. The name Anne was extremely popular and was often combined with Mary, giving rise to such charming diminutives as Nannerl, Marianderl, Mariannerl. Girls who bore it were given presents and sometimes serenaded by their lovers on the occasion of their patron saint's day. At the beginning of the nineteenth century it was fashionable to send the Annes and Annettes of one's acquaintance greeting-cards decorated in the sentimental style of 1830 with feathers and lace, with piquant or ardent mottoes. They were also offered fans, embroidered handkerchiefs, comfit-boxes. Tradesmen vied with one another in producing the most ingenious and elegant boxes, 'adorned with appropriate mottoes, bearing the person's name inside a wreath of flowers and real pearls'.

On that day there was dancing in pleasure-gardens or sumptuous public ballrooms, according to one's taste, for dancing was accepted as an inseparable and necessary feature of all religious festivals. In the interval between Mass and Vespers, parties would settle down in the fields surrounding the most popular sanctuaries, all or nearly all of which stood on the border between suburbs and countryside. Then they would take out of their baskets the provisions they had brought, which were always abundant and delectable, for the Viennese liked to associate good fare with religious ceremonies. And then until the bell rang for afternoon service, the young people would dance while their parents dozed. Everyone, that day, wore the costume of his native province; the multitude of many-coloured dresses and scarves floating to the rhythm of the dance made a charming spectacle, which was particularly noted by the Comte de la Garde, a participant in the Congress of Vienna and its self-constituted historian.

On this occasion La Garde saw for the first time Tyrolese in national costume perform their highland *ländler*, and was struck with admiration. These Tyrolese, who had emigrated to the capital, worked there as watch-makers; they remained closely united, and foregathered every Saturday to sing and dance together. On St Anne's Day and St Bridget's Day they performed their leaping, whirling steps amidst the other dancers, accompanied by shrill cries and songs. The beauty of their voices, the originality of their Alpine melodies, the piquancy of the mimed love-making which formed the basis of their dances, aroused, on one occasion, the interest of a theatrical entrepreneur, proprietor of the great Apollo dance-hall where thousands gathered every night, and who was always on the look-out for new 'attractions' to draw and hold his public. Once the Tyrolese had been discovered, the Theater an der Wien wanted them too, and incorporated them in a rustic opera which was immensely successful.

Everybody knew them, and when they happened to sing in chorus in the streets, crowds gathered and followed them to listen, to such an extent, so the Comte de la Garde tells us, 'that the police were sometimes alarmed, and kept watch from a distance in case trouble should ensue'. The most distinguished salons tried to wrest them from the theatres, and the Tyrolese, now all the rage, were engaged for a tour in England, where their talents and their simplicity were greatly appreciated. It is said that one of the women singers was so pleased with the compliments graciously paid her by King George that she gaily flung her arms round His Britannic Majesty's neck and kissed him on both cheeks.

St Bridget's Day

The Feast of St Bridget was the occasion for even more numerous and popular merrymakings, if possible, than that

43

of St Anne. 'There are people who, all the year round, never set foot outside their own district,' writes the Austrian novelist Adalbert Stifter, 'but who would think themselves disgraced if they did not make their way to the Prater on May 1, St Bridget's day, even if they have to pawn their beds and the very linen they're wearing.' St Bridget's was the great springfestival, just as St Anne's was the great summer festival.

The enduring popularity of these festivals was due to the fact that they fell at the loveliest seasons of the year, and thus provided an opportunity for those outings which the Viennese loved so dearly that they would seize on any pretext to go off into the country.

They had not far to go to enjoy rural delights; these awaited them just outside the city gates, and the moderate heights of the Wiener Wald were within reach of the laziest walkers. What unwritten law, what custom of unknown origin obliged all the inhabitants of Vienna, unless confined to bed by sickness, to rush off towards the Prater on May 1, there to be jostled by the crowd and possibly crushed by the carriages that galloped at full speed, unless the seething mass held up their progress?

At the beginning of *The Poor Musician*, an admirable tale by Franz Grillparzer, there is a picture of the Feast of St Bridget which exactly reproduces the atmosphere of that day, at the end of which one would go home exhausted, covered with dust, with aching limbs and clothes soiled and often torn, to sink on one's bed with mingled feelings of weariness and regret that it was all over – that sort of melancholy that overwhelms one when the last firework has been let off – and yet longing for next year's May 1 and a new St Bridget's Day. And that nostalgic gaiety, which is inherent in the music and painting of Vienna as well as in its literature, suggests this atmosphere of post-revelry, the return to the workaday world after the enchantment has faded, after the dream has once again given place to reality. Because St Anne's and St Bridget's days fell amidst the clear bright days of spring and summer, they were tinged too with the enchantment of sunlight, as though the elements themselves were in collusion with human passions and sensations.

There was indeed an infectious magic about these rustic religious festivals, these bourgeois bacchanalia, and many a maiden, forgetting the austere saints in whose honour they were held, flung her bonnet over the windmill in the arms of some plausible student or handsome officer, with the connivance of the Viennese night, of the music in the air and of Mother Nature, most ancient and deep-rooted of all divinities. As the Eipeldauer's letters quaintly put it: 'It's the same year after year, a crazy throng, unbridled gaiety and almost always, to end up with, everybody gets a bit drunk, for which the women are even more responsible than the men.' The Eipeldauer meant no doubt that women were the main cause of this intoxication, and that their charm and prettiness went to their companions' heads even more potently than the *heuriger* of Grinzing or Hungarian Tokay.

The anonymous author of *A Week in Vienna*, writing in 1830, estimated at 40,000 the number of visitors to the Brigittenau; all classes, all ages were represented and there was entertainment to suit all tastes. One would stand watching short-skirted Tyrolese girls spinning like tops, another whirled round in a breathless waltz, a third settled down at a confectioner's to stuff himself with cakes. The air hummed with music from every sort of instrument, from barrel organs to the fiddle of the wandering violinist who came there to earn a few florins. On trestles were grimacing dwarfs, leaping monkeys and dogs that stood on their hind legs. Ingenious trainers displayed learned birds that distributed horoscopes to the girls in the audience.

For this vast merry-making, circuses and menageries foregathered at the Brigittenau, packed so close together that the parading clowns exchanged their quips over the heads of the gaping crowd. Agile thieves slipped through the throng, feeling pockets, stealing bags, while simple-minded spectators marvelled open-mouthed at the fire-eater, the sword swallower and the human pyramid of acrobats, at the summit of which an intrepid child brandished a flag. Before long, permanent pleasure grounds were set up all round the Brigittenau, and these eventually stayed open all the year. The most monumental of these was the Colosseum, which well deserved its name; Bermann's picturesque description of this, in 1834, is quoted by Reichsl,[3] to whose work one must constantly refer when studying Vienna in the Biedermeier age. For ten kreutzers, which was a very moderate sum, one was admitted to all forty-four attractions of the Colosseum: switchbacks, roundabouts, swings, shooting booths, games of skill of every sort, boating, horseback riding. The Colosseum had the wherewithal to satisfy every whim, to fulfil every desire: puppet shows, joking clowns, menageries. Those who sought wonders could consult an oracle, an old man in homespun robes, with a long beard, hidden in a highly romantic hermitage; or else they could try their skill at archery with the very crossbow used by William Tell. Lovers of the waltz thronged into a huge barrel-shaped ballroom, while billiard players found tables at their disposal. To all these marvels was added in 1840 a miniature railway.

Fanatical devotees of St Bridget gave up two days to her festival, spending the night in the neighbouring meadows or parks, and one can think of no more picturesque or delightful sight than that joyful crowd, camping out under the stars and sleeping little, for songs, laughter and dance music went on uninterruptedly all night; and for all that there was never the slightest disturbance or brawl.

The art of pleasure was so highly developed by the Viennese, and to a pitch of refinement unknown elsewhere, that a vast number of people, gathered there to enjoy themselves, and freely seeking refreshment at the counters of wine-merchants and brewers, retained a sense of decency, good nature, and gaiety without vulgarity, which made the people of Vienna the most civilized in Europe. It was not until the revolution of 1848, which so profoundly altered the character and customs of the Viennese, that the authorities found it necessary 'in view of these unprecedented and exceptional circumstances' to put an end to the pious junketings of St Bridget's day, which brought such entertainment and seemed so necessary to the very existence of the people of Vienna.

It is easy to understand why everybody flocked to the Brigittenau on May Day, either to take part in the rejoicings or to watch the curious spectacle that they presented.

Grillparzer's 'poor musician' also took up his post on the road along which people drove or walked, to collect a few groschen in his old hat, and he watched the endless procession of carriages of every sort file past, the humblest passing close to the grandest without any sign of jealousy or envy. Class hatred was something unknown in Vienna before the revolution of 1848 which, through its excesses and the harshness of its repression, began to form a gulf between rich and poor; and so it might happen that these carriages would jostle or even collide with one another without provoking anything more than a smile of amusement, a gesture of apology; when drivers eventually exchanged insults they did so without conviction, out of habit, in a joking vein. And it can be imagined how hard it must have been to keep in check fiery horses amidst a crowd so dense that carriages could scarcely force their way through it, while the procession of devotees and onlookers, men and horses, could advance only at a snail's pace.

A Viennese proverb says that in this city the coachmen drove like demons, while foot-passengers paid little heed and made no attempt to get out of their way, and none the less there were never any accidents.

Elsewhere, enormous popular gatherings such as were held on St Anne's and St Bridget's Day might have provoked brawls and even riots; in Vienna all difficulties were resolved with a smile, by a smile, and once the incident was over life would begin to flow again, to glide by smooth and unruffled. On the narrow thoroughfare of the Prater where carriages sped towards the Brigittenau, the crowd was a cheerful, sociable, affable crowd. They had come there to enjoy themselves and so must carefully avoid anything that might spoil that enjoyment for themselves or other people.

City Pleasures

People went into the country as often as they could, yet the city had its attractions too; one of its advantages which was particularly appreciated by the Viennese was the large number of cafés – an institution admirably suited to a sociable people, neither gregarious nor misanthropic, seeking the presence of others to enhance thereby each one's pleasure. The café is a very different place from the *salon*, where convention requires one to obey all the rules governing social behaviour like a formal dance; at a café you can be alone or not alone as you choose, sit in solitude with your cup of mocha or your glass of wine or, if you prefer, take part in your neighbours' conversation, join them at cards or chess. In a café, a man feels perfectly free, free from family responsibilities and social duties; and it was in order to enjoy his freedom to the full that the citizen of Vienna went to the café. He did not go there to drink, or rather, if he drank it was because he liked good wine and considered the light, clear vintage of the Austrian hillsides conducive to gaiety and witty talk; he took no delight in getting drunk; what he enjoyed was that superficial intoxication that removes any sense of oppression and gives a sparkle to the intelligence and to witty sallies.

In certain cafés tobacco was forbidden, as though the smoke of pipes and cigars might cloud men's brains. The other oriental product, coffee, was adopted with enthusiasm, because it is conducive to lightness and lucidity; tobacco and its heavy fumes were, for a long time, banished not only from the company of women, needless to say, but also from any gathering where it might prove unwelcome. Princess Metternich was once travelling by train when one of the occupants of her carriage, wishing to light a cigar, asked her if she objected to smoke. 'I don't know,' she replied coldly, 'nobody has ever dared smoke in my presence.'

Smoking was forbidden in streets and restaurants, and it was only in the lowest class of tavern that devotees of pipe and cigar-smoking could indulge their passion freely. Yet it was to the interest of the Austrian state not to restrict the use of tobacco, for it held the monopoly of its manufacture and sale, forbidding the import of any foreign tobacco, and meanwhile making the consumption of Austrian cigars obligatory in the Italian provinces under its sway, much to the annoyance of Piedmontese and Lombards; one of the first signs of emancipation and insurrection in these provinces, later, was to be the boycott of Austrian tobacco.

Foreigners often found it trying only to be able to get

Austrian cigars; as we see by reading Heinrich Laube. His
'*Journey through the Biedermeier*'[4] clearly reflects this attitude.
He liked everything in Vienna, except having to give up his
favourite Havanas.

> 'I'm curious to see' (he writes) 'what I shall eventually say
> about Vienna, this city which is an earthly Paradise without
> figleaves, serpent or tree of knowledge. Probably all my
> opinions will be highly favourable, for my stomach has been in
> perfect order the whole time. I think I shall stay in Vienna,
> where I shall become a martyr, for I shall have to give up wit,
> liberalism and Havana cigars, none of which are to be found
> here. But that's what makes Vienna Vienna; after a few weeks
> you don't want anything that's not Viennese and you cease to
> feel the lack of anything.'

The first public place in which mocha was distributed to
all and sundry and which was therefore christened *café* was
opened in 1683, the very year when the Turks besieged
Vienna. The institution quickly became popular, for cafés
multiplied and became one of the town's special features.
They undoubtedly correspond to a need and a tendency of the
Viennese people, for they have remained through all social
transformations one of its characteristic elements. One might
write an interesting analysis of capital cities by describing the
nature of cafés in each country, and one would obtain at the
same time a considerable source of information on the
psychology, the habits and feelings of different races by
examining what a café means for each of them.

The Viennese café, favourable alike to solitude and
sociability, naturally reflects every alteration in taste and way
of life. It becomes more luxurious in its equipment and
decoration when the upper classes begin to frequent it. It
usually provides music, except for certain taverns reserved
for those rare citizens who are not fond of music. The class
of each café depends on the drink served there; the lowest,
on the whole, are the beer shops; I don't mean the great
bierhallen, which have splendid rooms, and gardens with
music and entertainment, but the taverns in the lowest
districts frequented by Danube sailors and workmen.
Taverns selling wine are of a better character. The majority

49

of the Viennese are wine drinkers: the taste for beer only developed fairly late and never seriously threatened the sale of Austrian and Hungarian wines.

What chiefly characterizes wine- or beer-shops, however, is the fact that the customer comes there primarily for the pleasure of drinking. He has to put up with noisy neighbours, the quarrels of tipsy sailors, and a room thick with tobacco smoke. The coffee drinker, on the contrary, seeks a quiet place where he may enjoy '*luxe, calme et volupté*'. Talk in cafés never goes beyond the bounds of good manners. When the waiter has brought you a cup of mocha, a glass of water and a huge pile of newspapers, you can stay there all day if you choose and all evening till closing time; the waiter will solicitously renew your glass of water and your newspapers, according to a rite more than two centuries old, without which Vienna would no longer be Vienna.

There have been famous cafés in Vienna; some have disappeared, others have long kept up their old reputation; the favourites have always been those where people foregather after the theatre, and where spectators may be lucky enough to see at the next table the actor or singer who has been the star of the evening's entertainment, and who naturally goes on playing the star role in everyday life.

Joseph Richter, author of the witty *Eipeldauerbriefe*, sang the praises of one of the most characteristic cafés of the late eighteenth and early nineteenth century: the Café Hugelmann, built close to that bridge that joins the city to the suburb of Leopoldstadt, which stands on one of the islands in the Danube – the Ferdinandsbrücke, a busy thoroughfare for everyone going to or coming from the Prater. The Café Hugelmann had on this account a wide clientele, attracted moreover by all the advantages it offered: in the first place – since that was what one saw before entering the house – by a great garden where tables were set out.

Many people liked open-air cafés such as Hugelmann's because of the charm of the natural setting. Situated at the river's edge, it offered customers the delight of watching boats float down the Danube, sailors in Greek or Turkish dress and bathers without any dress at all. You could see pleasure boats and heavy barges mooring, you could trace the delicate wake left by ferrymen's boats making their way as best they could between the bridges. Among the customers one might see poets and musicians, painters and actors.

Hugelmann's was also famous for its 'academy'. This was not an academy of literature, art or science but simply a Billiards Academy. This game was all the rage, and adepts foregathered at this café to compare their exploits. In its modern form (there had certainly been earlier variants), the game was widespread in eighteenth century Vienna, sufficiently so, in any case, to cause some anxiety to the authorities, who in a regulation dated 1745 forbade the establishment of billiard rooms except on ground floors, fearing no doubt that the weight of the table and the throng of spectators might make floors collapse.

Billiards champions were as famous as actors, which is saying something: so much so that they were a great attraction for Hugelmann's clients, who knew them by name and jostled one another to watch them play. 'People go to see the best billiards players at Hugelmann's as they go to see the actors at the Crown Theatre,' writes Franz Fräffer.[5] 'There was the great Reich and the famous Untel, and Hungarian players so skilful that they played three games at once. This was still the golden age of delightful innocence, of happy ignorance, before the discovery of the *coup sec* which was to astonish the world ... Hugelmann's was the seat of the University of Billiards which has now moved to Adami's.'

In other cafés, people went to hear music. I say 'hear' and not 'listen to', for the pleasure to be got from tavern virtuosi was not comparable to that enjoyed by music-lovers at the morning concerts in the Orangery at the Augarten, where Mozart and Beethoven played. Café musicians have at all times excelled in creating atmosphere rather than in giving true aesthetic pleasure; they provide the sort of thing Erik Satie called 'furniture music'. It might be either very good music like that of the Strauss family, or else some old tune scraped out on makeshift fiddles by street musicians. Some innkeepers, furthermore, tried to provide genuine attractions for their customers: such as the band of harpists which a

Frenchman who kept a tavern on the Prater road had fetched from Paris as a 'curiosity' and which in fact drew crowds.

Elsewhere, people went to listen to improvisers. One of the most curious features of the early nineteenth century was the extraordinary vogue for these poets who, on a theme provided by a spectator, immediately recited a long and sometimes really beautiful poem, such as those which Mme de Staël ascribes to her Corinne. We know from the *Mémoires d'Outre-Tombe* that Chateaubriand used to send for improvisers to enliven the soirées at his Embassy at Rome, and Hans Christian Andersen has written an excellent novel of which the hero is an Italian improviser. For Italy was the home of these astonishing virtuosi who were equally popular in high society and among the masses in the public square. From Italy, probably, the vogue for improvisers passed into Austria; they were all the rage in the Viennese cafés and suburban inns, and various memoirs of the time commemorate the fame of Ferdinand Sauter, whose mischievous couplets, the Gzantzeln, delighted the audience.

Sauter, a poorly paid clerk in an insurance company who had decided to swell his budget by going from tavern to tavern reciting verses on topical themes, improvised with extraordinary *brio*. He was rewarded with enthusiastic applause, a few kreutzers and innumerable glasses of wine, which before long ruined his health. Dressed in dirty, tattered clothes, muddy boots and a rag round his neck by way of cravat, he delighted his audience by the mocking good-nature with which he made fun of himself and his appearance. This bizarre entertainer, who looked like some hero of Hoffmann's tales, this inexhaustible improviser was to die in the cholera epidemic of the tragic year 1854, which claimed so many victims. The mass of his poems have disappeared, naturally, since they were invented on the spur of the moment; they lingered for a while in their hearers' memory and then faded, but enough of them have survived to give us some idea of the verve of this whimsical poet, so essentially Viennese in character and talent, whose inspiration was the 'tavern muse'.[6]

Singers, both male and female, violinists, zither players,

acrobats and conjurers entertained those who sat drinking in suburban inns and the garden cafés where the Viennese came to spend their leisure hours. When they had not time for an excursion into the Wiener Wald, which took a whole day, since one must never take one's pleasures hurriedly, they would go and sit under the trees, or in the shady arbours, which in the humblest taverns were replaced by pots of flowers standing on posts.

Country Walks

It was almost a daily necessity for the Viennese to go walking in gardens, with the inevitable halt at some place of refreshment; failing the forest drives of the Wiener Wald, the sanded paths and the lawns of the Prater, the Augarten or the Volksgarten satisfied that thirst for 'nature' which all Austrians feel so insistently. The Comte de Sainte-Aulaire notes this characteristic in his memoirs, to the credit of the people of Vienna.

'Country walks, music and dancing in the fresh air, always accompanied by good fare, are habitual among all classes of the population. At the end of the day, if time allows, the suburban artisan takes off his working clothes and puts on a neat suit; with his wife and children he goes to eat fried chicken in one of the innumerable small inns scattered over the rich countryside through which the Danube flows. The bastions and glacis of the city provide superior restaurants for the lower middle class and well-to-do artisans; in the public gardens which form a green belt round the town, the avenues are copiously supplied with refreshments and solid viands. In the centre of the gardens a huge space is always set aside for dancing, and numerous bands, which have been conducted by Strauss and Lanner themselves, play waltzes and operatic selections.

'It is delightful to see this crowd of men and women of all ages enjoying life so calmly and appearing so well content with their lot; there is never the slightest disturbance, no sound is heard save the clink of knives on plates. Everyone talks quietly to his neighbour, the walkers process two by two round the space reserved for dancing; sometimes couples, abandoning their tranquil pace, break from the ranks of the spectators, dart into the whirling crowd and spin round in the waltz with an

53

impetuosity for which the gravity of their demeanour and the seriousness of their expression had not prepared the foreigner.'

This urge to leave the town, which struck all visitors, and which took possession of the entire population, was a trait peculiar to the Viennese. Love of nature was the primary cause of that daily exodus towards the countryside and the gardens, and also the desire to set aside part of the day from professional duties, to make a break in the succession of habitual actions. The Viennese knew the value of that gesture of rest and relaxation. They would return from their ramble with mind and eyes refreshed and cheered by the grace and beauty of all they had seen, and go home with lungs filled with fresh air.

Since the enjoyment of fresh air was the legitimate right of all classes, no rules of priority governed the exodus of the joyful crowd towards the Prater when, in fine weather, nobody would consent to stay at home once his daily task was done. In the throng of pedestrians and carriages, everybody kept to his own place. Sainte-Aulaire admired this discipline, which could probably not be seen anywhere else.

'From five o'clock in the afternoon onwards, during May and June, the city dwellers, who change their customary mealtimes at this season, hasten to leave their gloomy dwellings; all the streets that lead to the Rothen Turm are crowded with carriages and with men and women on horseback. The line of vehicles begins at the little bridge over the Danube, and goes on all along the Jaegerzeile as far as the entry to the Prater. Up to then, the carriages go at a walking pace in single file; none must get out of line. There are no privileged exceptions. I have seen the Emperor and Empress themselves obeying the rule and after a long wait, seeing no hope of reaching the Prater before nightfall, giving up their expedition and turning back towards the city.'

An incident such as that caused by the daughter of the Russian Ambassador was so unusual that the French diplomat tells it in full in his memoirs, and relates the extraordinary vicissitudes of the lawsuit between Count Esterhazy and the city council. They are minutely described in the chapter entitled 'Viennese Entertainments'.

The banks of the Danube, that famous Blue Danube which is blue only in Johann Strauss's imagination – really jade-coloured and rather muddy, at any rate as it flows through Vienna – also provided delightful excursions. Sailing and rowing boats were available to those who sought a river trip, and the landing-stages were always full of tumult and excitement, with fluttering scarves, cries of delight and gasps of fright. Elsewhere one might see a herd of calves brought from Enns, terrified by their crossing, or else the cargoes of clay that the famous porcelain factory in Vienna consumed in large quantities. People would sit drinking on inn balconies and enjoying this lively and ever-changing scene.

Pleasure boats, painted in every conceivable colour, their bright sails flapping merrily in the wind, had been introduced by an officer who, during his campaigns in Italy, had enjoyed the delights of leisurely sailing on the lakes of Lombardy; on his return he had had the happy thought of bringing to the Danube and its canal the industry of the boatmen of Como and Stresa. This experiment was highly successful, and the author of an interesting guidebook which describes the neighbourhood of Vienna for twenty leagues around[7] informs us that pleasure-sailing had become one of the favourite pastimes of the Viennese, some gliding along the water driven by a good following wind, while others sat at the terraces of the riverside inns, raising their glass of wine or beer to toast the bold mariners. The restaurant called the Golden Rose, at Nüssdorf, specialized in serving fish and shellfish dressed in the most picturesque and exquisite fashion; a letter in Bauerle's Journal, in 1829, signed by 'a friend of the good inns of our country', sings the praises of the Golden Rose, with its two great balconies overlooking the river, its fine garden, its excellent cuisine, its moderate prices, and the privilege enjoyed by customers of choosing their own fish or shellfish from the tanks where they are kept alive.

Foreigners were sometimes astonished by the fact that, for the Viennese, a good meal was an invariable adjunct to a country outing. The bookseller Nicolai, whose harsh criticisms we have already quoted, notes with surprise that after

E

five o'clock in the afternoon all the gardens are full of working-class people; he had never seen such a thing, either in Berlin, his native city, nor in any of the other towns he had visited, and he stresses the way these good folk flocked to the bowling alleys, so numerous that in one single garden he counted thirty-eight. When they settle down round a solid oak table, or squat on the ground in front of the food spread out on a napkin, they behave, he says, 'as if God had created them merely to eat. In Bavaria the common people eat a good deal; in Swabia they eat a great deal, in Switzerland too; but nowhere do they eat as much as in Vienna, and they seem to have attained their heart's desire when they have eaten their fill.'[8]

The importance attributed by the Viennese to the pleasures of the table seemed natural to people of the lower and middle classes, but it sometimes irritated artists, who were distressed to see their fellow-citizens too strongly drawn by material pleasures at the expense of things of the mind. The Englishman Edward Schulz describes, in the London magazine *Harmonicon*, his encounters with Beethoven in 1823. He had made long excursions on foot in the composer's company, in the neighbourhood of Baden, not far from Vienna, where Beethoven was then living; for, he tells us, 'Beethoven is a good walker and enjoys going on long expeditions, lasting several hours, especially in wild and romantic country. I have heard that he sometimes walks all night long, and that he has even stayed away from home for several days.'

They stopped to take their meal in an inn, in the open air, which delighted Beethoven; the menu, however, pleased him less. 'Viennese meals are famous throughout Europe,' writes Schulz, 'and the one which was prepared for us was so luxurious that Beethoven could not resist commenting on this waste. "Why so many different dishes?" he exclaimed. "Man sinks almost to the level of an animal when eating becomes his chief pleasure." '

Music

It was unjust to imply that the Viennese were so obsessed with food that they neglected the joys of the mind. Music has always taken first place in their minds, to such an extent that even their meals would not have satisfied them completely had they not been enlivened by the presence of a flautist, a violinist, a zither player, an improvised trio or quartet who would settle down on the lawns of the Prater itself, within hearing of the diners, and delight them with airs often borrowed from the operas of Mozart and Haydn, and later from the works of Lanner and Strauss; as for Schubert's *Lieder*, they were so closely attuned to the general sensibility, to the romantic and melancholy moods of every Viennese, that every boy or girl in Vienna whose ear was good and whose voice was true would sing them all day long, to their families' delight.

Our picture of Schubert would seem incomplete without those joyous rambles in the Vienna woods; equally, these very rambles would lose their charm without the joyful or nostalgic songs that echoed through the woods. For, as the English traveller Dr Charles Burney noted on a visit in 1773, in Vienna even the stone angels carved over the doors sing.[9]

CHAPTER THREE

THE CAPITAL OF MUSIC

In the Heart of the City—Music as a Unifying Factor—The Court Orchestra—The Cage of Nightingales—'Here Lived . . .' —Great Moments of Music—Vienna and its Musicians

---

In Vienna, music has always been something far more important than mere entertainment or even aesthetic enjoyment; it was a sort of vital necessity. And that not merely at a certain moment of its history, but during its whole lifetime; its whole character is so strongly steeped in music, pervaded and moulded by it, that the town and its musicians are inseparable from one another; they explain each other, and if the personalities of Schubert, for instance, or Johann Strauss represent in the highest degree the Viennese atmosphere to which they owe much of their character and genius, they have in return left an ineffaceable imprint on the city itself; we cannot think of Vienna without thinking at the same time of the author of the *Unfinished Symphony* or of *The Blue Danube*.

Music is indissolubly connected with Vienna, because it reaches deep into every class of society, because it has its place in every family; because it is an indispensable element in home life and in street life. Thus its effect is shown in the intimate everyday behaviour of all Viennese, and this phenomenon recurs so persistently and so enduringly, through the centuries, that we must really consider it as a constant factor in the national temperament. Other cities have known brilliant and fertile periods, when art has flowered dazzlingly, but these have been brief, like all flowerings. Thus there was one period when the Neapolitan opera set the fashion for the whole of Europe, and a virtuoso was obliged to serve his apprenticeship there if he wished to make his career in his own country. Mannheim possessed, in Mozart's day, an orchestra which was unequalled in any other country, and the Mannheim period of the composer of *The Magic Flute* was thus one of the major moments in the flowering of his genius. Dublin enjoyed, in the second half of the eighteenth century, a renown so great, and drew so large and so distinguished an audience of music lovers, that illustrious works such as Handel's Messiah were first performed there. During the romantic period there were Dresden, Düsseldorf and Hamburg, as there had been Leipzig in the days when J. S. Bach was cantor of St Thomas's church there. But when we think of these towns, they are musical capitals only in retrospect, however fine may have been the orchestras they possessed in the years following their glorious heyday, or those they still possess.

In the Heart of the City

Things are otherwise in Vienna; here, music dwells in the very heart of the city. The meanest houses, the narrowest suburban streets are imbued with it. The same is true, to some extent, of almost all German and Austrian cities, and there is no Germanic town, however small, where when you walk at evening after the din of traffic has died down, you may not hear drifting from some open window the notes of a Haydn trio or a Mozart quartet, or even a Beethoven septet performed, not without faults and weaknesses sometimes, by parents and children united by the same passion round the same music-stands. For the passion is what counts; I know that in Viennese homes the performance of a symphony arranged as a duet is not always faultless, that in a sonata, piano and violin sometimes have a scramble to reach the bottom of the page together; I realize that the poor vagrant musicians often murdered masterpieces on their fiddles, but it sometimes happened – remember Grillparzer's excellent tale, *Der Arme Spielmann* – that they were, if not actually virtuosi, at any rate reputable violinists and good flautists, who had not been fortunate enough to secure a place in some orchestra (for, though orchestras were numerous, the number of applicants for vacant places was greater still), or who, like Grillparzer's hero, preferred this life with all its risks, uncertainties and hardships to bourgeois comforts, to the security of a fixed salary and the boredom of a monotonous and commonplace existence.

To the question: which sort of music did the Viennese prefer? (and there were many sorts, from the whine of barrel organs to the admirable choral singing at the Hofmusik-kapelle) one must reply that they loved them all equally. And, in fact, the band to which hundreds of couples waltzed under the chandeliers of the Apollo ballroom, glittering like a fairy palace, was as necessary to their happiness as the trio of wind instruments that performed under the arbours of the rustic inn at Grinzing, where new wine could be tasted, or the great morning concerts of the Augarten, or the score deciphered by parents and children when the supper-table had been cleared and the instruments taken out of their cases.

Equally *necessary*: that was the essential thing. For each hour of the day, every circumstance of life, every emotional mood needed its own special music. Even the military bands that marched at the head of those fine glittering regiments, wearing Chinese hats with many-coloured plumes and tinkling bells; the silver drums, stamped with the Emperor's initials and borne by a white horse that pranced to the rhythm of the march; the big drum of the infantry regiment, standing on a little cart drawn by a lively pony which followed the trombones and tubas – all these delighted the populace and the connoisseur alike, for the scores of these marches were often signed by famous names, and, after all, military music has its own objects and its own emotive power, just like church music. Or like tavern music, I would add, if I were not afraid of seeming disrespectful; and, because only good music existed in eighteenth and nineteenth century Vienna, people did not get their pleasure from vulgar or crudely sentimental tunes. And that for the simple reason that Viennese music, whether that of Mozart, Schubert, Lanner or Strauss, has never ceased to draw inspiration from popular sources.

In the whole history of Vienna and its music there has

never been that deplorable rift which elsewhere, with few exceptions, has always formed between the people and the so-called élite. In certain countries and at certain periods this rift has become irreparable, for the purveyors of music who supplied the needs of the people have deliberately striven to debase their taste, on the idiotic and criminal pretext that 'it's good enough for the masses'. The élite of music lovers, on the other hand, have withdrawn into a hermetic art that confers on the rare listeners who can appreciate it the comforting conviction of being among the elect.

Nothing of the sort ever happened in Vienna; artistic snobbery was as non-existent there as was social snobbery. Such a thing was out of the question during the fortunate period with which we are concerned, when Vienna lived cheerfully under the easy sway of its emperors; snobbery is a result of democratic régimes, and was used by the bourgeoisie to compensate for the aristocratic titles it lacked. Just as a prince is always perfectly simple, accessible to all and friendly to all, a great nobleman knows nothing of snobbery which creates artificial, arbitrary barriers between the different categories of society. It is an undeniable fact that music was one of the most potent factors giving unity and homogeneity to the people of Vienna, who included the Imperial family as well as the suburban artisan. When milliners' assistants and young clerks could go and waltz at the Palace, when Archdukes dined more or less incognito at rustic inns in the Viennese forest, and, when the time came to settle their bill, were forced to confess that they had no money, since Highnesses do not need to carry cash in their pockets, then was the reign of true democracy founded on mutual sympathy and trust, and not on envy, hatred and fear.

It is a remarkable phenomenon that bad music did not exist in Vienna, nor indeed in any other European town, at this period; music was more or less sophisticated, more or less scholarly, more or less easily understood by those who could not play an instrument or read a score – and there were few such in Vienna – but, however popular a work might be in inspiration, composition or performance, it was still good music. It was good even if it was popular – perhaps

particularly if it was popular. Music is only bad if it is deliberately contrived in a spirit of vulgarity or pretentiousness, and
thus imposes on the people something alien to their true
taste. Note with what spontaneity and harmonious perfection
classical and popular music are associated and combined in
the work of those typical Austrian composers, Mozart and
Schubert. They are accessible to all because they speak the
language of the heart, which is always the same in all men;
and if there are different Mozarts and different Schuberts,
according to the listener's degree of musical taste and his
capacity for discovering and understanding the reasons of
genius, connoisseurs and the great mass of instinctive lovers
of music are deeply at one in the shared experience of
listening.

Music as a Unifying Factor

It is by no means paradoxical to assert that, at a period when
the court was still governed by the strictest and most repressive etiquette in the Spanish tradition, and in a city
where the common people, though exceptionally good-
natured, well-behaved and civilized, could be touchy where
their independence was concerned and, when the occasion
arose, disrespectful towards authority, music was – even
more than their attachment to the Hapsburg monarchy and
far more than the dynastic principle – the principal factor
making for unity in the social and political life of the Viennese.

If we turn for a moment from the particular half-century
we are studying to the present day, we see that the reopening
of the Vienna Opera House, the destruction of which was
part of the irreparable damage done to this loveliest of cities
during the war of 1939–45, was celebrated as a real national
festival, an event that was magnificent, solemn and joyful at
the same time, in which everyone participated as in a family
festivity, as if the Opera had been the city's safeguard and its
reconstruction were the pledge of an era of prosperity, peace
and joy. I am certain that such a thing could happen only
in Germanic countries – save perhaps at Milan, with its
Scala. In that immense crowd, as they stood devoutly rapt,
moved even to tears, experiencing the shared emotion of

love for their city and for music while listening to *Fidelio* being broadcast from loudspeakers at every street-corner of the brilliantly illuminated city, which seemed to have become a vast concert hall, there may have been some who had never been to the Opera and perhaps would never go there; but they felt certain, and rightly so, that the Opera belonged to them, because it was the shrine of music, just as St Stephen's cathedral was the shrine of religion. Even the Viennese who do not go to Mass consider that St Stephen's belongs to them, as the ancient cradle of Viennese Christianity, as much as if they went every day to hear Matins and Vespers there.

We have already noted to what complex aspects of the Viennese character this unanimous passion for music corresponds, what qualities and also what defects of that city it satisfies. But the dominant feature is this: music is never superimposed on the life of the people, as it often is elsewhere, in France or in England for instance, despite the great number of music lovers in those countries and the remarkable quality of the music to be heard there.

Each time the Paris Opéra has been burnt down, which has occurred several times in the course of its history, its resurrection from the ashes has never assumed the importance of an unforgettable date in the city's history, and I do not suppose that Londoners have felt more strongly about Covent Garden. In Vienna, on the contrary, the absence of the Opera – or the makeshift means by which this absence was more or less made good – seemed a national bereavement. No one who really knows the Austrians can imagine Vienna ceasing to be at the head of European music, and we shall see a fresh proof of this in the fact that the prodigious revolution which has renewed the whole of modern music – the invention of serial music, the twelve-tone scale – was born in Vienna, with Schönberg, Alban Berg and Webern.

The 'Court Orchestra'

In the eighteenth and nineteenth centuries, and right up to the fall of the Empire, the seat and summit of Viennese musical culture was to be found in the Hofmusikkapelle, or

Court Orchestra, which combined all the elements of a church choir, a symphony orchestra, a lyric theatre, and a conservatorium. That is to say, it gathered together all the artists who took part in the religious ceremonies of the Imperial chapel, who played during meals, at feasts and balls, who gave private or public concerts and who accompanied operas. At the same time gifted children who could sing and play one or more instruments were accepted there, to complete their musical training by taking part in the performances given by virtuosi. There were a number of 'music colleges' but this one was famous, and justly renowned for the quality of its teaching. Here certain great musicians, notably Schubert, acquired not indeed the rudiments of their art, for only advanced and talented students were admitted to the Hofmusikkapelle, but the major principles, at any rate, which were to perfect their technical and theoretical musicianship.

The Hofmusikkapelle was one of the finest and most fruitful creations of the Hapsburg passion for music. It was founded as far back as the reign of Maximilian I who, in 1498, laid down the rules of the institution, and entrusted the directorship to the organist Georg Slakonia. The Hofmusikkapelle played so important a part thenceforward in the life of Vienna and the court that Albrecht Dürer includes it in the set of wood engravings representing *The Triumph of Maximilian*. He depicts the choristers grouped round their masters Slakonia and Ludwig Senfl, riding on a splendidly decorated chariot, while on another chariot the organist Paul Hofaimer is shown seated at his organ while an assistant blows the bellows.

The poet Wolfgang Schmelzel, who taught in the Scottish convent, composed in 1548 an ode in praise of Vienna in which he pays great tribute to the Hofmusikkapelle. 'I praise Vienna,' he writes, 'above all the cities of this country, because of the profusion of singers and instrumentalists who may be heard there, come from all parts of the kingdom and often indeed from abroad. Nowhere, assuredly, are so many musicians gathered together.' The court orchestra was a small one to begin with, particularly as compared with the ever-increasing number of instrumentalists and singers summoned thither subsequently by Ferdinand III, Leopold I, Joseph I and Joseph II.

Conceived of originally as a choir school for sacred and secular music, this 'chapel' – the name itself shows the ecclesiastical origin of the institution – consisted of forty-seven singers, plus twenty-four children; the orchestra was limited to a brass ensemble, plus six trumpets and timpani. The organ played a preponderant rôle, as was to be expected at a period when the Netherlandish school of organists were the leaders of musical culture even in Vienna.

The cult of music, natural to the Viennese, was further fostered in each successive generation thanks to the material and moral support given by music-loving sovereigns. The princes, the Empress, the Emperor himself spent several hours each day studying one or more instruments. These illustrious personages were not mere dilettanti, half-hearted amateurs; their teachers had given them a serious, almost professional training. Ferdinand I, for instance, although a passionate addict of the chase, devoted a great deal of time to music, under the direction of the Italian Valentini, who had been appointed Director of the Hofmusikkapelle in 1619. Valentini aroused the Emperor's keen hostility to the Netherlandish style, and a strong liking for Italian opera; this was the period when Imperial princes married Italian princesses, spoke Italian, and went to Italy to complete their cultural education. Ferdinand III, successor to Ferdinand II, wrote poetry in Italian and founded a literary Academy on the model of those existing in the peninsula.

The Emperor's brother, the Archduke Leopold Wilhelm, knew that he could pay no finer tribute to Ferdinand III than by writing, in an Italian poem composed in his honour: 'His sceptre rests on the lyre and on the sword.' This conjunction of material strength with the spiritual strength represented by music is characteristic of the Austrian monarchy, and it was to remain the finest tradition of the Hofburg until the middle of the nineteenth century. Whatever may have been the merits of Ferdinand III as a composer of oratorios and operas, which are by no means worthless and indeed show real originality, we must hold it against him that he

65

caused a cleavage between *serious* and *popular* music through the very measures he took to protect musicians, showing his hostility to those whom he called 'mendicant musicians' who had not been trained in musical colleges nor subjected to the sound discipline of the Hofmusik.

Leopold I, under whose reign were waged the Turkish wars that led to the siege of Vienna, suffered from a typically 'baroque' form of melancholy – that of Hamlet or of Sigismond in *La Vida es Sueño* – and he might have said, like Shakespeare's Jessica, 'I am never merry when I hear sweet music.' He loved sad music, to suit his mood, which did not prevent him from enjoying magnificent shows at the opera, which had grown increasingly spectacular, nor from having a vast and splendid theatre built by the great baroque architect Burnacini and equipped with the most ingenious machinery. His taste for the grandiose is seen, too, in the material expansion of the 'chapel' which under his reign reached the figure, never surpassed since, of a hundred singers and two hundred instrumentalists.

At the beginning of the eighteenth century the 'chapel' was still under the almost exclusive domination of Italian composers and executants; Joseph I, who came to the throne in 1706, made no alteration in this respect to what had been done since the musical hegemony of Italy had taken root at court, under Ferdinand II. Joseph I was the most richly and variously gifted of all this dynasty of artistic rulers. He was an advanced student of mathematics, he had been initiated into architecture by the great builder of 'modern', i.e. post-siege, Vienna, Fischer von Erlach, and had worked with him on the plans for Schönbrunn. The music he wrote clearly shows the influence of Alessandro Scarlatti, which was then dominant throughout Europe, but that was no bad thing. According to contemporary witnesses he 'played the harpsichord to perfection, was a skilful flautist and performed with such excellence on various other instruments that professionals could not display more art, and they had only one advantage over him, that of being able to practise all day when they wanted to.'[1]

This was not mere courtiers' flattery. Even when they

could not give up their whole day to music, overburdened as they were by the responsibilities of power, the tyranny of etiquette and court life, the Austrian sovereigns spent several hours each day working at their singing and their instruments. From sheer love of music, not from vanity, and from a conviction that, however good a listener one may be, there is always something lacking when one is unable to perform. Thus Charles VI never missed a concert or an operatic performance, given at the Hofburg or at his favourite castle, the Favorita; and it often happened, according to Apostolo Zeno, that he would go up to the music desk and conduct the orchestra from the harpsichord, as was the custom in those days, to the great wonder of the audience, who admired his professional skill. He also accompanied his daughters, the Archduchesses Maria Theresa and Maria Anna, when they sang.

The welcome given by the Empress Maria Theresa and her court to the child Mozart, when he came to Vienna for the first time, proves how much this devotion to music was transmitted from one generation to the next, from one reign to the next, to the time of Ferdinand I who, as his portraits show, had a piano in his study next to his desk. This was one of the finest traditions of the monarchy, one of the happiest examples set by parents for their children to follow, and it is small wonder that even apart from the natural disposition of the Austrian people this example set in the highest places conferred on music an exceptional position among the occupations and passions of the Viennese.

The Cage of Nightingales

Moreover, the Hofmusikkapelle was not the only conservatorium where virtuosi or merely good musicians were trained. There was also the Stadtkonvikt, where a large number of musically gifted children were maintained and educated at the expense of the city; they received an eclectic education, just as in a school, but with the chief emphasis on vocal and instrumental music. This institution – not unlike the 'charity conservatoria' so numerous in Italy in the eighteenth century, particularly at Naples and Venice, and known by the charming name of 'nightingales' cages' – was intended to enable poor children to enjoy a complete musical training free, with all their needs supplied.

The Konvikt formed part of the University; it was housed in a dark and dreary building, a former Jesuit college, secularized when Joseph II expelled the order; but on summer days, when the windows were open, such floods of harmony poured forth from it that passers-by stopped to listen with delight to voices and instruments. It soon became a regular concert, and neighbours and tradesmen brought out chairs to enable music-lovers to listen at their ease.

The pupils of the Konvikt wore a half-civilian, half-military uniform, somewhat like that worn by members of the Imperial riding-school, which enjoyed exclusive possession of the wonderful white horses from the stud at Lipizza: a black tail-coat cut like a modern dress-coat, but adorned with epaulettes, black waistcoat, white cravat, white breeches, and a two-pointed cocked hat which some of them wore jauntily a little on one side. On leaving the Konvikt these children immediately found work in an orchestra, which was a very precious advantage.

At this period, when public concerts were still very rare – they did not really begin until the reign of Joseph II – people only listened to the music that they made themselves, or that they paid an orchestra to play for them. No doubt there was a good deal of proud emulation in the zeal with which the great nobles vied with the Hofburg and with one another in possessing the largest orchestras, the best companies of actors and ballet dancers, which they maintained, with selfish vanity, for the sole benefit of themselves and their guests. We read in the correspondence of the day that on their periodic visits to Vienna to pay court to the Emperor and take part in official festivities, these great nobles also brought their musicians; it is well known what quarrels ensued between Mozart, who lacked Haydn's docility, and the Prince Archbishop of Salzburg, who was less of a gentleman than Prince Esterhazy.

An exaggeratedly gloomy picture is often painted of the humiliating position of 'domestic' artists with respect to their patrons; we tend to forget that it was the only chance they had of enjoying a secure position with a regular salary, and the possibility of composing without being subject to the risks of material success or failure. If they ate at the servants' table, which was actually the secretaries', and not at their masters', this implied no shame, for the equality of classes had not yet been laid down as a dogma by the Declaration of the Rights of Man, and the people by whose side the musicians dined were no doubt quite as good as those who sat under the glittering chandeliers in the lords' banqueting hall.

It also happened very frequently that, from love of music as much as from delicacy of feeling and good manners, these noble patrons endeavoured by their kindness to diminish the gap and to treat as equals these subordinates who were so much their superiors.

The Austrian nobility of the eighteenth century and the first half of the nineteenth, illustrious by its rank and ancient lineage, has won enduring fame chiefly by its relations with the artists it employed. The families of Lobkowitz, Schwarzenberg, Esterhazy, Lichnowsky are known today above all through their relations with Mozart, Haydn or Beethoven, and the memory of the Russian Ambassador Razumovsky would probably not have been perpetuated were it not enshrined in Beethoven's dedication of his famous quartets to that diplomat.

The honourable welcome given to artists in the most exclusive aristocratic salons is shown by the rôle played in the life of Beethoven by Countess Thun, Count Fries and Countess Deyn. It was in the latter's palace that he met Theresa von Brunswick, who was to be his 'Immortal Beloved', and Giulia Guicciardi, to whom he dedicated the C minor sonata. His biographers are not in agreement, however, as to the identity of the 'immortal beloved'. Besides the traditionally accepted name of Theresa von Brunswick, those of her sisters Giulietta Guicciardi and Josephine von Brunswick have been suggested, as well as the singer Amalie Schald, Theresa Malfati and others . . . As if it mattered!

'Here Lived . . .'

Excellent concerts were also given in the *salons* of the upper middle class, who had attained an increasingly important social position, comparable to that of the aristocracy, between the reign of Maria Theresa and that of Ferdinand I. Doctors were among the leading Maecenases in the musical world, beginning with the celebrated Dr Mesmer, the discoverer of animal magnetism and the owner of splendid gardens in the neighbourhood of Vienna where on a fine summer's night, Mozart's *Bastien and Bastienne* was first performed in an open-air theatre inaugurated for the occasion. Dr Genzinger, Dr Frank, and particularly the Empress's physician Van Swieten, who possessed an extremely rich library of music, all entertained the most renowned performers and composers.

Excellent music was also to be heard at the homes of the botanist Jacquin, Mozart's friend, the printer Trattner, the lawyer Sonnleithner, whom Schubert visited constantly, and finally of certain publishers, responsible for printing the scores of composers, who were thus both their guests and their clients: men like Coppi and Artaria played a more important part than is generally believed in the life of Viennese music and musicians.

In spite of the transformations brought about in the middle of the nineteenth century by the modernization of the city and the piercing of the Rings, and in the present century by the appalling destruction due to the second world war, the presence of the great musicians of the past is still manifest today in the houses where they used to live. One can scarcely ramble through the streets of the inner city or its suburbs without coming across one of these houses which one might indeed call hallowed, where the presence of genius still lingers.

These are the homes of Haydn, Mozart, Wagner, Liszt, Weber, Schubert and Beethoven, and Beethoven's are the most numerous, for the composer's sombre temperament, his anxiety and that perpetual dissatisfaction which haunted him wherever he went impelled him to move house constantly. If we were to map the homes of famous musicians on the plan of the city, we should be surprised to note what a wide variety of dwellings they had, although they chose for preference some suburb or village where they could find what they longed for above all: communion with Nature.

Great Moments of Music

The great moments of music which are the glory of Vienna are innumerable, and the immortal masterpieces created there form part of her artistic diadem, even if, as often happens, the composer was too far in advance of his time to reap the unanimous applause of the public, which is invariably conservative. These great moments are those in which something authentically new is achieved in music, some form of expression revealing undiscovered paths.

We may instance the operas of Gluck which were given for the first time at the Hofburg Theatre, *Orfeo* in its original Italian version on October 5, 1762, and *Alcestis* in 1767 on the same stage; Mozart's *Magic Flute*, in Schikaneder's theatre, the Theater auf der Wieden, which, according to a contemporary, was a 'long rectangular building looking like a huge box'; *Fidelio*, on November 20, 1805, at the Theater an der Wien, at which Beethoven conducted from the piano to a scanty audience, the French army having just occupied the Imperial capital; Haydn's *Seasons* in April 1801, as warmly applauded as his *Creation* had been three years earlier, in April 1798, at the Schwarzenberg Palace.

Another great moment was the production of *Lohengrin* in May 1861, which was immensely successful. 'These enthusiastic and uninterrupted ovations,' Richard Wagner wrote, 'have been given me only by the public of Vienna.' Wagner was very fond of Vienna; he had come there for the first time when he was only nineteen, and had felt at home there. 'Vienna,' he wrote, 'meant to me, for a long time, creative activity; the musical and dramatic impressions I received there certainly had an enduring effect upon my mind.'

Other musicians, on the contrary, felt lost and unhappy there because their own character did not harmonize with that of the town and its population, because there existed a contradiction between the nature of their art and genius on the one hand, and the musical taste of the Viennese on the other.

Such misunderstanding is clearly shown during Robert Schumann's two visits to Vienna, which brought him nothing but disappointment, bitterness, the failure of his dearest dreams. He loved the town itself and the countryside, when he saw it for the first time in September 1838. He notes in his Journal:

'Vienna and the spire of its St Stephen's Cathedral, its lovely women and its luxury, Vienna enfolded by the winding Danube, which flows through a plain that rises by degrees towards ever higher mountains, Vienna which calls to mind the greatest German masters, must be a fruitful soil for the musician's imagination. When I looked down at the city from the hilltops I thought of Beethoven, who must often have raised his eyes towards the distant outline of the Alps, and of Mozart gazing pensively down the river, of Haydn shaking his head as he marvelled at the dizzy height of St Stephen's spire. The Danube, the spire of St. Stephen's, and the chain of the Alps in the distance, these are an epitome of Vienna. As I listen to Schubert's symphony I picture the city again, and I can understand how such works may be born in such a setting.'

Schumann was quite prepared to be on good terms with this charming town and to settle down there, provided he could find a means of livelihood. He had come on the advice of Chamisso, in spite of the reservations of his friend Councillor Vesque von Püttlingen, who was more sceptical regarding the welcome that Austrian music-lovers would give the fiery romanticism of the Saxon composer, whom even his compatriots, more genuinely 'romantic' than the Viennese, did not always understand and seldom appreciated. And in fact Schumann soon changed his opinion. 'Here they only like facile music, old familiar tunes, songs and dances, serious music is not at all to their taste.' At this period, it is true, the craze for the waltz had swept over the population; Johann Strauss was their idol, and crowds flocked into the huge glittering ballrooms, neglecting concert halls and the pathetic, anguished, disquieting music, so essentially un-Viennese, of this alien, who felt increasingly alien to them.

Schumann returned to Vienna a few years later, with his wife Clara Wieck, who gave concerts there; he still hoped to be appointed teacher at the Conservatorium, which would have provided him with a regular salary, the dream of all poor musicians in those days . . . But Vienna adored Meyerbeer, that empty, turgid, superficial composer whom Schumann had abused in his musical journal, and Meyerbeer was there, he was invited to everybody's drawing-room, and was most likely taking his revenge by denigrating the as yet unknown composer. Moreover Clara's concerts did not have the hoped-for success; the first barely covered its costs, for the second the hall was empty, and the following concerts only attracted an audience because Jenny Lind, the Swedish nightingale, took part in them.

Schumann therefore gave up the idea of settling down in a city which clearly did not want him – the city which gave a triumphal welcome to Weber, whose *Euryanthe* was performed with immense success in 1823, which greeted Liszt with rapture and which was to offer Brahms, in 1862, the refuge where he was to spend the rest of his life. It has been pointed out that public taste had changed, especially since the period of the Congress, which impoverished the city while giving it the illusion of prosperity, and which altered its way of life profoundly. 'The upper classes of society clung obstinately to the ways of the old régime, according to the tone set by Metternich, and thought it good policy to proclaim their predilection for the ideology of the Holy Alliance,' wrote Jean Chantavoine and Jean Gaudefroy-Demombynes.[2] Far from drawing closer to the masses, they created a gulf between them. The only ground on which music lovers of all sorts were united was the revival of Italianism. Bauernfeld, quoted by Ehrhardt, notes in his Journal the verdict current in Viennese drawing-rooms in 1816: 'Mozart and Beethoven were old pedants, the older generation were fools to enjoy them; until Rossini came we did not know what melody could be. *Fidelio* is rubbish; how can one bear to endure such boring stuff?'

There have always been, there will always be insensitive, pretentious fools who condemn what they are incapable of appreciating and loving, but it is hard to believe that the delicate taste of the Viennese had degenerated so far. The Italianism that reigned in the thirties was a recrudescence of that which inspired the Court Opera until the reforms of Gluck. Salieri was set up against Mozart; Schumann saw those whom he scornfully dubbed 'canaries' preferred to him; Liszt was admired for his talents as a virtuoso pianist rather than for his compositions. The transformations which took place in social classes, as we shall see later, as a result of the Napoleonic wars, the advent of the bourgeoisie, the development of industry, the hegemony of financiers, are all reflected in the alterations of musical taste.

The drawing-rooms in which 'music-making' went on during and after the Congress were no longer those of princely palaces but of bourgeois mansions. That is not to say that the music played there was inferior, nor the audience necessarily less qualified. The bankers Wurth and Fellner were among the first to offer their guests Beethoven's *Eroica* Symphony, and the musical soirées of other financiers, such as Pereira, Arnstein, Geymüller or Henikstein, attracted the élite of connoisseurs at the very beginning of the nineteenth century, and far more some thirty years later. Many artists, writers and high officials were to be met at Wertheimstein the financier's, as well as at Hammer-Purgstall the oriental-ist's or Prokesch-Osten's, or Privy Councillor Kiesenwetter's. Konrad Graf the piano manufacturer, a stout, clumsy man with a massive face, heavy in appearance but with a subtle mind and delicate tastes, invited the most famous pianists to perform upon his instruments. The same was true of the great industrialists, Schöller, Hornbostel, Arthaben, Miller-Aichholz, founders of bourgeois dynasties in which a love for music and a pride in artistic patronage were handed down from one generation to the next.

Vienna and its Musicians

It would be unjust therefore to say that Vienna had degenera-ted, and no longer deserved to be called the capital of music; the inevitable changes in the taste of its people do not entitle us to consider them as insensitive Philistines. If the advent

74

of the bourgeoisie marks the decline, if not the disappearance, of the aristocratic refinement of earlier days, this was a general phenomenon in all countries at that period, an inevitable trend towards democratization. Some critics have quite rightly stressed the benefits of aristocratic patronage in the eighteenth century, but it must be recognized that for all their sympathetic attitude these noble patrons were not always generous enough to their musicians to spare them the anxiety which money problems inevitably arouse in those who should not have to be concerned with them. Although he was fêted in princely salons, Beethoven was never well off and died in semi-penury.

When we study the life and works of Viennese musicians – and I mean by Viennese those who made their career in Vienna even if, like Beethoven, they were not born there – one may wonder whether that city was as much of a paradise for artists as it has been and still is for amateurs and music-lovers. In other words: has Vienna always proved worthy of the presence of the men of genius who have lived within her walls? Has she recognized them, encouraged and supported them adequately? Has this capital of music not proved, for many musicians, an unhappy place because they found neither the understanding, nor the sympathy, nor the material support which they needed, humanly and financially, in order to create?

To reply to this question one would have to study biographies anew, to establish a balance between what such artists have received from Vienna and what they have given her, one would have to take this opportunity of asserting and repeating that whatever the success enjoyed by a true artist, he always gives infinitely more than he receives; let concert audiences remember this, when they think that by paying for their seats and applauding they have discharged their debt towards the musicians, which is above all a debt of gratitude.

Did Vienna show herself worthy of Mozart? She allowed him to wilt away in a penury that exhausted his strength and hastened his premature death. The perpetual requests for money addressed by the composer to his friends at Salzburg

75

and his brother Masons, that constant and agonizing need for money that harassed him right up to the hour of his death; the pauper's hearse that bore his body to the common grave, the wretched expedients to which he had recourse in order to live, seem to prove that Vienna could not or would not provide him with that minimal livelihood which would have secured him peace of mind and allowed him to work in peace.

The perpetual neediness of the Mozart household was due less to Constanze's frivolous caprices, which were not exorbitant, as to the meanness of the families who paid him an absurdly low fee for his lessons, the indifference of the public who let his operas be failures or semi-failures, the dishonesty of publishers who cheated him of his royalties when, with his usual carelessness in money matters, he had neglected to make sure of them by duly signed contracts. And who was better fitted than Mozart to win the admiration and devotion of the whole people of Vienna, who none the less preferred Salieri and Martin y Soler and other composers vastly his inferiors?

On the other hand, composer and city were in perfect harmony in the mutual love match between Vienna and Franz Schubert; the two are so inseparable that one can scarcely imagine Schubert being born or working elsewhere than in Vienna, or the musical history of Vienna without Schubert. Why is this? Because it happened by some miraculous conjunction that a composer expressed the very spirit of a city, its nature, its character, its appearance, with a spontaneous genius of exceptional freshness, with the simplicity which sometimes conceals genius, a state of grace granted only to the elect, to the pure in heart. A few bars of Schubert are enough to call up some picture of Vienna, the courtyard of a suburban house with its wooden balconies and climbing plants, or a country pleasure-garden with its arbours full of singing-birds and the blue outline of the distant mountains, those distances which are so dear to the romantic imagination.

Johann Strauss, too, personified Vienna, but at a transient moment of her history only: the Vienna of the vast ballrooms of 1820 and the frenzy of the waltz, spurred on by the diabolical violins of Hungarian or gipsy bands. He does not represent the enduring element in Vienna; he is too much of his time to be for all time, and the distance between the father and the son, Johann Strauss I whose waltzes were meant to be danced to, and Johann Strauss II, whose waltzes were meant to be listened to, proves how much closer the second King of the Waltz was than his predecessor to the constant factor in Austrian life, even to the point of becoming a symphonic composer.

Johann Strauss stands for dancing Vienna, but Schubert stands for Vienna in love, Vienna enraptured by the sunshine, Vienna in joyful or tender mood, her emotions quickly stirred, her sorrows quickly comforted. But Schubert is a very great musician and far more than merely a Viennese musician; he is universal like all men of genius, and his character is as complex and as full of contrasts as any man's. His personality appears superficial only to those who fail to plumb its depths and are satisfied with a hasty label, so convenient for lovers of simplification. Schubert's contemporaries, his friends themselves, Schober, Vogl, Mayrhofer, Spaun, have left such a simplified and simplifying picture of him, primarily because a whole aspect of his genius, possibly the most important, escaped them. This is shown by the astonishment, almost disillusionment, with which they heard for the first time the *Winterreise*, that cycle of *lieder* written under the sway of violent physical and moral suffering, in which the tragic Schubert who is so often neglected develops his sombre and mournful sides. His friends can surely not have been unaware of this 'dark face' of his character, despite the sensitive discretion with which he concealed it from them; only a deaf man could fail to be profoundly stirred by those dark mysterious messages which we catch so often in his piano music, his songs, his quartets and symphonies.

It may seem paradoxical to say that Schubert is unfamiliar to concert-audiences, since his works are so often played; but they are always the same works; out of the 600 *lieder* he composed how many are known – except by connoisseurs, of course – and are those most frequently heard the most important for one's knowledge of the essential man?

In his excellent book on the Viennese composer, Robert

Pitrou[3] points out quite rightly that, like Schumann, he is closely akin to the Hoffmann of the *Fantastic Tales*, where the cloudy magic of darkness abounds. He was not one of those charming unconscious geniuses who create as a bird sings; that commonplace insipid image, popularized by tradition, of a Schubert tossing off his *lieder*, humming a new melody between a couple of jokes, is far from taking into account the infinite sum of anguish and suffering which was in him and which finds expression in his music. In the first place, he foresaw that he would not live long, and he died at the age of thirty-one. And he was twenty when he wrote in his friend Hüttenbrenner's album: 'Nature has allotted us a limited span of days, but an immense span of glory.' Beethoven recognized in him the divine spark, and the youth himself knew what he was called to do when he said: 'I am only in this world to write music.'*

Like Schumann, who admired him so much and called him 'my one and only Schubert', he might have written that 'to compose means to enter the kingdom of dreams'. But for him, and in this he was truly of Vienna, there was no contradiction between the world of dreams and the world of reality. The simple pleasures that delighted him, country rambles, evenings spent round a few bottles of wine or a bowl of punch, not for the sake of getting drunk but to give a keener edge to the joys of friendship, in company with a few good friends, gay, exuberant, affectionate, talented – these were enough; the petulant, tender-hearted little fellow, who had been nicknamed 'little mushroom', asked nothing more, save indeed love, in which he always showed himself over-timid, diffident, always enamoured and always undecided.

He had loved Therese Grob, daughter of a baker who wanted a wealthier son-in-law than this needy, unknown

---

* 'Those who only know Schubert through his legend – which is expressed nowadays through films, operettas and romantic biographies – see him as a creature of sentiment, naïve, pure and somewhat foolish, a sort of Parsifal of the *lied*, in short a heavenly simpleton who produced his melodies as a tree bears its fruit. No doubt Schubert, as a man, had the virtue of humility. He sought out neither worldly fame nor honours and preferred family affections or the joys of intimacy to everything that satisfies vanity.' – Marcel Schneider, *Schubert* (Paris, Editions du Seuil, 1957).

musician. He had resigned himself to giving her up, although their love was mutual. As he told Hüttenbrenner, 'for three years she hoped that I was going to marry her, but I was unable to find a job which would be adequate to support us both. Then, at her parents' wish, she married another, and this was a great grief to me. I still love her and since then no other has ever pleased me as well or better. It seems that she was not destined to be mine.'

These few sentences teach us a great deal about the character of Schubert, too timid to overcome the obstacles dividing him from the woman he loved, and too much obsessed by his genius, too, not to consider that music came before everything and deserved the sacrifice of his love. Here, too, we find the proof that, even for an artist who had already acquired a certain fame in musical circles, Vienna could not provide a means of livelihood that would enable him to get married. Like Mozart, like Beethoven, Schubert was always short of money, not that his tastes were extravagant, poor fellow! but because the position of artists without private means was always risky and difficult. The compulsion of having painfully to earn their daily bread tormented these great artists till the day of their death. The public is always more or less ungrateful, particularly towards men of genius, less accessible than the mediocrities who enjoy all its favours, and the public of Vienna was ungrateful too, unconsciously, through carelessness, and because the lighter music was the more the public liked it. Beethoven had already complained of this to the critic Rellstab, a poet and the author of certain lines set to music by Schubert in his *Schwanengesang*: 'Since the Italians have taken such a hold here, the best art is in jeopardy. The nobility has no eyes for anything but ballet, no feeling for anything save race-horses and dancing-girls.'

If popular favour and wealth were denied to Schubert, who in any case did not seek them, he enjoyed on the other hand the greatest delights that friendship can offer. He radiated friendliness, and one of his close acquaintances said that all his friends loved one another in Schubert. Their affection for him was so great that on the day of his death one threw himself out of the window, wanting to die with him. Sociable by nature, like a good Viennese who loves the company of his fellows and is happy in a café, in the street, wherever there are crowds, Schubert dreaded solitude, for there he would meet again his anxieties, his nostalgia, his sufferings. His gaiety revived in the company of his friends, and he would dazzle them by his talent, his wit, his good-natured mischief, his kindliness. Thus he loved to spend his evenings where he knew he would meet the poets and painters, singers and actors whom he liked to have around him. 'They were a band of joyful youngsters,' wrote Dahms, 'who got all the pleasure they could from life in the good old Imperial city. An exuberant zest for living helped them to rise above the trivialities of existence. What united them was not only their common awareness of the rich harvest germinating and blossoming within them; their enthusiasm for art and science was what, in spite of the diversity of their minds, linked their hearts together by the strongest of bonds.'

Thus the young Viennese élite of the twenties, closer perhaps to the people than to the 'upper classes' of society, although several of them belonged to the aristocracy or the *grande bourgeoisie*, dreamed of the glittering future awaiting their talent. It was there, in some pretty rustic inn or in the white-and-gilt rooms of city cafés, that the real spirit of Vienna dwelt, that musical spirit which errors of taste – if an excessive predilection for things Italian can be so called – never completely perverted.

That Vienna gave birth to Franz Schubert would in itself be a title to fame, even if she did not always provide him with the means to work in peace, untroubled by cares. Perhaps Schubert's glory needed, for its completion, the halo of an early death. No other town would have given him the atmosphere his personality required and although genius is independent enough to develop anywhere, when the wind of the spirit blows, we cannot imagine the composer of the *Winterreise* in Paris, Milan, London, Dresden or Berlin, however much these capitals may be entitled to call themselves, too, capitals of music. The air of Vienna was indispensable to Schubert as it was to Schwind, to Stifter, to

Grillparzer. 'No other music speaks of the Austrian landscape, reflects the Austrian sky to such a degree,' writes
Annette Kolb.[4] This intimate alliance with music is the key
to the problem of Schubert, for there is such a problem.
Fate is kind, even when it allots suffering, if it lets an artist
be rooted in the milieu when his genius can best prosper.
Even though one should not carry too far Taine's theory of
'the milieu' as applied to the typical Viennese artists of the
early nineteenth century, the 'stars' of Austrian painting,
Austrian poetry, Austrian fiction, Austrian music – Schwind,
Grillparzer, Stifter, Schubert – one cannot deny that they
would not have been what they were, what they had to be, if
chance had forced them to live anywhere but in Vienna.

CHAPTER FOUR

THE THEATRE

---

*Schikaneder's ideas—Literary Drama and Popular Drama—
The 'Burgtheater'—Realism on the Stage—Nestroy and
Satirical Drama—Raimund and Poetic Drama*

It was a great day for Vienna when the amazing Emmanuel
Schikaneder, whose immortal fame rests on his share in the
libretto of *The Magic Flute*, came to settle in the capital.
This ingenious impresario had grasped precisely what sort of
theatrical performance appealed most to the Viennese: that
blend of music and fairy pantomime, or music-hall, which
was to bring fame to a producer who had started his career
amidst poor vagrant musicians. Schikaneder, once he had
grown rich and famous, described this existence, with all its
hazards and hardships, in an operetta called *The Merry
Beggars*. And indeed the actor's lot was a hard one in those
days, when there were no theatrical buildings and no regular
performances, and when companies set up their stage for a
few days, or a few hours, in some inn yard to give their shows.

Schikaneder's Ideas

These companies had excellent material in them; the actors
had to display a variety of talents, for their repertory included
drama and comedy, opera and operetta, even farce . . . and
each had to play a multiplicity of rôles. Since a new show
was put on every night an actor had to be able to sing, dance,
spout tragic tirades, or keep his end up in a knockabout act;
Schikaneder was celebrated for the *brio* with which he played
juvenile leads, noble fathers, tragic heroes and comic yokels.

Schikaneder knew what the public wanted, and he supplied
it; he was above all a man of the theatre. To those who
reproached him with his use of facile 'effects', which always

82

impress the gallery, he replied: 'My sole aim is to work for the box-office and to see what is most effective on the stage, so as to fill both the house and the cash-box.' Knowing the public's love of variety and amusement, this innovator of genius devised sumptuous sets that gave an illusion of reality by the use of machinery and huge crowds.

When he put on Miller's drama *Count Waltron* he added marching troops and battle scenes which were doubtless compatible with the subject but which the author had probably not demanded nor even imagined, accompanied by stage music with all the effects of a military fanfare. He arranged all this so skilfully that 'at some moments the music seemed to come from very far off, then suddenly rang out from behind the curtain, startling the spectators and creating around them that atmosphere of terror and anxiety which befitted Miller's somewhat gloomy play.'[1] This did not prevent him from including in his repertory the great romantic dramas of the time, the works of Lessing and Schiller, Shakespeare's plays and even Voltaire's *Semiramis*.

With these great authors he probably hesitated to take such liberties as he did with a drama by Torring, *Agnes Bernauer*. The actor Wellerschenk, who played the villain, Vicedom, had entered so thoroughly into his part and played it so convincingly that he incurred insults in the street and was almost massacred in a tavern, so closely did the public identify him with the character he played. The most effective scene was one in which Agnes was thrown over a bridge and drowned. One evening the spectators could no longer bear to see the innocent victim's death and they began to shout: 'Save her; drown Vicedom.' Faced with this tumult, Schikaneder, who would do anything for the sake of peace and popularity, came on to the stage and announced that that evening as a special concession to the public, Vicedom would be drowned instead of the lovely Agnes, which won him cheers and applause.

Schikaneder inaugurated the heyday of the Viennese theatre by his unfailing instinct for what the public wanted. He put on fine plays: *The Brigands*, *The Barber of Seville*, *King Lear*, *Othello*, *Hamlet*, *Romeo and Juliet*, *Clavigo*,

Minna von Barnhelm, but he always managed to produce something spectacular by his insistence on stage settings. For Johann Ewald's drama *The Death of Baldur* he produced a 'ride of the Valkyries' of astonishing ingenuity, and for *The Great Provost* he showed the astounded audience a tournament on an island.

Open-air spectacles provided an opportunity for manoeuvring crowds of 'extras'. He staged *Count Waltron* with cavalry charges, a camp with two hundred tents, and such a huge company of actors that they apparently outnumbered the spectators. He even composed an operetta in which the principal character was a balloon, piloted by its inventor Lutgendorf, who (unfortunately for the box-office) never succeeded in taking off.

The master-stroke of this daring and inventive producer was his association with Mozart in the composition of *The Magic Flute*, with fantastic Egyptian settings which probably impressed the audience far more than did the music itself.[2] He appeared in person in *The Magic Flute*, playing Papageno. He also created a quaint and delightful 'type', Stupid Anton, with which he triumphed in a play by Schack and Gerl. Anton immediately became so popular that he dethroned the Kasperle who had made Marinelli famous, vied with Kurtz's Bernardon and drove from the stage the traditional Hanswurst who had for centuries delighted the Viennese.

The Austrians were fond of recognizing themselves – in part at any rate – in some comic character, both mischievous and foolish, who simulates foolishness, perhaps, the better to practise his mischief: a buffoon in the style of Scapin, the Spanish *gracioso*, Arlecchino or Truffaldino. Born in the puppet theatre no doubt, Hanswurst inevitably featured in every performance, dramatic as well as burlesque. He brought to these an ironic wit and a rustic commonsense which made of him the critic of the hero's actions, the *vox populi*. Inseparable from the Viennese stage, Hanswurst became a man when living actors replaced puppets. Immortal, like all such types which personify the essential character of a nation, the Flemish Til Eulenspiegel, the Spanish Sancho Panza, Hanswurst became transformed during the course of centuries; he changed his name, but though he was called Anton or Bernardon he retained his original personality, adapted to the spirit of a new age, and the Man from Eipeldau of whom we have already spoken appears as a variant of Hanswurst, based on Joseph Richter's yokel.

Nothing so well expresses the character of a nation as the dramatic or comic characters which are its collective creation: witness Pulcinella and Guignol, Punch and Judy, Karagheuz and Urvinek. One might even discover notable differences between the German Hanswurst and the Austrian Hanswurst, and particularly the *Wienerische* Hanswurst created by Josef Anton Stranitzky in his fairground theatre in the New Market. He had the honour of playing before the Emperor, despite the radical separation existing at the beginning of the eighteenth century between the 'cultured' stage, represented by the Court theatre and by the private theatres of great nobles – for there was as yet no public playhouse – and the 'popular' stage, which showed its farces and melodramas in public squares and fairgrounds.*

Literary Drama and Popular Drama

Two currents can be clearly traced in the evolution of the Viennese theatre, two currents which meet with Schikaneder and are thereafter harmoniously amalgamated in the work of Raimund and Nestroy. The cultured, literary current arises here, as in many other countries, from the performance of plays on sacred themes, or those drawn from classical antiquity, in Jesuit colleges from the sixteenth century onwards.

* Haydn's recently rediscovered comic opera, *Das abgebrannte Haus* (The House That Burned Down), written and first performed at Esterhaza in 1776 or 1777, was, according to *The Times* of June 14, 1961, 'one of the last of the famous "Hanswurst" comedies in which the laughable, warm-hearted, downtrodden, sympathetic figure of Hanswurst (literally Hans Sausage) is the central figure . . . It is a Hanswurst comedy at its funniest and its earthiest, also at its most touching . . . Hanswurst's speciality was to appear in various disguises; in this opera he shuffles on the stage as a beggar woman, prances in as a cavalier (with pompous music in A major), swaggers in as a soldier, and finally wins his Colombina away from the advances of Leander, the city slick, who like all the characters of better station speaks not in dialect but in *hochdeutsch* . . . Hanswurst is given arias with tunes so popular and so ear-catching that they all sound like folk melodies.' (Translator's note.)

In the seventeenth century, the college of the University possessed a theatre seating three thousand, and in 1667 Burancini, the great baroque architect and stage designer, constructed on the bastion of the castle a theatre seating five thousand, with a stage three storeys high: a clear proof of the antiquity of that passion for the theatre which has always been so strong among the Viennese. At the same period, following a general tendency of the Counter-Reformation, there were given a series of 'acted processions', spectacular and moving, well calculated to touch the feelings and imagination of the people by their representations of religious or historical subjects. The 'cultured' theatre, at Court, included in its repertory only ballets, operas, oratorios, cantatas and Spanish comedies. Visits from English companies revealed to Austria, as they had to Germany, Shakespeare and the Elizabethans.

The popular theatre was far more varied, more alive, closer to what we call theatre today, than the court repertory; the latter was slow to adopt the English plays which for a long time appeared only in puppet shows and on the trestles at fairgrounds. One of the critical dates in the history of the Viennese theatre, before Schikaneder took over the Theater an der Wien of illustrious memory, was the installation of Stranitzky at the Käntnertor Theater. Stranitzky had started as a medical student, then he had become a quack doctor, and the habit of astonishing his audience by his patter and jokes encouraged him to take up acting; this was his true vocation. This theatre was the first public playhouse, built by the municipality of Vienna in 1708 for the entertainment of the citizens. As a city theatre, it had many advantages; it was independent of the court; it was not forced to close on the frequent occasions of official mourning; it was equally at the disposal of nobles and populace. It was upon this stage that Stranitzky displayed, in the character of Hanswurst, the innumerable resources of his talent, for Hanswurst appeared in every play in the most varied rôles: sighing lover, chamberlain, warrior, seducer, highwayman, duellist, spy, doctor . . . and many others. He even became Dr Faustus, strange as this may seem; hitherto he had merely acted as servant to the celebrated magician, but with Stranitzky he became Faust in person, without ceasing to be Hanswurst, a somewhat paradoxical combination.*

Strangers as well as Viennese thronged to applaud Stranitzky in the role of Hanswurst. This actor had a very lofty conception of the dignity of his profession. He used to tell his company: 'The theatre is as sacred as the altar, and a rehearsal as sacred as the vestry.' But he was capable of the most bewildering inventions; as when in *Amphitryon*, he played Jupiter as a burlesque figure falling from heaven through a skylight and, in the guise of Amphitryon, running into debt and causing outrageous scandals.

Stranitzky, that prince of the theatre, imitated royalty in one respect: he appointed his successor when he said farewell to his public: Gottfried Prehauser, who inherited the rôle of Hanswurst. It must have been a highly touching scene when the popular and successful actor announced that he was leaving the theatre; fortunately Prehauser changed grief into gaiety when, having thus been 'invested', he fell on his knees, mimicking grotesque terror and imploring the spectators to be indulgent to him and laugh at his buffooneries. Prehauser was clever and lucky enough to surround himself with excellent actors, whose names have remained famous in the annals of the Viennese theatre:[3] Harlequin and Columbine, played by Nuth and his wife, and the versatile Weiskern, a scholar and topographer renowned for his maps of Austria, who had given it all up to play comic fathers and second lovers in Prehauser's troupe.

The immortal Hanswurst of tradition underwent a fresh metamorphosis, thanks to the genius of Joseph von Kurz, creator of Bernardon. Kurz adored fairy pantomime; a precursor of Schikaneder, he transported his audience from

* 'The Viennese Faust, represented by Hanswurst, conceives of the problem of the world with far more simplicity, clarity and even depth than does Goethe. The Viennese Hanswurst represents with a purity which is unsurpassed in any of the world's literature the aesthetic concept of the comic as opposed to the tragic, the down-to-earth as opposed to the sublime, the naïve as opposed to the sentimental, the natural as opposed to the refined. The Viennese Hanswurst is the comic *an sich*, the essentially comic element in the world and in human life.' Kralik, *History of Vienna* (French translation, Paris, Peyot, 1932).

the Greece of Orpheus and Endymion to the sands of Babylon. Wonder, *la maraviglia*, that essential feature of the baroque, inspired all his work, which had in it elements of the Arabian Nights, of old wives' tales and of classical mythology. He also staged, equally well, Goldoni and Molière, the Commedia dell'Arte and the farces of the fairground; he himself always and only played Bernardon, and the audience never tired of watching him and laughing at his sallies.

The 'Burgtheater'

The creation of a national theatre being a necessary item in the enlightened despot's programme of reforms, Joseph II dreamed of sponsoring such an undertaking, which his predecessors had never considered. Maria Theresa did not despise the theatre, but for her it was merely an accessory of Court life, and nothing done outside the Court deserved the name of theatre. Leopold I, who composed operas and oratorios, was more interested in music than in stage production as such, and knew nothing about comedy or drama. Joseph II, for his part, imitated the organization of the Comédiens-Français, who had given a series of performances in Vienna in 1776, and he also followed the principles of Lessing, whose *Dramaturgie* had revolutionized the German theatre; he had talked to the author of *Nathan the Wise* when Lessing visited Vienna in 1775.

The famous and immortal Burgtheater was the fruit of Joseph II's desire to make of his 'national theatre' a political instrument, a means of bringing unity through culture to the different peoples of his Empire. Excellent producers such as Brockmann, Schroeder, von Braun ensured the vitality and success of this theatre, which had all the essential features of a modern theatre: permanent premises, a resident company, regular performances, an established repertoire.

Joseph Gregor has rightly described Joseph II's undertaking as a 'political use of the theatre'.[4] It also had the advantage, which he had surely neither foreseen nor intended, of arousing a keen spirit of emulation and rivalry in the suburban theatres, which were immensely influential in developing Vienna's theatrical tastes; modest popular playhouses such as that at Leopoldstadt attained a remarkably high standard and competed successfully with the official Burgtheater.

Entertainment of high quality, moderate prices which enabled theatre-going to become a habit rather than a rare luxury, frequent changes of programme alternating literary drama with farce and pantomime, such were the essential objects of the directors of suburban playhouses. These became so numerous at the beginning of the nineteenth century that a keen struggle was waged between impresarios, who competed for the favours of the public by lowering the price of seats and using all sorts of methods to attract audiences. And not only 'popular' audiences; for the spectators at Schikaneder's theatre, An der Wien, and Marinelli's at Leopoldstadt – the two principal rivals – also included members of the cultured classes and the aristocracy.

On May 9, 1808, in honour of the Emperor's birthday, Schikaneder put on an extraordinary production of Gluck's *Armide*, which was talked about for a long time after. Great blazing torches lighted the way from the Burgtor to the door of the theatre, and soldiers lined the streets. Seventeen hundred places had been distributed to high-ranking officials, leading personages of the town and distinguished foreigners, as Geusau tells us in his *Historisches Tagebuch* (Vienna, 1810).

Classic operas were produced with great taste but, since it was essential to please everybody, other attractions were put on, often more startling than artistic. The Theater an der Wien having organized a concert of mechanical instruments that played by themselves, Marinelli retorted by engaging for Leopoldstadt an ensemble of 'chamber virtuosi' who were adept at imitating birdsong and the notes of every instrument in the orchestra.

Marinelli also put on a play in which the hero and chief actor was a dog – the very play that cost Goethe his position as Director of the Weimar theatre, for he had refused to insert it between a tragedy by Schiller and a play of Shakespeare's.[5] Schikaneder retorted by offering his stage to a 'miraculous marvel', the incombustible Spaniard, Niklas Isidor Roger.

Roger was an Austrian, but the vogue for things Oriental had put Spain in the fashion, and so Roger appeared in a dazzling torero's outfit. How did this human salamander succeed in protecting himself from the flames which would have burnt anybody else? He submitted to examination by doctors and learned scientists, who were forced to admit their ignorance. Josef Prechtl, who witnessed his performances with admiration, declares[6] that Roger set half Europe marvelling without anyone being able to discover his secret. Countess Thürheim tells us in her memoirs that he demonstrated his incombustibility during a fire in St Petersburg by dashing repeatedly into a blazing house to rescue the inhabitants and emerging quite unscathed.

Roger was also the inventor of a universal counter-poison. He offered to sell it to the Emperor Francis, but his Majesty refused, saying that he ran no risk of being poisoned. Napoleon, on the other hand, asked for it, and it was said to be Roger's antidote that saved him on one occasion at Fontainebleau when he had swallowed an overdose of opium.

Realism on the Stage

This constantly changing variety of entertainments was the best way to attract and hold audiences that wanted to be amused and would have wearied of an exclusively serious repertoire. Tragedies and operas were followed by pantomimes, ballets and farces, and the visual side of a play, even of a masterpiece like *The Robbers* or *The Magic Flute*, remained one of the chief attractions of the performance. This almost childish demand for diversity obliged theatrical directors to vary their repertoire continually. Thus the Theater an der Wien, which had witnessed the creation of *The Magic Flute* and the first performance of *Fidelio*, did not think it was lowering its standards by putting on a pantomime with cavalry charges, mountain storms and shipwrecks. Schikaneder also prided himself on presenting interesting personalities to his audience; the name of Mozart having retained its popularity in Vienna, he organized an 'academy', i.e. a concert, by the son of Wolfgang Amadeus, introduced as Mozart Junior, on Palm Sunday 1820. He also staged an early work by a young composer of great promise, so the poster said: *The Twins*, by Franz Schubert.

Any means were justified, and a producer would not hesitate to borrow exotic animals from the menagerie at Schönbrunn and bring them on to the stage to enliven the show. In the case of *The Dog of Montargis* the play had been expressly written by the animal's trainer to show off his pupil's talents; but whenever an episode in any play took place in the East, or in Egypt under the Pharaohs, which was very fashionable at that period, camels were brought on; these delighted the Viennese and looked most effective, rigged out in Oriental draperies, in Etienne's opera *Gulistan*.

Contemporary newspapers also tell of a magpie which, for some months, eclipsed all the actors, so much did the public delight in its mimicry and its clever tricks. Josef von Sonnleithner aptly describes the kind of show which was all the rage in the capital: 'As long as it's spectacular enough the Viennese will like it.'

The anxiety of the police authorities was eventually aroused by the scale of the realistic battle scenes which delighted audiences in suburban theatres. Schikaneder, as we have said, manoeuvred whole regiments and fired cannon; some regulation of these fusillades became necessary, and they were eventually forbidden. The Theater an der Wien, directly affected by this ban, begged for an exception in its favour, pleading that the firing of cannon and rifles had never caused the slightest accident, that the utmost precautions were taken when loading, and that certain plays could not be performed if gunfire was forbidden.

The police retorted that these explosions seriously affected ladies' nerves, that there was a risk of setting fire to the woodwork and furnishings of the theatre, and that the actors themselves were exposed to considerable danger. This firing of cannon, rifles and pistols was something quite new; nobody had felt the need of it before, and the worst part was that it had now become the main attraction of the entertainment, that people went to the theatre for that sole reason, and

that it had even become customary to announce beforehand
the number of shots that would be fired during the performance, in order to ensure a box-office success.

This minor war between the theatres and the police ended
in the latter's victory. The use of powder in theatres for
fusillades or fireworks was forbidden by order of the
Emperor in 1807; it was allowed in the open air, which was
doubtless one of the reasons why Schikaneder began building
enormous stadiums where his squadrons and batteries could
be displayed even more freely than in his Theater an der
Wien. This, which he had rebuilt in 1801, was described by
Johann Pezzl as 'the largest and finest in the whole capital'[7];
five hundred men and fifty horses could move freely about its
stage.

This predilection for realism was one of the chief characteristics of the Viennese theatre: we recognize it, right at the
end of the nineteenth century, in Alexander Girardi's
touching and truthful characterizations of the humbler
townsfolk, such as the cobbler Valentin in *Mein Leopold*, a
piece of acting that has remained famous in the history of the
European stage. The art with which he cleaned windows,
cobbled soles, or brought a letter was deservedly admired,
and his style has rightly been compared with that of
Stanislavsky's Russian actors.

The citizen of Vienna loves life; he does not consider it
monotonous or boring. Life in itself is an entertainment for
him; he wants the stage to reproduce for him that reality
which he cherishes because it is always new and interesting.
Every aspect of life, the commonest as well as the most
exceptional; he can only enter into the spirit of the play if it
gives him the illusion of reality. At the same time, he likes to
see this reality touched with a certain magic, for in his mind
magic and reality are not mutually exclusive. One reason for
his delight in the supernatural is that he sees no radical
opposition between it and the world of reality.

And so Grillparzer's historical dramas, dealing with such
remote figures as Libussa or Ottokar, appeal to him as
strongly as the peasant comedies of Anzengruber which
transport the whole village, just as it stands, on to the stage.

And for the same reason the two favourite dramatists of Viennese audiences during the first half of the nineteenth century were the famous actor-author Johann Nestroy and the delightful, 'unique' Ferdinand Raimund, whose fantastic fairy-tales, like those of Gozzi, were none the less deeply rooted in the life of the people of Vienna. And one of the best ways of getting to know the city of that period is to watch it move and hear it speak in the plays of these two writers, so different, but so closely akin because so profoundly Viennese.

Nestroy and Satirical Drama

There is nothing tedious about the fifteen volumes of Johann Nestroy's works.[8] His writing is always fresh, piquant and amusing, even for us, who lose much by not understanding the topical allusions. We miss Nestroy himself too, since any actor-playwright writes a part for one man and one man only. If Nestroy's plays are rarely put on, they can still be read with pleasure, for the period element in them blends with what is universally human. His style is easy and graceful, making full use, as perhaps only an actor-author can, of telling repartee. Nestroy's *mots* always have a moralistic point, and this romantic shows himself akin to the French eighteenth century when he writes: 'I have always despised the Prodigal Son, not because he kept swine but because he went home.'

Nestroy rose above topical satire, which he treated in masterly fashion, to attain a real philosophy of life. He writes with a disillusioned smile: 'I expect the worst from any man, even from myself, and I am seldom disappointed.' That remark sums him up. A sceptic in politics but respectful of the established order, rational but capricious, sentimental as befits the Biedermeier period, but with an irony that mocks and parodies romanticism. He will cap a broad joke with a philosophical reflection, and slip between a couple of light-hearted lines such powerfully harsh remarks as this: 'There are few bad men in the world, and yet there is much unhappiness; most of this unhappiness is caused by the many, the very many good men who are nothing more than good men.' He adored women, and drew some exquisite figures of *ingénues* and women in love, but he summed them up in a memorable description as having 'cobweb nerves, a heart of wax and a little iron head.'

This embittered satirist, who could be so merry and so biting at the expense of himself and his fellow-citizens, never, like poor Raimund, fell victim to any 'little iron head'. He dominated his period and his circle, and remained one of the representative figures of this transitional phase of the Viennese theatre, between romanticism and realism.

Nestroy's origins help to account for the diversity of his character and talents. Belonging to a Polish family which settled in Vienna after living in Bohemia, he is a perfect example of that felicitous mixture of races that made up Austria. His father was a lawyer, his mother came from a wealthy tradesman's family. He was born on December 7, 1801, and was christened in St Michael's church, close to the Jordangasse where his parents lived and which was then a fairly fashionable district. The bourgeois atmosphere in which he was born and spent his childhood left its imprint on his talent, even after he had broken free of it. He studied at the Scottish College, where the élite of Viennese youth were educated and which produced diplomats like Metternich and artists like Moritz von Schwind. No profession attracted him except the stage, and his dramatic gifts had already been noticed when he acted in school plays and sang in drawing-rooms, for he was a singer as well as an actor. He made his debut in 1822 as Sarastro in *The Magic Flute*, at the Känt-nertor Theatre; then, since his manager paid him badly, he left for Holland where he played some fifty rôles, including that of Kaspar in *Der Freischütz*. He was entirely dedicated to his exacting but magnificent profession, and to the strange career that was a dramatic singer's in those days.

The range of the repertoire obliged the same artist to sing, dance, play pantomime, farce and tragedy. The most diverse talents were required of him; he must excel in buffoonery, move the audience to tears in melodrama, sing a grand aria impeccably and put across vaudeville couplets with wit. Nestroy possessed the Protean qualities needed by a Viennese actor of the early nineteenth century; he could declaim Kleist and Schiller, sing Mozart, Meyerbeer, Rossini, Weber and Auber, and moreover interpret with dazzling verve the traditional character of Kasperle, a wittier successor to Hanswurst, played at Leopoldstadt by Martinelli himself.

By dint of acting in other people's plays Nestroy evolved the idea of writing his own, of inventing situations where his imagination could display itself with most brilliance, and made-to-measure parts exactly fitted to his capacities and his ambitions. He began by adapting foreign plays to get his hand in; then he gave rein to his original genius and put on his first comedies, which took the public by surprise, Vienna being then under the spell of Raimund. Success was slow in coming, for his satire was too violent, too direct to be fully appreciated by a public which did not like being roughly handled. He first triumphed in the rôle of the non-commissioned officer Sansquartier, which won immediate and enduring sympathy, in a play called *Twelve Girls in Uniform.* Here caricature was broad and truculent; too much so, perhaps, to win the favour of those who were, or thought themselves, sensitive. Nestroy had become a popular favourite, but the critics still looked askance at him, displeased by these extravagant caricatures. Having been abused by two critics in particular, Saphir and Wiest, he revenged himself on the latter in a way that reminds one of the Commedia dell'Arte, and shows what liberties actors sometimes took with their text. One evening when he was playing the part of a servant bringing in the cards for a game of whist, he added to his usual remark a phrase that delighted his audience – for the public was fascinated by the war between Nestroy and the critics: 'It's surprising that the most intelligent of games should be called after the stupidest man in Vienna.' This bold witticism earned him five days in jail, but he had definitely won the hearts of the Viennese.

He was equally successful as author and as actor. In 1832 he won great applause in both capacities, playing a highly farcical parody of a fairy-tale, *Nagerl und Handschuh,* and in the following year the immortal *Lumpacivagabundus,* where, with a verve that set the seal on his fame, he played the unforgettable rôle of Knierim the cobbler. He respected nothing; he turned Schiller's dramas and Wagner's operas into farces, but people did not mind, they accepted it all, for as Princess Metternich declared: 'You can take anything from Nestroy.' Raimund was forgotten. The Theater an der Wien and the Leopoldstadt theatre fought for Nestroy as author and actor, and the spectators filled whichever house he performed his plays in.

He wrote them, and learnt his parts, with prodigious speed. He composed eighty-three comedies, produced them and acted in them, without ever ceasing to observe the foibles and vices of his contemporaries and to collect in his notebooks the remarks which were subsequently to be included in some play, or which suggested some character; the bureaucrat Tratzchmiedl, the Gaugraf in the parody of Tannhaüser, or the worthy charwoman who brought him one of his greatest and most enduring successes. Like most of his fellow-citizens, he was not greatly interested in politics; the revolution of 1848 merely furnished him with a pretext for a few satirical comedies, like *Liberty at Krahwinkel* or *Judith and Holofernes*; impartially, he made fun equally of the insurgents and the government against which they were rebelling. Bourgeois by origin and education, he was both rebel and conservative; he refused to take part in the civil war, which remained for him merely the theme of a comic play.

His works are not all of the same quality; several of them never had more than a topical interest, and they are scarcely even of documentary interest to us today, but many of them on the other hand are extremely alive. It must never be forgotten, however, when reading them, that they were written solely for the stage. Nestroy was primarily an actor, with the qualities and faults of his profession, considering everything from the point of view of the stage and with little regard for critics or men of letters who would know his plays only from reading them. He cared so little about these that he did not bother to get more than a dozen plays published during his lifetime, indifferent to the fate of the rest once the footlights no longer shone on them.

He was typically Viennese, like Peter Altenberg and

Arthur Schnitzler in more recent years; he was the precursor of the famous Viennese operetta of Strauss, Lehar, Kalmann and Fall; but above all he was Nestroy – a reasoner who doubted the power of reason, a man of feeling who distrusted sensibility, a sceptic who longed to believe, a tender-hearted mocker of all things and primarily of himself. Otto Forst de Battaglia, in an excellent study,[9] has described him aptly. 'Nestroy,' he says, 'is German in his depth and diversity, Latin in his clarity and logic, Austrian in his taste and tact, his flair for the right expression in the right place.' He remained faithful to the formula of 'popular' art according to the Viennese character, but he stripped it of all vulgarity, and he associated fantasy and realism in such skilful proportion that he moves from fairy-tale to farce with unexpected modulations. Between him and the artist who preceded him in Vienna's favour, Raimund, there is an immense difference of character, but an equal degree of talent. A comparison between these two actor-authors is highly instructive for the study of the history of taste in the early years of the nineteenth century, or of the social and psychological evolution of Vienna during the same period.

Raimund and Poetic Drama

Ferdinand Raimund died in 1836, when Nestroy's star was in the ascendant. Nestroy was to live nearly thirty years longer, enjoying considerable wealth and great renown, at any rate within the limits of his own country, which was all he desired. Nestroy's farewell performance on October 31, 1860, was an apotheosis; he appeared in extracts from his most popular rôles, Sansquartier, the philosophical cobbler Knierim, Jupiter in *Orpheus in the Underworld*, the Gaugraf in *Tannhäuser* and Willibald in *The Rascals*. Raimund was barely forty-six when he took his own life in a fit of deep depression, grief and despair, banished from the stage by his fortunate rival, forgotten by the public who had once idolized him. 'I can't do anything about it,' he commented hopelessly. 'People like what he does, I myself have laughed when I've seen him. My plays and I are done for. Everything is pointless.'

97

Why had the Viennese changed their allegiance so radically? It was no longer merely a question of theatrical taste but of a deeper, broader transformation, which shows its results in every sphere of life. Raimund was a man of the Romantic movement, of that romanticism that began with Mozart; he was born two years before the composer's death; he belonged to what one might describe as the old régime. He lived, moreover, in a world where magic and reality were indissolubly intermingled. He was a poet, whose airy fancy was grafted on to everyday life; he was not at home in the industrial era or under the reign of the moneyed bourgeoisie, and his characters are midway between heaven and earth, not, like Nestroy's, firmly rooted in everyday reality. When the public became aware of class antagonisms, and when, moreover, it began to prefer realism to fantasy, it inevitably deserted the poet for the satirist. This happened in Vienna between 1820 and 1835, as it had happened in Venice during the previous century, when Goldoni's realism brought about the decline of the Commedia dell'Arte and the twilight of Carlo Gozzi, creator of lovely fantastic *fiabbe*.

Raimund is akin to Gozzi in his choice of subjects and his manner of treating them. His delight in the marvellous is in the folk-spirit, but is given a baroque or rococo turn of mind. This charming, delicate, fantastic writer, barely earthbound and yet never cut off from reality, belongs in fact to the Viennese romantic school. He represents, too, the 'biedermeier' type of romanticism, so original, so curious, so essentially Austrian (and even more Viennese), which has no equivalent elsewhere and whose charm is unequalled.

Born of a humble family, brought up on fairy-tales in a poor home in the Vienna suburbs, Ferdinand Raimund made his debut in the theatre by selling sweets in the foyer during the interval. As he performed this modest rôle to perfection, occasionally putting on an act to persuade possible customers, he was transferred from the house to the stage, and became an actor. His ambition to belong wholly to the theatre was still only half satisfied, for he dreamed of writing plays. Providence came to his aid when he met an author who was in despair because he could not finish a comedy he had begun;

young Raimund helped him out of the difficulty, then, considering that if he could write comedies for other people he could do even better for himself, he began composing plays in which he acted himself.

An actor-playwright, like Nestroy, he naturally gave free rein to his taste for fantastic realism, that blend of truth and whimsy which was his individual secret, and which delighted popular audiences as well as connoisseurs. He was a close acquaintance of Moritz von Schwind, Schubert's friend, who also combines in perfect proportion a sort of delicate naturalism, wholly free from vulgarity, with the spirit of old folk-legends; Raimund satisfied the Viennese love for a certain type of 'the marvellous', surprising enough to be different from everyday life and yet giving the impression that, after all, such wonders weren't completely improbable. A play like *The Peasant Millionaire*, one of his best-known works, is an exaggerated but significant reflection of Viennese optimism, which likes to think that fairies or genii intervene in life as in legend to help men out of tight corners from which they would be unable to extricate themselves unaided.

The portraits he sketches in a comedy of character like *The Spendthrifts* are truthful but at the same time kindly. He touches lightly on failings and absurdities, and there is nothing savage in his satire on manners. He has no wish to moralize, and never indulges in spiteful or bitter taunts as does Nestroy. His tender, mischievous good-nature is akin to that of his contemporary fellow-citizen Franz Schubert. He was probably influenced by the Italian drama, notably that of Gozzi, whose *fiabbe* always have a happy ending after fantastic adventures; so much so that he might be called a Viennese Gozzi, with the atmosphere of the Austrian capital replacing that of Venice.

In these fairy plays, with their pageantry, their lavish use of mechanical devices, transformation scenes and supernatural characters, the baroque and romantic are mingled; *The Elf-king's Diamond*, *The Barometer-maker in the Enchanted Isle*, *The King of the Mountains* and *The Enemy of Mankind* seem to have been written for grown-up children by a delightful, unpretentious comic actor, a man of 'popular' inspiration in the best sense of the word.

He suffered from his popularity; the Viennese public, having idolized him for a few years, presumed to control his personal life. During the whole of the nineteenth and part of the twentieth centuries, actors were considered public figures almost to the same extent as the Imperial family; their slightest actions were known, discussed in the newspapers, commented on round café tables. Raimund, having rashly got engaged to a woman whom he soon discovered he did not really love, wanted to break off his engagement; he would have done so had not public opinion taken up the affair with such intransigent passion that the poor actor had to carry the thing through so as not to disappoint or vex his public. The same public, after his disastrous marriage had broken up, forbade him to marry the woman he loved, Toni Wagner – which in any case, being a good Catholic, he could not have done.

It was a high cost to pay for a triumph which was short-lived, since the rise of Nestroy spelt failure, despair and suicide for poor Raimund, less fortunate than his own Peasant Millionaire, who married his beloved in the end. Ephemeral affairs, backstage flirtations and his unhappy passion for Toni never brought Raimund that full emotional maturity that only happiness can give. This teller of carefree stories with happy endings was basically a melancholic; the nervous depression that led him to take his own life crowned an inability to cope with the sorrows and misfortunes of life.

Like a good Viennese, as long as he could refuse to admit sorrows and misfortunes he gave the appearance of enjoying complete happiness. He played the part at which so many of his fellow-citizens also excelled, probably because it was their natural line, that of Watteau's 'Indifférent', who shrugs off all difficulties with a smile and a pirouette. Thus so many decent folk who have nothing to do with the stage live their lives as if they were acting in a play, avoiding asking themselves the question: what is true, what is false? lest they should destroy the dream, the mirage, the lifelike illusion which they have instinctively adopted so as not to be crushed or disheartened by life.

They liked their drama lifelike, they dramatized their lives; that was the price the Viennese paid for peace of mind and heart, for their happiness. They had to pay it, and not scan too closely the contradiction between reality and fiction. On the stage, everything is real and false at the same time. And in everyday life too, if one is to find it bearable . . .

A certain poetic realism – that is to say a sort of unreality – in the theatre, and in life that magical brilliance which, though artificial, can create an illusion for those who are willing to accept it: probably no nation, not even the Italians or the Irish, have proved so adept at bringing nature on to the stage and drama into their lives. 'We are such stuff as dreams are made on': never did this seem so true as in Vienna, during this happy Romantic age.

CHAPTER FIVE

SHOWS AND ENTERTAINMENTS

*Oxen, Bears, Monkeys, Giraffes, Elephants—Menageries—
Puppet Shows—Conjurers and Automata—Musical Freaks and
Mesmerism—The Eskimos—Fireworks—The First Railways*

One characteristic of the Viennese, due partly to the Latin streak intermingled with the Germanic in their nature and partly to inherited Italian influence, was their tendency to consider all happenings, whether ordinary or extraordinary, as a pageant which they instinctively watched with unvarying enjoyment. One could not spend all one's life at the opera or the play; and even if mountebanks, puppet showmen and trainers of performing dogs solicited spectators in the open street, they had to contend with the busy life of the street itself, which for the Viennese was an inexhaustible supply of surprises and delights.

Like the Parisian, the citizen of Vienna is traditionally given to sauntering wide-eyed through the town, watching everything, ready to be amused at any incident which he sees. For him the everyday life of the great city is an infinitely entertaining spectacle; one would be a fool indeed not to take advantage of the thousand opportunities for laughter and astonishment provided by the behaviour of passers-by, the patter of cheap-jacks, the quarrels of coachmen, with their extraordinary wealth of scurrilous language. The pretty barefooted flowergirls in many-coloured aprons, the goatherd lasses offering glasses of warm milk, the swaying carts of the water-carriers, the hawkers with their trays of trinkets, the rustic tumult of the markets, all provide so many excuses for delighted dawdling.

Oxen, Bears, Monkeys, Giraffes, Elephants

This passionate love of pageantry of all sorts, from the changing of the guard outside the palace or the solemn welcome of a foreign monarch to the performing dogs and clowning mountebanks at the street corners, made life a perpetual holiday for the Viennese. They were interested in everything, even in the lamentable procession of oxen being driven to the slaughterhouse, whose passage through the streets was accompanied by a sort of carnivalesque cortège. Hungarian oxen were particularly admired, and their arrival in the Imperial city invariably aroused great excitement among the populace. The authorities had laid down strict rules so that no danger or damage should result from the passage of these animals; obscure complications ensued also from the fact that the butchers of Vienna, jealously attached to their privileges, claimed an exclusive monopoly, for which their rivals contended, sometimes violently, in street scuffles which added yet another attraction to the spectacle.

The cattle market was held at the Ochsengries, close to 'Hungarians' Street', in a suburb encircled by the river on three sides, on the left bank of the Wien, the stream that gives the town its name. Around 1760 a new market had been built on the right bank, near the Stubentor bridge. Everybody wanted to see the exciting ceremony of the Hungarian oxen's arrival. Franz Gräffer, who has left such fascinating pen-pictures of popular life in old Vienna, thus defines its attraction for the Viennese: 'It's a holiday, and it doesn't cost a kreutzer.' In order to avoid disaster, the owners of houses in the streets along which the oxen were to pass were urged to close their doors and put up the shutters over their shops; indeed, householders and shopkeepers left their homes to throng on the pavements with their wives and children. The 'cattle parade' was preceded by a regular military march past: dragoons on horseback, their swords drawn, encircled the animals and opened and closed the procession, with a great sounding of trumpets and drums. Butchers' boys goaded the oxen, mastiffs snapped at their legs to urge them on and barked ferociously at laggards. It sometimes happened that one of the animals, terrified by all the shouting, would take

H

flight, possibly knocking over one of the dragoons' horses. Then there was an exciting chase, horsemen brandishing their sabres and infantrymen their bayonets, after the black, bellowing, fierce and frantic creature which, dashing far from its allotted course in search of liberty, scattered the crowd before it. When the rebellious animal was finally captured, it was slaughtered on the spot with sword and bayonet, to prevent any further such incident, and its carcase was carted away.

The cattle parade was such a popular entertainment and so eagerly awaited that we read in a book published in 1812, entitled *Komische Gedichte über die Vorstädte Wiens*, a humorous quarrel between two friends about the advantages of their respective homes; the one who lives in the district through which 'the Hungarians' pass mentions this as being one of the pleasantest features of his street. As often as this event, ordinary enough in itself, took place, so often did the whole population delightedly leave workshop and counter, and put on its Sunday best to watch the passing of the cattle, with the secret hope that some untoward accident might add fresh piquancy to it.

We may find it hard to believe that such kindly, gentle people as the Viennese could enjoy watching scenes as savage and bloodthirsty as these cattle parades too often became. And yet there were many among these peaceable, good-natured folk who went to watch executions; the same is true, however, of London and Paris, which were not considered particularly savage or cruel on that account. The ladies of the French court scuffled for places to watch Damiens being torn in pieces, and London tradesmen paid high prices for chairs on which to climb, the better to see a man being hung for the theft of a handkerchief; and yet seventeenth century France and England do not stand condemned thereby. There is some bestial and sadistic instinct in the mob of any race and of any city, which clamours for such spectacles. Thus, right up to the end of the eighteenth century, there was a special theatre in Vienna where, as in Roman circuses, the populace could watch animals – wolves, lions and bears – tear one another to pieces for its delight. This theatre was fortunately destroyed by fire, and the Emperor Francis I forbade its reconstruction, so as not to perpetuate what he described as 'a ferocious and dishonourable custom'. Although admitting that he was right, the population protested and displayed open discontent, perhaps because the custom was a very old one, dating back to the Middle Ages, or even to Roman Vindobona, and so deeply rooted in their way of life that its horror no longer struck them.*

None the less, the Viennese were fond of visiting wild animals in their city's various zoological gardens. When menageries were on show, theatrical newspapers reported on them as well as on the latest opera or fashionable comedy. The menageries were usually lined up along the Jaegerzeile, where their posters promised all sorts of wonders to the curious crowd. A trainer from Augsburg, in 1812, brought a 'school of acrobatic monkeys' which was enormously admired for a long time. In a neighbouring booth could be seen another monkey which danced on a tight-rope and played on various musical instruments, fast or slow as requested. A performing hare was all the rage for a short time, so well trained to overcome his native timidity that he would stare unflinching at the pistols aimed at him and never twitch an ear when they were fired.

The greatest sensation in the sphere of rare and surprising creatures was caused in 1828 by a giraffe which had been presented to the Emperor by the Viceroy of Egypt. From the time the animal embarked at Alexandria, the Viennese newspapers kept their readers informed daily about the progress of its journey. Some anxiety was felt when the *Theater Zeitung* of July 3, 1828 published the following bulletin: 'We learn from the Agram Journal that according to official information, the arrival of the giraffe at Fiume will not take place at the anticipated date, since the boat has been delayed by a storm; we will publish further news on this subject as soon as we receive it.' When the giraffe was at last comfortably installed in the menagerie at Schönbrunn, bourgeois and working-class thronged to admire it, and

* The composer Gluck himself had interests in an enterprise of this sort.

scholars examined it and discussed what name it had gone by in antiquity. According to Dr Ludwig Fitzinger, it was the Biblical *Zamer* ... For several years, fashions in hair-styles, scarves, and so on, were all *à la giraffe*; it was pictured on snuff-boxes, glove-boxes and (in miniature) enamelled rings; actors who specialised in topical satire made great play with it. Raimund wrote a comedy about it, and the ingenious owner of the great ballroom *Zur Blauen Weintraube* organised balls *à la giraffe*; a new 'giraffe's gallop' was danced there, in which there took part, wearing his turban and Turkish slippers and smoking his narguileh, the Arab who had escorted the animal from Cairo to Vienna and who had become a fashionable figure, much in request in all places of entertainment. As a souvenir of the Giraffe's Ball, Perl, the owner of the Weintraube, graciously distributed to all ladies present a bouquet of flowers in the middle of which was a sugar giraffe, to be eaten or piously preserved according to taste.

This fondness for rare animals was one of the oldest and most respected customs of Vienna. In the castle of Ebersdorf which he had built, Maximilian had installed a huge pheasantry and a pen for wild sheep, including a rockery on which they climbed, just as in a modern zoo. In 1552 the Emperor had provided the Viennese with an unprecedented and fantastic spectacle, the ceremonious arrival of an elephant; this event was celebrated by poets and scholars, and the memory of it was enshrined in the many houses which chose an elephant for their emblem and were known by its name – the last of these, on the Graben, was demolished in 1865, as we learn from Friedrich Reichsl, to whose valuable book *Wien zur Biedermeierzeit* reference must constantly be made by the historian of old Vienna. At the same time as the elephant, the Viennese were presented with 'Indian crows' which were actually parrots brought from America by the Spaniards.

At what period did the custom begin of keeping deer and bulls in some of the dykes surrounding the town, of using others as fish-pools, and of housing bears, tigers and lions in carefully segregated ditches? It probably dates back to the time when feudal lords who could not keep their moats filled with water put wild beasts there to act as sentinels and warn the soldiers of any nocturnal attack. Among the staff employed at court, on a regular salary, were monkey-trainers, singing- and talking-teachers for parrots and even a 'lion-purger'.

Accidents sometimes occurred when imprudent visitors went too close to the cages; the Viennese tell the sad story of a girl known as 'the lion's bride', in the menagerie at the Belvedere castle belonging to Prince Eugene, conqueror of the Turks. The man in charge of the lions had a daughter who brought her favourite lion its food every day; on her wedding day, wishing to fulfil her usual task, she entered the lion's cage in her wedding dress with the bowl in her hand. Suddenly the wild beast rushed at her and tore her in pieces, whether because it did not recognize her in her unfamiliar dress, or else – and presumably this was the more popular hypothesis – because it considered its young attendant as its own bride and preferred to kill her rather than give her up to a man.

Menageries

The zoo in Schönbrunn Park, formed in 1752, was immediately thrown open to the Viennese people, who delighted in it. The purchase of the private menagerie of an Italian, Albi, and the gifts of foreign sovereigns quickly made of this garden a much-admired resort. On Sundays whole families would set off to the castle, with baskets of provisions on their arms, to picnic on the lawns and walks and then visit the pavilions full of astonishing animals. Joseph Richter, who in his *Eipeldauerbriefe* relates with charming irony, in Viennese dialect, the wonders and curiosities of the city, does not fail to describe these Sunday excursions to the Imperial menagerie. He lets us see 'the two monkeys perched on a pole, surrounded by other monkeys watching them open-mouthed all day long,' the 'gigantic birds' (probably ostriches) 'who hold their heads even higher than my lady wife does; with their bare feet, they walk about as proudly as the ladies in the great avenue of the park.' The picnic basket also held a bottle of wine and some great hunks of bread for the elephant, nuts and apples for parrots and monkeys, and rolls for the fishes, birds and bears.

'Little Father Elephant,' Schönholz[1] tells us, 'filled the park at Schönbrunn as a good actor fills his theatre. Peaceable and cunning, a wise old creature, though somewhat proud and moody, he lived a contented life in his garden.' He was the people's favourite, which did not prevent him from showering dust or water over them with his trunk if the fancy took him. When he fell ill people eagerly read the bulletins about him in the Wiener Zeitung, and his death was mourned as a national bereavement.

This love of animals, this interest in everything rare and strange, this typically Viennese desire to be perpetually amused and surprised by some unexpected sight, were highly profitable to travelling showmen. Many districts of the town became permanent fairgrounds, where mountebanks, quacks, clowns, exhibitors of trained beasts shouted one another down in their efforts to attract passers-by. To get an idea of the zeal and ingenuity shown by these organizers of popular entertainment, one should read some of the posters that were displayed outside the menageries, all along the avenue formerly called the Jaegerzeile and later the Praterstrasse, which was reserved for them. They were fortunate in being established along such a busy thorough-fare, which led towards the park where the Viennese found all the delights they most enjoyed: fine romantic trees to dream under, shady groves for lovers, bowling alleys, taverns, roundabouts, dance halls, games of skill . . . The passer-by found it hard to choose between so many menageries, each boasting its superiority; he had to be attracted, and persuaded, by alluring promises such as the following announcement, which appeared in a newspaper in 1818:

'On the Jaegerzeile, in the first booth on the left past the church, there may be seen a number of enormous and curious beasts, offering the greatest interest: comical monkeys and a great number of fine parrots. The owner of this booth is Mme Denebecq, widow of the famous director of the Metamorphoses Playhouse which was well known here a few years ago. On the stage of this former playhouse there may be seen a pair of dwarfs, husband and wife, extremely graceful and well-made, who take part in a puppet show with highly diverting effect. The most remarkable members of the menagerie are the lion, the lioness, the great Royal Tiger and an armadillo from South America, who came here a year ago; the first armadillo ever to be brought up in captivity. The lion is truly admirable in his beauty, force and majesty; the only regrettable thing is the way in which he condescendingly allowed his mate to rumple and tear out his mane when they were together in one cage. The lioness is the fiercer of the two, and roars uninterruptedly. He joins in only when he is hungry; in the presence of these animals one experiences every kind of excitement and alarm. Before devouring his meal, the Royal Tiger prowls round his cage holding between his teeth the huge piece of meat he has been given, showing that he is quite capable of swallowing it. The armadillo is like a rhinoceros on a small scale.'

In August of the same year a Frenchman, Dominique Ferrand, newly arrived from Paris, announced that 'with the consent of the authorities he hopes to display to the public a considerable company of monkeys, thirty-four in all, of the most diverse races, and also a collection of rare and surprising birds, which will be shown at the same time as the monkeys. The owner offers these animals to anyone wishing to buy them. This show will take place in the Jaegerzeile, next to St John's Church, in the large building used as a booth.'

Since the public enjoyed these menageries as much as plays, theatre critics devoted articles to them, sometimes displaying a certain talent, as for instance in a note published by the *Theater Zeitung* in 1829. The menagerie in question is that of Ferdinand Exinger, installed opposite the Jünglingskaffee. It is interesting to discover from this article that Exinger had abandoned the ordinary methods of display in favour of those picturesque panoramic effects inaugurated at Hamburg, which have been imitated in all zoological gardens since.

Amongst the inhabitants of Exinger's zoo there were four crocodiles, a great many snakes, cobras and pythons, a giant walrus, together with more familiar animals such as pelicans, Canadian swans, moose, and golden Chinese pheasants. But what our chronicler praises most highly is the fact that the animals are not in cages, but in open air pens, behind high fences, so that 'the visitor is not troubled by the stench which usually arises from the excrement of animals in an enclosed space.' Here is to be seen, he writes, 'one of the most charming and ingenious sights that one can imagine. We suddenly behold jagged rocks, grey stones covered with vegetation, and we are transported on to Alpine summits, at dizzy heights, where avalanches roll by with a noise like thunder. This landscape, however, is not unpeopled. Agile chamois dart through space, delighting us with their leaps. Snow-hares, quaint and timid, perch on the cliffs, and in the dark crannies eagles and vultures make their nests. This lifelike and faithful image of nature will surprise and delight all who see it.'

Puppet Shows

Denebecq's Metamorphoses Theatre, to which we have just referred, showed such diverse curiosities as ballets performed by dwarfs and puppets playing and dancing together, and those 'optical effects' of which the late eighteenth century was so fond because of the varied and violent emotions they aroused in the spectator. The romantic passion for ghosts and supernatural apparitions had reached the fairground; magic lanterns projecting phantom figures, mysterious winds stirring the curtains and the moan of lugubrious voices gave the unsophisticated an uncanny thrill and the delicious pleasure of being frightened for a moment, and then returning, a moment later, to the green arbour of some pleasure garden, with its foaming beer and new wine.

The combination of dwarfs and puppets on Denebecq's stage must have created a disturbing ambiguity, an uncertainty that might become acutely painful; when a man imitates a puppet's movements so well, and the puppet is so skilful that it seems human, where does the limit lie between illusion and reality? Marionettes were enormously popular in Vienna; they came from every province of the empire, and from abroad; Venice and Sicily sent their most agile *burattini*, Bohemia brought its rough rustic *pupazzi*, given to broad clowning and grotesque gambols. There was Pulcinella from

Italy and Hanswurst from the Germanic provinces, while Kasperle was a product of Czech fantasy. Diverse races and peoples foregathered on the puppet stage as in a miniature League of Nations.

These puppet theatres abounded. The simplest were in caravans which moved from one district to another; they were the humblest but the most natural, and probably the most amusing. In regular buildings, plays and operas were performed with the help of excellent singers, actors and instrumentalists; the marionettes vied with these and sometimes eclipsed them, which suggested to Heinrich von Kleist his admirable Treatise on Puppets, certainly the most complete and profound study of the subject.

One of the most popular puppet shows in Vienna was the Krippenspiel of Mme Godl, landlady of the Golden Eagle Inn where these performances took place. As her prospectuses proudly announced, Mme Godl had several times displayed her dancing and singing dolls before Their Imperial Highnesses, who had graciously expressed their satisfaction and admiration; this did not, unfortunately, prevent the censor from banning certain of the plays, which all had to be submitted to it. The police, constantly vigilant, dreaded any sort of subversive propaganda, and since the apparently innocent puppets made their appeal directly to the crowd, to the mass of the people, careful watch was kept by the censor over the plays thus put on.

Mme Godl's Krippenspiel, however, had no subversive intention; the plays shown there were chiefly fairy-like spectacles, for instance *The Creation of the World*, from the appearance of the stars in the sky to the creation of Adam and Eve in an earthly paradise where trees grew in a few seconds and flowers burst open on bushes. There were also astonishing light effects, storms with thunder and lightning, and the destruction of Sodom by fire miraculously streaming down from heaven. The Biblical scenes shown during Advent and Carnival concluded with the destruction of Jerusalem, with Roman 'cannon fire' shattering its walls. But the rarest, subtlest and most accomplished technically of these effects were the visible transformations to be seen in *The*

Seasons, with flowers blossoming under the spectators' eyes, cuckoos singing in the forest, harvest festivals, autumn hunting scenes, and finally winter's snow covering everything to the strains of melancholy music.

Mme Godl's show was immensely successful, but success always stimulates competition and imitation; clever speculators, according to the Eipeldauer, quickly copied the marvels of the Krippenspiel, and taking advantage of the interest which novelty always arouses, they won over Mme Godl's audiences, and her theatre was deserted; she found herself bankrupt; her settings, her puppets, her delicate and ingenious machines were all put up for auction. Puppet theatres, which were still forbidden by decree in 1770, multiplied at the beginning of the nineteenth century; the most curious and interesting was, in 1804, that of Maximilian Sedelmayer, who gave his performances in the Holzplatz, in the courtyard of a house which he first roofed over with glass to protect the spectators from the weather.

Ludwig Böck, who published in 1919 an excellent work on puppet shows in Vienna, describes this little makeshift theatre with its benches crowded with turbulent schoolboys, its three-dimensional stage sets, for Sedelmayer would not rest content with canvas backcloths, and the harpsichord accompaniment played by a distinguished musician, Simon Sechter. Much praised, too, was the Krippenspiel of the painter Schönbrunner, who, having grown almost blind and being unable to paint, had taken up the art of marionettes as a means of livelihood. The magnificence of his stage sets was particularly praised, and for a long time people talked about his extraordinary Jacob's Ladder on which the angels went up and down, and the royal retinue that accompanied Joseph, eclipsing even the carriage-and-six that had been poor Mme Godl's pride and joy.

This delight in puppet shows was not confined to rustic and uneducated audiences; it was shared by the great, and there were puppet theatres in many palaces and castles. Prince Nicolas Esterhazy had one set up in the magnificent residence which he had built in 1766 on the banks of Lake Neusiedler. Of this residence a French traveller, Risbeck, wrote after visiting it in 1784: 'Apart from Versailles, there is perhaps no place in France which can be compared in splendour with Esterhaz.' The park was full of devices in the fashion of the day, hermits' grottoes, Chinese pavilions, labyrinths, 'philosophers' walks', and Temples of Love.

The puppet theatre, opposite the Opera house, which held four hundred spectators, and the café where singers and players went to refresh themselves during the intervals, were decorated in the most enchanting fashion; and the shows (which were probably accompanied with music by Haydn, since he was director of music to the Esterhazy princes) were no doubt comparable in elegance and artistic quality not with fairground booths and popular Krippenspiele, but with the Imperial theatre itself.

Conjurors and Automata

Puppet shows on the whole formed an innocent entertainment, but one which might in certain cases arouse uneasy and even painful sensations in the spectator, as for instance when human beings mingled with marionettes at Denebecq's. This ingenious master of illusions created other fantastic effects in his Metamorphoses Theatre, akin to those which won universal fame for the Belgian engineer Eugène Robert and were immensely popular in an age avid for wonders. The visit to Vienna of the illusionist Robert, who in order to conform with the current fashion for things English had altered his name to Robertson, has been perpetuated in the newspapers of the early nineteenth century by articles reflecting the enthusiam and terror felt by all spectators. Thanks to an ingenious mechanism of projectors and mirrors, Robertson called up sinister apparitions in a darkened room, hung with black, where the whole performance was accompanied by bloodcurdlingly funereal music. Lugubrious wails were heard, gusts of dank air chilled the spectators. And even if one did not really imagine oneself transported into the nether regions one had the feeling of living in a nightmare surrounded by monsters of every sort.

I do not know whether Vienna gave Robertson the same enthusiastic reception as did St Petersburg, where the

Russians, possibly more superstitious than other nations, firmly believed that this magician was able to make skeletons dance and call up the spirits of the dead. Why, you could see their faces, hear their voices, feel the touch of their icy fingers! The Viennese, more sceptical, played at being frightened, but the illusion was so cleverly created that their fright was often genuine, and several times, it seems, women were carried off fainting. Of course they knew that this was only a fairground show, somewhat more sophisticated than the rest, but none the less the citizens of Vienna left the black-curtained room paler than they had gone into it, and hastened to fortify themselves at the café over the way with plenteous draughts of light wine, beer and coffee.

Displays of automata, too, aroused the same kind of emotion as that felt at Robertson's, the impression of being in the presence of an extremely adroit and knowledgeable charlatan, with an underlying suspicion that this charlatan might also be a magician, able to command supernatural forces. Of all mechanical contrivances, the automaton is in this respect the most disturbing: it sets one wondering whether, in his arrogant ambition to compete with his Creator, man has not in fact acquired certain divine attributes in this domain, by making living beings with his own hands.

The history of automata, which is fascinating and which moreover has been told with great skill and learning by M. Alfred Chapuis, includes all the attempts made by man since the days of antiquity to create an artificial being, with the gifts of speech and movement, and giving the effect of 'natural' life.

The illusion was occasionally so complete that amongst the celebrated automata with which the dukes of Burgundy, in the Middle Ages, peopled the park of their castle of Hesdin, there was a hermit who walked about the alleys, who was greeted by passers-by because they thought him alive, and who returned their greetings.

Waxwork collections like the Musée Grévin in Paris or Mme Tussaud's in London were among the favourite diversions of the Viennese: the best were Dubsky's in the

Prater, and that of the 'Iron Man', Dubsky's neighbour and rival: and the wonderful 'mechanical theatre' of Calafatti. In the Prater, too, was the booth of Sebastian von Schwanenfeld, popularly known as the Prater Magician, in front of which pretty women queued up from early morning to consult the 'Turk'. The throng of simple-minded folk who hoped thus to fathom the secrets of the future, to learn the hidden thoughts of a faithless lover or a cruel mistress, was so great that the police frequently had to be summoned to keep order amongst the turbulent addicts of the supernatural.

Reichsl gives a delightful description of the magician himself, dressed in a great robe embroidered with mysterious symbols, a turban on his head, his magic wand in his hand, sitting enthroned at the entry to his Sibylline cave, while a chirping flock of tame canaries fluttered round him. Until 1845, when he died, Sebastian von Schwanenfeld, whose origins were unknown in spite of his impressive name and who had gone through all sorts of adventures before setting up shop as a magician under the great trees of the Prater, remained one of the idols of the Viennese populace, because of the messages of hope and encouragement distributed by 'the Turk' to the poor distressed folk who were such ready listeners.

What was the secret of Schwanenfeld's Turk? How could he give the right answers to everyone who consulted him? Was this a mere hoax imposed on the simple-minded, or was the Turk an exceptionally successful example of the ancient and difficult art of constructing automata?

In any case, he had a dangerous rival in the automata of Mälzel, who had made a complete orchestra of mechanical musicians, which he showed, with what success one can imagine, at the Theater an der Wien in the early years of the nineteenth century. The director of this playhouse had been deeply humiliated by the success scored by his rival of the Leopoldstadt Theatre with a concert given by an orchestra of birds which not only sang with their natural voices, but furthermore were able to imitate the sound of every instrument. Through what miracle was this accomplished? Were these birds unbelievably well trained or, even stranger, were they mechanical birds such as had never been heard before? The secret was well kept. As regards the automata, there is still some doubt today about Mälzel's famous 'chess player', of whom nobody can say whether he was an incredible masterpiece of mechanical ingenuity or an imposture, since a dwarf might have been concealed under the Turk's robes – the loose garments of Turks and hermits were very convenient for hiding machinery or accomplices – to play chess with those bold enough to challenge him.

Mälzel's famous Turk has been immortalized by E. T. A. Hoffmann in a celebrated tale called *The Automaton*, written at Dresden in 1814. Hoffmann had certainly encountered the 'chess player' and Mälzel's other disturbing creations during his travels, and, attracted as he was by everything that might be fantastic and supernatural, he made the Turk the central figure of a dramatic story. From the description he gives of Mälzel's booth we can well imagine that the Viennese felt a shudder on entering the cabalistic closet where the Oriental sat.

'The talking Turk,' (he writes) 'created a sensation and set the whole town astir; for young and old, rich and poor came from morning till night to listen to the oracles uttered in a low voice, in reply to their curious questioning, by the rigid lips of the wonderful figure, who seemed alive and dead at the same time. It is true that everything about this automaton was so skilfully designed that everyone felt drawn towards it, quickly recognizing the difference between such a masterpiece and the toys usually displayed at fairs and festivals.'

Mälzel had started by building mechanical military bands, which were the great delight of the late eighteenth century and were to be found, at this period, in almost every castle; the finest and most complete of those still in existence is the one at Charlottenburg. Marches were played by mechanical instruments concealed in a kind of baroque castle of gilded wood. As if there were a real fanfare in the room, you could hear trumpets, drums and cymbals; there were even cannon shots. Mälzel actually succeeded in introducing up to sixteen trumpets in one of these 'bands', ancestors of the mechanical music of present day fairgrounds.

Mälzel, who was an excellent musician as well as an incomparable engineer, set up in his own home, to delight his visitors, a septet of 'robots', to use the modern term, who performed their parts to perfection in very difficult compositions. This remarkable man had also studied surgery and knew how to make artificial limbs for cripples. He was equally learned in optics, acoustics and mechanics, and he astonished the Viennese one day by presenting before them Haydn's *Seasons* in a sensational décor with appropriate transformations. In winter, the snow fell, and the shepherds' huts were buried by avalanches; in summer the rain streamed down, the thunder rumbled . . .

This naïve and yet ingenious accompaniment to the famous score aroused immense curiosity, as may well be imagined, and soon Vienna swore only by Mälzel. Many people, however, suspected him of black magic, particularly after the wonders he had worked on the day of Napoleon's wedding with Marie-Louise, in 1810. He had installed on his balcony an automatic singer who warbled epithalamia in honour of the young couple; but his mysterious masterpiece, which roused the anxiety of the police and clergy, was the appearance in a darkened window of his house in the Kohlmarkt, of the Imperial pair, who suddenly emerged as if they had really been in the magician's dwelling, bowed to the crowd – who of course responded with wild cheers – and then disappeared as silently and solemnly as they had come. People who had actually seen the Emperor and his bride at the palace could have sworn that they were there in the flesh and blood, at the same moment, at Mälzel's window.

Amongst the strange and cunning inventions of this man who was the talk of all Vienna and who, in other days, might have been burnt at the stake with his automata, was the 'self-protecting desk', which is described in the *Theater Zeitung* of 1829. This was an ordinary-looking piece of furniture, so planned that anyone who tried to open a drawer without having previously manoeuvred a secret device would immediately find his wrists grasped by iron hands which held him prisoner, while the deafening din of what the advertisements of the time called 'janissary music' would bring everyone rushing round the culprit. A Hessian cabinet-maker who made use of Mälzel's invention added a ruthless contrivance: six loaded pistols which fired at the unfortunate burglar if in five minutes he had not succeeded in getting free of the iron hands.

Mälzel had a brother, even more extraordinary than himself, who was said by the Viennese to have made a pact with the devil, and who had emigrated to America; it was in Boston that, according to the *Theater Zeitung* of August 2, 1829, which regrets that Vienna was not the privileged city, he presented an orchestra of forty-two automata, capable of performing works as difficult as the overtures to *Don Giovanni*, *The Vestal* and *Iphigénie*. Mozart, Spontini and Gluck were played without a single fault, the newspaper adds . . .

Musical Freaks and Mesmerism

The passion of the Viennese for musical toys was quite incredible. They had to have music everywhere! One was awakened musically by the cuckoo-clock in one's bedroom, and every action during the day was marked by a musical *ritornelle*. The chiming clock played a solemn air every hour, and marked half-hours with minuets, quarters with gavottes. If one opened a work-case or a box of sweets, floods of harmony streamed forth. From the lid of a snuff-box there sprang up a humming-bird that sang loudly every time one took a pinch. And the desire to be constantly surrounded with music – 'bring forth your music into the air,' as Shakespeare says – made them hang on trees and houses Aeolian harps from which the slightest breath of wind drew unexpected melody, while in a storm they uttered wild moans and ominous wails which duly stirred romantic souls.

Mechanical organs, the construction of which required great skill, aroused the interest of the most illustrious musicians. Mozart himself wrote a few pieces for this instrument, which was akin to some of Mälzel's magical inventions. The *Theater Zeitung* of 1830 recommends to the Viennese, with what success I do not know, the musical bed invented by a Swiss, Firnhamm. It was so fashioned as to encourage sleep and, at the same time, to prevent one from over-sleeping. Thus a fondness for comfort and a taste for activity were equally satisfied. The musical bed functioned thus: as soon as you touched it, a lullaby sounded, then, when you were lying down, muted horns induced drowsiness, but when the time was up, a clatter of instruments broke out, so noisily that however deeply you were asleep you had only one desire, to take immediate flight from the couch thus transformed into a 'musical hell' suggestive of that painted by Hieronymus Bosch on the panels of his picture in the Escurial.

Landlords of cafés and places of entertainment also adopted the 'musical billiard table' which had appeared for the first time in London at Clovis's restaurant. Whether or not it satisfied music-lovers, it must have been extremely embarrassing for billiard players. According to the descriptions of this strange contrivance given by Viennese newspapers, sweet airs sounded throughout the whole game except when somebody made a mistake; this set the apparatus whistling and laughing to mock the clumsy player; the victor, on the other hand, was greeted by a triumphant fanfare of trumpets and drums.

Musical freaks without number were invented in this music-mad city, from the bird-cage whose hanging wires were so tuned that when the bird clung to them spontaneous melodies broke forth, to the 'soothing soundbox' of the dentist which, when the patient was about to endure the most acute pain, sang sweetly in his ears: 'Let me come closer to your mouth and gaze at your pearly teeth!' There was no end to the rare surprises offered, in the most unexpected circumstances, to the insatiable Viennese. It had become an obsession, and Schönholz reports that you could not open a door, touch a table, seize any object or even look at the clock without some spring immediately releasing floods of harmony.

Charlatans and swindlers, who abounded at this period almost more than at any other, knew how to use for dubious ends those optical and acoustical inventions of which the Viennese were so proud. When mirages and illusions left the domain of the fairground to feature in the sessions of secret societies, the thing ceased being a joke and became serious. Neither Mälzel nor Robertson had claimed to exercise power over supernatural forces: fantastic as their creations were, they could, in theory, be explained, and there was nothing miraculous about them, except the extraordinary talent of the inventor, the mechanic and the illusionist.

Unfortunately these prodigies were also made use of by those strange adventurers of whom the late eighteenth century seems to have been more prolific than any other period. When Cagliostro summoned apparitions and other-worldly voices to amaze and terrify his visitors it was presumably through trickery rather than black magic, although in those days it was very hard to distinguish the 'initiate' from the impostor. The fanatical worshippers of the Goddess Reason, in that 'age of enlightenment', were susceptible to every sort of superstition, even the crudest, while the Romantics of the early nineteenth century avidly sought out whatever was strange, irrational and supernatural; and whether genuine 'magi' or charlatans were involved, the illusionist accessories invented by scientists and engineers, at a time when mechanical science was making extremely rapid progress, encouraged every sort of skilful faking.

*   *   *   *

Magnetism, too, was all the rage, and Mesmer was one of the most remarkable figures in late-eighteenth century Vienna. In his castle near the city, whose open-air theatre was inaugurated with a performance of Mozart's *Bastien and Bastienne*, Mesmer received all the eminent and notable personalities of Vienna. From the famous tub which was reputed to cure all ills, to the trick experiments which he performed to the amazement of his visitors, Mesmer practised every sort of cunning allurement. If he attracted to his home the élite of city and Court, as well as all distinguished foreign visitors to Austria, who longed to meet a man famous throughout Europe, it was because the discoverer of animal magnetism knew how to assume in turn the grave demeanour of the scientist and the laughing mask of the mountebank.

Mesmer understood how to deal with this society, with its blend of naïvety and refinement, the simplicity that underlay its pompous Spanish ceremoniousness, and its happy combination of formality and familiarity. Versailles was far stiffer than Schönbrunn, and this was one reason why Marie Antoinette had some difficulty in adapting herself to France and the French, and in bowing to petty tyrannies of etiquette which she had never known at the court of her mother, the Empress Maria Theresa. This typically Austrian amalgam of distinction and good humour, reserve and friendliness, was part of the very atmosphere in which the children of the Imperial family were brought up. Two stories relating to Mozart's childhood illustrate this fact. The first time the little musician was received at Schönbrunn, when he was barely six years old, he slipped and fell down in a passage; one of the archduchesses, Marie-Antoinette, picked him up, comforted him and sat him on her lap; so that when he left her the child declared: 'I'm going to marry her when I grow up.' Next year, in Paris, Mozart was introduced to Mme de Pompadour; innocently, he tried to climb on to her knees, but she snubbed and rebuffed him almost roughly. The child was hurt, and retorted proudly: 'Who are you, that you refuse to kiss me? The Empress Maria Theresa kisses me when I go to see her.'

These are a child's remarks, of course, but none the less significant, revealing the virtues and faults of the Austrian character. For the Empress's kindness to the child prodigy, which was perhaps not very different from the amused curiosity one feels towards a performing animal, did not prevent her, some years later, when Leopold Mozart was seeking a position for his son, some princely patronage which might protect them both from the cruel hazards of an artist's life, from advising her son, then Grand Duke of Tuscany, against taking them into his service. It must be remembered, too, that Mozart's amazing success at Court when he appeared for the first time in Vienna as a child prodigy vanished the moment he stopped being a child, and that his subsequent life was a continual story of disappointment, injustice and misfortune, for the lighthearted Viennese did not really understand the true genius of Mozart any more than, half a century later, they understood that of Schumann.

The Eskimos

The incredible frenzy that possessed the inhabitants of the Imperial and royal capital (imperial for Austria, royal for Hungary) for musical toys of the kind we have described, and the popularity of magnetism, are evidence of that almost puerile thirst for amusement, that childish delight in surprises, that were characteristic of the Viennese. Many examples might be quoted of this, but one of the most amusing is undoubtedly the story of the Eskimos in the Belvedere. Why were these inhabitants of the Polar regions in the exquisite and splendid castle built in 1713 by J. L. von Hildebrandt for Prince Eugene of Savoy? In 1825 a certain Captain Hadlock had brought back from his explorations in the far North a couple of Eskimos, in order to show his compatriots what the inhabitants of those distant continents were like in appearance, customs and behaviour. It was impossible, of course, to reconstruct Baffin Bay, from which the sailor's promises of fame and fortune had lured them; but it was decided to instal them in the park of Belvedere Castle, next to the big lake on which people skated in winter, where they might feel at home.

There were crowds of curious visitors, and the Eskimos soon became as famous as the giraffe; everybody wanted to see them, and rushed to the Belvedere to gaze at this extraordinary spectacle. An eye-witness, Realis[2], describes the astonishment he felt on seeing the Eskimos' sports on the big lake. He writes:

'On August 4, in the afternoon, one of these inhabitants of the Pole, in his national costume, could be seen paddling his canoe, a sight never before witnessed in Vienna. The speed with which he paddles is indescribable. To see him overturn his canoe with sudden daring and roll over with it, diving and coming up again in the same place, one no longer wonders how these Polar folk can brave the storms and icebergs of their Arctic seas in their frail craft. He sat in his canoe as firmly and confidently as a snail in its shell. His skill at shooting with bow and arrows and at throwing the javelin was extreme; he unfailingly hit all the geese that flew above the lake, and finished them off with a sharp bite on the head.'

This way of finishing off wounded game seemed particularly astonishing to the worthy Viennese who came on Sundays to marvel at the Eskimos; and for a long time after the city remembered the presence of these inhabitants of Polar seas, who had been all the rage for a while and whose doings had been endlessly retailed by the newspapers.

* * * *

In ordinary times it was a favourite custom to sail in gondolas on the lake at Belvedere, or in the pleasure boats that travelled up and down the Danube. Pleasure trips were also made in the boats that journeyed along the Neustadt canal, which had been cut originally for practical ends, in order to facilitate the transport of provisions to the capital. In 1715, barely a year after its opening, it was already used by 1500 boats carrying 573,906 cwt of merchandise.[3] These boats, built specially for this purpose, could occasionally serve as 'river coaches'; powerful horses drew them trudging along the bank, while a sailor held the rudder with casual ease. When the canal was frozen and the boats had to be put up in their sheds, skaters took over, and ladies rode in sledges drawn by their beaux, each fur-clad and muffled up to the eyes.

Fireworks

Fireworks were the great speciality of the two Stuwers, father and son; the Viennese doted on such displays and seized every opportunity to indulge their passion. Birthdays and anniversaries of members of the Imperial family were pretexts for elaborate and fascinating combinations of figures, initials and allegorical emblems that caught fire at a given moment and burst into showers of flame. Fireworks proved a means of expression for the baroque genius which, though unfortunately transitory, was none the less characteristic. Eighteenth century Vienna, that baroque city, demanded pyrotechnic displays of particular brilliance; providentially, the Stuwers were there to supply the need. It must be remembered, too, that even when some aristocratic anniversary provides the occasion, a firework display is essentially a popular entertainment, since everybody can watch it. In order that the entire population might enjoy his shows, Stuwer set up his pieces not only on the Prater, where the number of spectators, although large, was limited, but also on the city walls and even on the mountain of Maria-hilfe. Religious festivals, notably that of St Anne and St Theresa, were accompanied by sumptuous firework displays in which everybody could thus participate.

A Viennese author at the beginning of the nineteenth century points out that fireworks had given rise among his compatriots to the birth of a new word, or rather a new way of pronouncing the word *bravo*; the spectator, gasping with wonder at the rockets and Catherine-wheels, cries out not bravo but 'bravóh', either because his head is thrown back or because by drawing out the final o he follows with his voice the fiery trail that speeds through the night and dies away in the darkness. 'And this is the only circumstance' points out the ingenious philologist, 'in which it is pronounced thus.'[4]

The newspapers of the early nineteenth century gave reports of firework displays and announced them beforehand, just as much as stage shows. The *Bäerles Zeitung* of 1832 uses a complex and subtle terminology to describe the various 'pieces' and their effects. Among the most successful of these it mentions a fiery streamer held by two doves, bearing the inscription: 'To our amiable spectators,' and above all the amazing representation of the celebrated Dr Faustus at supper, accompanied by demonic music.

This was the only time, to my knowledge, that the character of Faust – so often made the subject of operas, tragedies, farces, operettas and even of a comic ballet (by Heine) – was introduced into a firework display. The *Bäerles Zeitung* thus describes the astonishing picture. 'Faust was seen drinking one cup after another, to the sound of diabolical music and of thunder-claps. The black, terrible shapes of dancing demons, surrounded by red flames obtained with chemical powders, produced a most fearsome effect.'

The episode of Faust was followed, the same evening, by an equally extraordinary scene: the representation of an island fortress besieged by a squadron of ships, which fired their cannons at it; the movement of the vessels tossed by the waves was, it seems, rendered with incredible realism.

Vienna, therefore, had every right to claim that she possessed the king of fireworks, but this king did not always distribute his largesse gratuitously. Certain displays were reserved for a 'paying audience'; on such occasions, the access to the Prater meadows where they were held was strictly guarded by the police, to prevent an influx of curious spectators as well as to avoid the accidents that might be caused if some imprudent person ventured too close to the machines.

Gaheis described, in 1808, in his picturesque *Wanderungen und Spazierfahrten*[5] the precautionary measures taken by the police.

> 'Soldiers on horseback' (he writes) 'maintain order and discipline amidst the throng of vehicles. The Prater alleys are watched over by guards, and the great meadow along the Jaegerzeile is surrounded with nets like those used for hunting, alongside which cavalrymen patrol. In front of the entrances there are huts where you can take your tickets. The charge for entry is twenty-four kreutzers, and if you want to sit in the galleries, you have to pay another twenty-four kreutzers to enter the second gallery; places in the first gallery cost one florin twelve kreutzers. Children below the age of nine do not pay, provided they come with their parents ... The possibility of bad weather has been foreseen, and 'insurance tickets' valid for another performance are distributed ... When the first explosion is heard, all the people sitting in the Prater cafés rise up and rush towards the scene of the display. When the third sounds, a solemn silence falls, and the performance begins.'

Adalbert Stifter, whose novels describe Vienna in the Romantic period, has described this crowd watching in rapt attention as soon as the first rockets soar whistling up, people pressed so close to one another that the meadow seems to be paved with faces, enjoying, spellbound, the long-drawn-out delight of the slowly-dropping parachute rockets, and the thrill of the tremendous burst of multicoloured showers of sparks which seem almost to engender one another, up there in the night sky. The popularity of the Stuwers was immense, and they made a fortune by selling to private individuals the pyrotechnic set pieces which the latter delighted in setting off in their own gardens. Ever since the seventeenth century this had been one of Vienna's favourite amusements, and it was not until the revolution of 1848 and the consequent upheaval in the life of the people that firework displays dwindled in number and in splendour and, without completely disappearing, were restricted to a few exceptional and official occasions.

As well as manufacturing fireworks, the Stuwers were also interested in the development of science, and of that particular branch of science which might lend itself to spectacular display: aeronautics. The exploit of Pilâtre de Rozier, who had made an ascent in a balloon, aroused the spirit of emulation in these pyrotechnical experts. Vienna wanted to have her balloon too, and Johann Georg Stuwer provided one. The newspapers of the time are full of thrilling stories announcing and describing that extraordinary event. The news that Stuwer was going to build an aerial ship 'capable of lifting him above the towers of St Stephen's and carrying him up into the heavens' set the whole population agog. In the yellowed pages of the *Wiener Zeitung* and the *Wiener Provinz Nachrichten* one can read enthusiastic articles devoted to this experiment: the canvas cylinder 'as tall as a four-storey house' with a wooden car suspended below it, in which was maintained a fire whose smoke inflated the balloon and made it rise . . . Stuwer had had the graceful idea of prefacing his ascent with a firework display rich in allegorical compositions, which paid homage to Montgolfier, his predecessor.

As a precaution, the balloon was secured by ropes during the first ascent, that of March 20, 1784, but the great success of this and the impatience of the public, tantalized by the sight of a captive balloon, decided Stuwer to attempt another flight, this time in a free balloon, on August 25. Unfortunately the experiment was a failure. The wind being violent, the balloon crashed at a little distance from its point of departure, on the opposite bank of the Danube. A third attempt having met with no better success, Stuwer renounced aeronautics and devoted himself exclusively to pyrotechnics.

His successors in the art of aerial navigation, the brothers Ensslen, merely entertained the Viennese with enormous blown-up bladders representing comic figures; the Frenchman Blanchard, that daring and learned pioneer in aerial navigation, achieved in 1804 the first flight worthy of the name, from the Prater as far as Gross Enzersdorf, and the same year, before the astonished eyes of an immense crowd, a self-taught and somewhat eccentric mechanic, Jakob Degen, presented his flying ship, which combined, according to Reichsl, the principle of the balloon with that of the aeroplane; if we are to believe the authors who have dealt with this question[6] it was completely successful.

The First Railways

The Viennese, like most Frenchmen, did not take the invention of the railway seriously nor believe in its practical usefulness. The worthy citizens of the Imperial capital considered it at first as a novel amusement which would enrich the attractions of the Prater and serve to carry them and their families, gasping and delighted, round the park on a Sunday; something like the miniature train in the Paris Jardin d'Acclimation. And as though with the deliberate intention of amusing the public and giving this new means of locomotion the character of a fairground attraction, the first experimental journeys took place in the Prater, arousing, one imagines, enthusiasm, scorn, scepticism, but principally astonishment. One thing was certain, however; the first train built in Austria by Franz von Gerstner, in imitation of the English trains of which he had made a lengthy study, moved; and it moved so fast, according to some people, that this speed constituted a serious danger to the health of its passengers.

This happened in 1823. According to its inventor and the authorities who supported him, the first purpose of the railway was to establish communication between the two great navigable rivers, the Moldau and the Danube, on which traffic was enormous. Various lines were built, that from Linz to Budweis in 1829, that from Linz to Gmunden shortly after. In 1838 a line was laid at last, to the great delight of the Viennese, between Florisdorf and Wagram; the journey only lasted an hour, there and back; the carriages were comfortable, and according to the newspapers of the day, 'lacked for nothing as regards elegance and convenience.' The smoke and smuts from the engine obliged the travellers to keep the windows shut, but this did not prevent them from admiring the landscape, and they could recover from their excitement by going to eat and drink in the 'buffets' which ingenious innkeepers had installed without delay in the new stations. For lovers of statistics, we mention the fact that during the first six months of its life the Florisdorf–Wagram line carried 176,000 passengers; very few of these used the train out of necessity; most of them, almost all in fact, enjoyed chiefly the novelty of the thing, the excitement of its departure, for which a detonator gave the signal, the hazards of a journey which might be full of incident – it sometimes happened that the engine, carried away by its uncontrollable ardour, ran off the rails – and there was nobody in all Vienna who was not eager to make use of this fatal invention which was much inveighed against by the owners and drivers of coaches and diligences.

Indeed, there were many who felt their interests threatened by the appearance of the railway train. If the townsfolk found it thrilling to ride in padded coaches over jolting lines, well-informed people, principally at Court, categorically declared that the railway had no future. After his visit to the station at Vienna, Archduke Louis asserted that the whole thing was exaggerated: 'It's very pretty,' he said, 'but too big for Vienna.'[7] As for the satirically-minded, they indulged themselves to the full, and took a malicious delight in telling the worthy folk climbing into their carriages that all precautions had been taken for their safety, that doctors and surgeons had been engaged, and that priests, in fact, were posted at every station with all that was needed to administer extreme unction to the victims of the terrible iron machine. Close to the Prater, they would add, an immense hospital was being built for casualties, and the railway company had thought-fully decided that travellers should pay on arrival and not on departure; thus the dead would be spared the unnecessary expense; as to those who had not lost their lives during the journey, they would only be charged in proportion to the number of limbs left intact. With typically caustic wit the wags of Vienna announced with mock gravity that the authorities, to show how considerate they were, had en-trusted the running of the line to a celebrated English engineer, the same who, on the inauguration of the Birming-ham line, had caused the death of the Minister of Trade.

Such were the taunts flung at the first railways, its engineer and at those who had financed it, the Rothschilds, who certainly had not the reputation of willingly engaging in unprofitable adventures. But for all the gibes and laughter, the Viennese bourgeois with their top hats and umbrellas, their boys and girls beside them and their wives walking in front, cheerfully set off for the station that was 'too big', to take their tickets for a journey during which they would experience the powerful emotions of explorers and audacious innovators.

CHAPTER SIX

VIENNA AT WAR

National Mourning—Napoleon in Vienna—The French Occupation—The Return of the French—The Sacrifice

---

It was not only because their beloved archduchess Marie-Antoinette, daughter of Maria Theresa, who, disastrously for herself, had become Queen of France, was directly threatened by the events of 1789, that the Viennese viewed the Revolution with genuine horror, but chiefly because they detested any sort of violent uprising, any disturbance which must inevitably affect their lives adversely. Securely settled within the rigid framework of a Spanish-style monarchy, less open to new ideas than other nations, and on the whole averse to any sort of abstract thought or ideology, the Austrians, as we have said, were rather like children who put complete trust in their parents; quite ready, with their natural turbulence, to make fun of their masters, but never going so far as to question the legitimacy of their authority.

Some of the reforms undertaken by Joseph II, that 'enlightened despot', had met with little approval from the people of Vienna. They thought him petty-minded because of his lack of decorum; they preferred more theatrical monarchs in sumptuous attire. He was suspected of being a 'crowned revolutionary', and therein lay the basic cause of that misunderstanding which increased, throughout his reign, between this well-intentioned monarch and his subjects, who thought he was going much too far. A short time before his death he had so clearly realized that most of his reforms were unpopular that he had suppressed them in order not to provoke further discontent. How deeply moving is one of his letters to his brother, written in one of those frequent moments of discouragement when he questioned the soundness of the edifice that had cost him such great efforts to build:

'Sunk in the grief that I feel at my own misfortune and that of the State, I am now the most distressed of mortals. Patience and resignation, such is my motto. You know my fanaticism – the word is not too strong – for the public weal, to which I have sacrificed everything. The little renown I have enjoyed, the small esteem the monarchy has acquired, all are lost! Pity me, dear brother, and may God preserve you from such a fate.'

It was perhaps because Joseph displayed such fanaticism, to use his own term, that the Viennese failed to appreciate some of his measures. He was a good and generous man, however, and amongst the measures proposed by this monarch who had so many intelligent and *modern* ideas and who took such pains to transform them into reality, there was one which should have won him the heart of all Viennese: that which related to the protection of nightingales in the public gardens. Perhaps with the unconscious cruelty and naïve selfishness of so many musical obsessionists, the Viennese who liked to keep songbirds in cages had never stopped to think whether the singers did not sometimes long for liberty and need it for their song.

Because there was something doctrinaire and dogmatic about his political thought, Joseph II was lacking in the flexibility necessary to those who govern, that opportunism which tempers severity. This highly intelligent man failed to understand that there was no single way of making a nation happy but a hundred different ways, and he was distressed when people misunderstood him. Kralik's[1] judgment is correct: 'Joseph was rightly irritated at the universal folly of nations. The French rise up because they are refused liberty and equality, the people of Brabant and Hungary revolt when they are given what the French demand so clamorously.' He could not understand why the French preferred revolution to the war against Turkey in which he tried to involve his brother-in-law, whose crown and head this expedition might have saved. On the other hand the Turkish war had aroused the jealous anger of Prussia, which had united with the maritime powers against Austria, so little importance did they attach to the threat from the East. The Viennese, however, could not forget how narrowly they had escaped, thanks to the energy and boldness of Prince Eugene, at the time of the Great Siege, when the Prophet's standard had been raised for so long in front of the city's bastions.

Joseph II died on February 20, 1790; he had had time to see the French Revolution grow and consolidate itself. His more prudent successor and brother, Leopold II, considered it useless to try and make people happy in spite of themselves, against their will, by offering them a kind of happiness which they had not themselves chosen and for which they felt nothing but aversion. Leopold deliberately strove to efface as far as possible the 'revolutionary' element in his predecessor's actions, in particular suppressing the unproductive and unpopular taxation which Joseph had somewhat chimerically adopted.

The anti-revolutionary temperament of the Viennese would thus serve to explain the fury which events in France aroused in their hearts; they resented too, the fact that the French had called their queen 'the Austrian' as if it were a term of abuse; indeed, her Austrian nationality was one of the major reasons for Marie-Antoinette's unpopularity. It is no doubt an exaggeration to assert, as Kralik does,[2] that the series of Revolutionary wars was primarily a duel between Paris and Vienna; but there was far more hostility in France towards Austria than towards her other enemies, a hostility which, from the moment Marie-Antoinette arrived in Paris, created an atmosphere of mistrust towards the Austrian princess, whose qualities were resented even more than her faults. It is therefore not surprising that the Viennese, with an emotional ardour that took little cognizance of the political issues, championed an unhappy queen whom they had seen playing in the alleys at Schönbrunn and dancing so prettily in Court ballets, dressed as an angel or a cupid.

National Mourning

The city therefore consented to a sort of national mourning proclaimed by Francis I when he came to the throne in March 1792. He requested his people not to indulge in the

costly rejoicings which were customary in such circumstances, since this was no time for merrymaking, and also
because, as he said, the sums wasted on ephemeral festivities
would be better used for improving the town's amenities.
The money usually spent in erecting splendid triumphal
arches, which were promptly pulled down after the procession had passed through, leaving only a brilliant but
evanescent memory, was devoted to a town-planning project
which the romantically inclined will deplore, since it deprived
the city of a picturesque and fascinating medieval element;
the clearance of the ground around St Stephen's Cathedral.
Until 1792, in fact, the church had been surrounded with
buildings which, in the old tradition, huddled close to its
buttresses and cluttered up the square.

The neo-classicism which dominated Vienna, as well as
every other capital, at this period, could see no beauty in the
Gothic or, rather, had no appreciation of the paradoxical
and teeming beauty of medieval cities on which town-planners
had not yet ventured to lay impious hands. The discovery of
Greek, Roman and Etruscan antiquity had encouraged the
spread, throughout Austria, of the Louis XVI and Directoire
styles, which embody the revival of 'the antique' considered
as an ideal of absolute beauty, and the repercussions of which
are manifest in interior decoration, furniture and fashion:
particularly in feminine fashions, for straight floating tunics
and picturesquely-wound turbans had a flattering charm
which quite superseded the dated elegance of rococo styles.

To clear the ground round St Stephen's and to free the
square in front of the church from the clutter of houses which
interfered with a view of its soaring, sturdy and yet delicate
spire, was a happy thought inspired by a quite modern feeling
for space and perspective. If we compare the view of the
cathedral painted in 1832 by Rudolf von Alt, that charming
chronicler of early nineteenth century Vienna, with the older
engravings of the same subject, we cannot deny that the view
has gained in dignity what it has lost in picturesqueness, and
that from this angle at any rate, when the clearance was
completed, the councillors and bourgeois of the city were
justified in dedicating this new square to 'the Roman

Emperor who showed, by thus enlarging and embellishing it, that he set the beauty of his city and the comfort of its citizens above any triumphal arches.'

The relative austerity which Francis I had prescribed for the celebration of his coronation implied that Vienna was bound to share wholeheartedly in the sufferings of Marie-Antoinette, and to proclaim its abhorrence of the Revolution. When the Assemblée Nationale declared war on Austria to punish her for the help given to the émigrés and to their intrigues, Vienna gladly took up the challenge. The September massacres, in which perished several Viennese who had accompanied Marie-Antoinette to Paris, stirred up popular wrath still further: Vienna could not but fly to the help of her children, victims of the ruthless Jacobins. This feeling is clearly reflected in the *Eipeldauer Letters*. On the day when the guillotine severed the head of the unfortunate queen, the duel between Paris and Vienna reached its acutest phase, for certain crimes could not be expiated, and the humblest citizen of Vienna felt at one with the writer who declared:[3] 'the noble daughter of great Maria Theresa will be remembered when the French state has vanished and the site of Paris is looked for in vain on the banks of the Seine.' For, if the Revolution was born in Paris, the seat of anti-revolution was in Vienna.

* * * *

It was one of the weaknesses of the Empire that it consisted of an aggregate of nations whose ideals were widely different. The Poles, for example, whose unity had been brutally destroyed by a criminal partition, were whole-heartedly for the French revolutionaries, who fully returned their sympathy. 'Long live Poland' was still a slogan of revolutionary France in 1830, in 1848 and under the Commune, as it was of radical France in 1900. The Hungarians, on the other hand, were perpetually clamouring for autonomy, and then there was Italy, still *irredente*, and the Balkan provinces arbitrarily attached to the Austro-Hungarian crown! It would thus be a mistake to think that the entire Austrian Empire was hostile to revolutionary France, hateful as the latter had become throughout all European countries through its bloodthirsty excesses; in Vienna itself, there was not complete unanimity; for Vienna had her own 'jacobins'.

These Austrian Jacobins could not have been very dangerous; they certainly included a number of Freemasons of the type of Schikaneder, Mozart, Gieseke, and Ignaz von Born, who was the technical adviser to the librettist and composer on the Masonic element in *The Magic Flute*.

Proscribed by the autocratic Maria Theresa, tolerated and perhaps even secretly encouraged by Joseph II, forbidden once more by Leopold, Freemasonry was not, in its essential doctrines, revolutionary: on the contrary, the fact that in the beginning it recruited its adherents through a strict system of co-opting from the upper classes of society proves that it intended to oppose the ideal of violent upheaval with one of progressive reform, orderly and patient. This humanitarian and philosophic movement, enamoured of progress but hostile to popular uprisings, seeking to accomplish its reforms in peace, legality and concord, in that true human brotherhood preached by Sarastro and not that of the French Jacobins with the ruthless challenge, 'Fraternity or death!' – this Freemasonry of kings and princes, of great artists and thinkers (the names of Mozart and Goethe shed sufficient glory on it) might have saved Europe from the blind violence and catastrophic excesses of revolution . . .

There were certainly, then, a number of Freemasons, idealistic liberals, intellectuals, civil servants, magistrates and teachers, among those Viennese Jacobins who would have liked to see the reforms of Joseph II brought back and totally applied; they probably wished to go still further along the road shown by the Encyclopedists and the 'men of '89'.

The chief ground of complaint about them was their connection with the Parisian Jacobins. Emissaries of the Revolution had found their way into Austria at the same time as the émigrés, sometimes, possibly, under the mask of émigrés; they worked on public opinion, as much from proselytizing zeal as to create a current of feeling hostile to relentless war.

But nobody who knew the Viennese could expect them to welcome French revolutionary propaganda at the very moment when the French revolution had just murdered an Austrian princess. The great majority of the Viennese were wholeheartedly with the volunteers who set off to fight against the Republican armies, and the common people, unwarlike as they usually were, joined in with enthusiasm. Those who could not fight gave what support they could. The Emperor having set the example by melting down his gold plate, the aristocracy and bourgeoisie sacrified their silver; the town corporations themselves brought to the melting-pot their ancient insignia, the chiselled cups, some of which dated back to the Middle Ages. A spirit of unity pervaded all classes of society, and children, workmen and humble artisans contributed their mite to swell the war treasury of the Empire.

Thorough-going patriots, always zealous in pursuit of suspects, traitors and spies, loudly demanded that justice should track down all Jacobins and massacre them to expiate the Viennese bloodshed in Paris. Great publicity was given to the *Souvenirs* of a certain Joseph Weber, who had been foster-brother to Marie-Antoinette and as such, summoned by her to Paris, where he had tried to defend his childhood friend. Having joined the Swiss guards, who had been massacred in the Tuileries, and having been saved by a miracle after the death of Marie-Antoinette, whom he had tried in vain to rescue, he had come back to Vienna and related his adventures. The tales of this eyewitness, describing the atrocities he had seen, confirmed the people of Vienna in their conviction that 'there was no possibility of an understanding with such men' and that the bad citizens who strove to promote an agreement with them and to weaken the national will to war deserved no pity and must be severely punished.

A public petition was therefore posted outside the door of St Stephen's cathedral, according to a very ancient tradition, demanding the death of all Austrian Jacobins. The strength of popular feeling decided the police authorities, who had hitherto waited on events, to take action against possible trouble-makers. An unfrocked monk, Martinovicz, who had been fomenting insurrection in Hungary, and who was known to be subsidized by the Jacobins, was arrested and condemned to death, as was also Lieutenant von Hebenstreit, in whose house were found subversive tracts and explosives, and who was in touch with the irredentist movement in Poland. The other accused were less severely treated, being sentenced merely to a term of punishment. Viennese Jacobinism, thus deprived of its leaders, died out of its own accord; it was only to recover its vigour half a century later with the revolution of 1848.

Napoleon in Vienna

In 1797, when Bonaparte declared his intention of striking at the heart of Austria by seizing Vienna, and advanced as far as Leoben, the whole population was afire with a passionate resolve to fight the French. Each social class adopted a military organization befitting its resources and aptitudes. The nobility equipped squadrons of cavalry, of which Prince Liechtenstein took command; the bourgeoisie gathered its cohorts. Amongst the artisans, the woodworkers showed themselves the most resolute; fifteen hundred of them banded together, swearing to die to the last man rather than surrender. The University, led by its Rector, the Professor of Medicine, Quarin, sought the honour of bearing into battle the flags of those regiments which had won fame in the war against the Turks. Art students, singing old ballads, followed their standard bearer, the engraver Schmutzer.

Sensational 'conversions' were welcomed, such as that of the historian Watteroth, freethinker, disciple of the Encyclopedists, cosmopolitan and left-winger, who spoke up for the most intransigent patriotism and joined the ranks of student fighters. In the *Memoiren aus meinem Leben* of the playwright Ignaz Friedrich Castelli, who had joined the university legion at the age of sixteen, we can read a picturesque and sincere account of the atmosphere of Vienna at that time. 'I cannot describe the enthusiasm with which all, young and old, rich and poor, great and small, offered themselves to defend their homeland,' he writes. 'I saw many of my friends weeping because they were too small or too weak to be taken.' This unanimity of feeling among the

Viennese gave the city the special appearance of a barracks humming with patriotic and warlike song.

Since in this most musical of cities, any important event in the national life had to be accompanied with music, composers set to work too. Beethoven wrote his *Austrian War Song* and his *Song of Farewell to the Citizens of Vienna*, on the occasion of the volunteers' departure, which the soldiers sang on the field of battle; old Haydn wrote his *Missa in tempore belli*. He also offered Count Saurau to write a national hymn, which had never hitherto been felt necessary; this grave and beautiful hymn was played for the first time on February 12, 1797, the Emperor Francis's birthday.

It was perhaps this valiant attitude of the Viennese which persuaded Bonaparte to accept peace, or rather to sign the peace preliminaries at Leoben. The city's danger had been averted for the time being; the troops came back in triumph as if they had actually fought and won. They had shown in any case, even if they had not yet received their baptism of fire, that Vienna had another ideal than that traditionally attributed to her and summed up in the title of a famous Strauss waltz: *Wine, women and song*. The students reaped full honours; each of them received a silver medal and the professors who had marched at their head a gold one. The Emperor reviewed all the troops on the glacis.

The war was not over, for all that; it was obvious that the French would not give up their intention of bringing republicanism into every country, either by force or by cunning. A skilful propaganda campaign run by the Directoire was to sow dissension abroad in order to promote French ambitions and to disorganize, internally, her enemies' will to resistance. These manoeuvres, cleverly carried out by secret agents, irritated the Viennese, and there was a real uprising on the day when the huge tricolour flag, hanging down to the ground, appeared on the house of the banker Geymuller, who was known to be a good patriot.

What had happened? The respected financier had certainly not gone over to the Jacobins, but General Bernadotte, who had come to Vienna as ambassador for the French Republic, had taken up residence in this fine house in the Wallnerstrasse, from which he had promptly flown his country's flag. The crowd considered this action an unforgivable provocation and gathered in the street, demanding, with angry shouts, that the hated emblem be removed. The chief of police hurried up and tried to calm the demonstrators, explained the incident and, appealing to diplomatic custom, begged his hearers to go quietly home. Of course they did no such thing, and to understand the attitude of these worthy Viennese one must remember that for them there was no difference between the Terror and the Directoire, that all Frenchmen seemed to them bloodthirsty monsters who murdered priests and aristocrats and had no greater pleasure than to see heads roll under the blade of the guillotine.

It was explained to Bernadotte that he would appease the crowd and put an end to the affair by withdrawing his flag; he refused to do so. Then the populace stormed the house, pushing aside the soldiers of the Imperial army who had been brought along to establish order, smashing windows with stones and crossing swords with Bernadotte's escort, who had taken up their arms. One bold spirit climbed up as far as the flag-pole and threw the banner on to the ground, where it was immediately torn up and burned.

A few demonstrators were wounded in the fray; that was enough to set the rumour flying round the city that the French were massacring the Viennese; after which the Imperial police, even with the help of hurriedly summoned soldiers, were powerless to control the rioters. They sacked the unfortunate banker's house, from which Bernadotte had hastily fled; he was said to have taken refuge in the Papal Nuncio's residence in the nearby Naglergasse and even the most hot-headed were reluctant to pursue him thither. Once the French had stopped resisting and Geymüller's house had been sacked, the crowd calmed down and the police were able to restore order.

The incident was not closed, however; from the Nuncio's residence, Bernadotte had written a letter of protest to the Emperor and demanded his passport back, describing the disturbance as an insult to France and its government in the person of the Ambassador; an insult for which the Austrian ministers were responsible, directly or indirectly, since they had been incapable of protecting him, Bernadotte, when his flag was desecrated. He demanded consequently that they themselves provide him with a new French flag and hoist it over the Ambassador's house; he insisted, finally, on the gravity of the *casus belli* which thus infringed the law of nations, and announced that Bonaparte would certainly wreak sensational vengeance if he were not given complete satisfaction.

The Emperor and the Minister of Police had no desire to provoke another demonstration simply for the sake of calming the Ambassador's wrath, particularly as, once their annoyance had subsided, the worthy Viennese had gone back to their everyday occupations; it was to be feared, however, that the sight of a new tricolour flag might provoke fresh disturbances. They therefore eluded Bernadotte's demands and gave him his passport, after which the indignant general, cursing Vienna and theatening horrible reprisals, left the town and went off to Rastatt.

These threats were empty; Bonaparte disavowed his envoy. He was preparing his Egyptian expedition at this time and had no wish to be involved in fresh war with Austria. The Viennese considered this a victory; but other dangers awaited them, new campaigns launched by Napoleon as First Consul and then as Emperor, with all the risks and dangers that war inevitably brings. They could be grateful, however, to the Emperor Francis for taking the precaution of securing strong allies for Austria, ensuring England's help by means of a firm treaty and Russia's by marrying the Archduke Joseph to a daughter of Tsar Paul.

The Viennese realized what useful assistance they would get from these powers, and watched with curiosity the crowd of foreign officers whom these alliances brought to their capital. The English admiral Nelson, greatly admired for his distinction and simplicity, was the most warmly acclaimed. They stared with some amazement at the illustrious Russian general Suvarov, recognizable – amidst staff officers in glittering uniforms and medals – by the almost coarse simplicity of his equipment. This audacious little man, highly-strung, intransigent and wild-eyed, wore a faded old coat and a sheepskin cloak like a mountain shepherd.

Strange things were told of him; dressed like one of his private soldiers, he ate like them from a mess-tin and slept on the bare ground; in the finest palaces he stayed in he had to have a thin palliasse laid on the floor; moreover all mirrors had to be removed or hidden before he arrived, for he smashed them in a rage as soon as he caught sight of his reflection in a glass; popular superstition explained this curious conduct by the fact that he had sold his soul to the devil, or rather his reflection – which is surely the same thing – in exchange for the victories which the Evil One had promised him. And in the rôle of a fantastic figure, the 'man without a reflection', Suvarov appears in Hoffmann's famous story *Saint Sylvester's Night*.

War had begun again, meanwhile, with varying fortunes. The citizens of Vienna learnt with grief of the humiliating Peace of Lunéville, which brought about the disappearance of the Holy Roman Empire; henceforward Francis II could no longer bear the title of Emperor of a non-existent Germany. He simply kept that of Emperor of Austria, and as such became Francis I. But Austria, even thus so reduced, still remained the target for Napoleon's attacks, now that, as Emperor of the French, he aspired to European hegemony.

Francis maintained his alliance with England and Russia, but certain German states, Bavaria, Baden, and Würtemberg, had made common cause with France, which brought the Grand Army terribly close to the gates of Vienna. The papers told sad news, the gravity of which they tried to tone down, about Allied defeats, the capitulation of General Mack at Ulm, the entry of Napoleon into Munich, his arrival at Linz. The capital was felt to be directly threatened, and defensive measures were hurriedly prepared. Since the defeat of the Turks no foreign foe had come within shooting distance of the bastions and the present threat came from considerable forces, flushed with victory, hardened by many campaigns and provided with powerful artillery against which the old fortifications might perhaps be useless.

Technicians were consulted, and pointed out that habitual

indolence and a prolonged period of security had caused the Viennese to neglect elementary precautions, and that the bastions which had checked the Turks would be easily demolished by French gunfire. There was not even any question of a siege; the picturesque old ramparts which provided such delightful walks would offer no defence to a city threatened by invasion. Only one course was left to avoid annihilation: Vienna must capitulate.

Having taken this decision, and wishing to spare himself the shame of so humiliating a procedure, Emperor Francis left for Olmütz, where he was to join Tsar Alexander. The public treasury, the most important archives, State papers and art collections were removed. Many citizens, fearing lest the arrival of the French might let loose a reign of terror, hastened to leave the town – that unfortunate town which had been saved from the Turks but which was to be handed over to barbarians, since Napoleon was, in fact, a revolutionary wearing an Imperial crown. The army retreated too; Vienna retained only a civic militia, responsible for keeping order if it could. Everyone secretly hoped that the Tyrant would accept capitulation, which would spare their beloved city the horrors of forcible occupation and its inevitable consequences, pillage, fire and slaughter. And so the Viennese awaited with anguish the return of their burgomaster and the city magistrates, who had gone to Puckersdorf to negotiate with Murat about the surrender of the city.

There was, however, no question of unconditional surrender. The Viennese plenipotentiaries agreed to capitulate only if their conqueror guaranteed the protection of their religion and their public buildings, together with the safety of the citizens and their property. Murat having refused to make any such promise, the delegation departed for Sieghartskirchen, where Napoleon was staying. The latter generously accepted the conditions suggested by the Viennese; after which French regiments prepared to take possession of the town, in which no foreign army had set foot for centuries past. Kralik tells us[4]:

'On November 13, about midday, Murat and Lannes entered the city through the Burgtor, at the head of the advance guard, fifteen thousand strong in battle array, with flags flying and bugles playing, while the civic guard paid honour to them. The French marched quickly through the town, by way of the Kohlmarkt, St Stephen's Square and the Red Tower; then, crossing Leopoldstadt, they reached the Tabor bridge across the great river. Austrians were still on guard there, ready to set fire to the wooden bridge as soon as the enemy came in sight. But the Frenchmen seized the bridge by surprise, as also the artillery park beyond the Danube, and thus seriously threatened the retreating Austro-Russian army; this decided the fate of the campaign.'

The French Occupation

The Viennese were thus enabled to behold almost daily the Corsican Ogre of whom they were so terrified. Napoleon used to gallop through the town escorted by marshals and aides de camp in gaudily braided uniforms. In the early days of the occupation, he had planned to live in the Hofburg, but, although the citizens seemed inoffensive, he did not feel at ease in the heart of an enemy city; he therefore moved out, a few days later, to Schönbrunn, that same Schönbrunn where his son, the 'King of Rome', was to spend the last years of his short life and meet his sad death. He reviewed his troops, he organized parades and marches, he watched performances of ballet, opera and tragedy given by Viennese companies augmented by a crowd of dancers, singers and actors from Paris.

These performances were invariably accompanied by the tumultuous and yet formal ceremonial which the Emperor had instituted, and which made so sharp a contrast with the mingled distinction, solemnity and simplicity of the Austrian court. Viennese society, reluctant to frequent the theatre in company with French officers, avoided such performances. Thus it happened that the first performance of *Fidelio*, which took place at the Theater an der Wien on November 20, 1805, had an audience consisting solely of French officers, most of whom were probably quite indifferent to music in general and could scarcely have appreciated Beethoven's masterpiece, although the ideas which it exalted were precisely those which had inspired the Revolution. They pointed out to one another, with amused curiosity, the great leonine head of the composer with its wild, untamed black curls. Beethoven conducted with all the fire and passion that possessed him as soon as he mounted the rostrum; this romantic vehemence disconcerted the indifferent and shocked the fastidious – for there were some of these even in Napoleon's army; nothing of this sort had ever been seen or heard in Paris, they said; what strange folk these Viennese were!

Although they were by nature inclined to put up with any situation, even the most painful or embarrassing, the people of Vienna found the French occupation very hard to bear. When citizens lived side by side with soldiers of the occupying army, unintentional clashes inevitably arose which frequently degenerated into street fights. Napoleon then threatened to inflict crushing penalties on the city and to take hostages, and this heightened that terror of the French which the Viennese had felt ever since 1789. And then, at the beginning of December, came the battle of Austerlitz, and at the end of the month the Treaty of Pressburg; peace was restored – for how long? nobody dared ask! – and in the middle of January 1806, the Emperor Francis and the Imperial family returned to their beloved city.

'They were welcomed in the Donauspitz by mounted guardsmen and by the Burgomaster. The suburbs and streets of the town, through which the procession passed, were decorated just as at Whitsuntide, but with branches of pine and fir. The City Council were all gathered at the Red Tower. The procession moved on to the Cathedral, where the Te Deum was sung, and thence to the castle. Two days later Archduke Charles, who had returned from Italy with the victorious army, was also given a joyful reception. The Emperor issued a proclamation promising "to raise up the State by the development of true intellectual culture, the prosperity of national industry and the re-establishment of public credit". Keen efforts were also made to strengthen the army. The civic militia drilled incessantly. The horrors of war called forth admirable acts of self-sacrifice from the men and women of Vienna.'[5]

The period during which the French armies, having invaded Austria, dwelt as conquerors in its capital was one of the most anxious and distressing in the history of Vienna. The memoirs of the time, notably those of the novelist Karoline Pichler, gave a vivid picture of the state of mind then predominant. The traditional optimism of the Viennese had been cruelly disappointed. They were so sure that 'things always worked out in the end', but experience had shown that things did not always work out as they wished, nor to their advantage.

This optimism had been severely shaken by the sight of the French Revolution, which the powers of this world, with the support of the powers above, ought to have crushed without effort; on the contrary, the Revolution had triumphed, and Napoleon, in spite of being an Emperor, was none the less a former Jacobin, the associate and possibly even the friend of that 'Robas-Boar', or Robespierre, who had aroused such horror and alarm in the hearts of tens of thousands of Eipeldauers. The sight of the French army astonished the townsfolk; the extraordinary uniforms of Murat's hussars, the Mamelukes of the Guard dressed like janissaries – arousing hateful memories of the Turks – the *grognards*, long-bearded veterans in shaggy bearskin caps, all this seemed a fantastic spectacle to the gaping crowd, used as they were to the Imperial soldiers clad in white and pink, light blue or fresh green. The astonishing story went round that some of Napoleon's marshals, covered with decorations, plumes and gold braid, were former artisans or inn-servants who had won their epaulettes on the field of battle. Their names were plebeian and lacked the noble ring of those generals' names familiar to Austrian ears, recalling all the glories of the Empire. The Viennese were naturally inclined to venerate anyone who bore a title. They readily dubbed any well-dressed gentleman *von*, Baron or Excellency without inquiring closely into his degree of nobility. This, however, did not prevent them, working-class and middle-class alike, from being well-informed on matters of rank and precedence in the aristocracy, and taking the greatest interest in all incidents in the life of great families.

Strollers along the Jaegerzeile would gaze with wonder on Sundays and holidays at the carriages that drove past on their way to the Prater, and when the vehicle slowed down enough for them to recognize the coat of arms painted on its doors they knew enough heraldry to tell correctly whose it was. The picturesque German term 'ermine flea' (*Ermelinfloh*), bestowed on anyone too much enamoured of titles and too eager to live in the wake of the nobility, as though clinging to a courtier's robes, can aptly be applied to the bourgeois of Vienna. They loved their Imperial aristocracy, they rejoiced in its existence, and when they were allowed to be present at its festivities, if only as spectators in the street, they felt as if they were taking part in these, and belonged, at least in the capacity of onlookers, to this splendid spectacle.

The French, on the other hand, had guillotined their sovereigns and their nobles, whose places and functions they had given to adventurers, people of low birth, whom the Revolution had enriched and of whom war had made generals and marshals. The bourgeoisie of Vienna gazed with suspicion at these upstart nobles, this unpolished soldiery, these counts and barons whose wives looked like *vivandières* or washerwomen. The pomp and the enormous scale of Napoleon's military parades merely made their heads reel without impressing them; Schikaneder's theatre did things better, they reminded one another, quoting the spectacular shows in which that producer of genius had displayed armed men in their thousands, fired cannon and sent up balloons.

The occupying army took up too much room and made too much noise. It brought the ill-mannered rowdiness of camp or barrack-room into the drawing-rooms of Vienna and even into the theatre, as Karoline Pichler shrewdly notes in her memoirs. This, for instance, was what happened at the Opera:

'When we reached the theatre, which is a charming, graceful building, we found the galleries full of noisy French soldiers in gaudy uniforms. The curtain had not yet risen, for they were waiting for the Emperor. After this had gone on for some time, enabling me to contrast it with the punctuality of our kind ruler, who was always careful not to keep the public or officials waiting, about eight o'clock there was suddenly heard a furious drum-roll which announced the Emperor's arrival. And again I could not help comparing this unfriendly din to the alarm-signals we use for exceptional and tragic happenings such as outbreaks of fire . . . He went into his box and sat down, a pamphlet in his hand; behind him stood his aides de camp, or something of the sort. So this was the man who had made earth tremble, the man who shook all the thrones of Europe and had overturned more than one of them. What was he going to do next, this man to whom nothing seemed impossible, in whose hands all our destinies lie? That was what I was wondering, during the performance of a one-act play by Sargine, followed by a slight entertainment to which my mind paid little attention, so absorbed was I by that terrible man up there in his box!'

This hostility to Napoleon caused the Viennese to welcome with warm sympathy the French royalists who visited their city, and it was because of her hatred for the Emperor and his army, rather than her fame or the beauty of her writings, that Mme de Staël, high priestess of the resistance movement against Napoleon, was fêted by the Austrians; she amply repaid them by praising, with her customary lyric eloquence, the beauty and charms of their capital. It is of the greatest interest to read her descriptions of Viennese scenes in *De l'Allemagne*, that book which introduced so many people to the Germanic world, its poets and its thinkers.

Her romantic sensibility is stirred by the sight of herds of deer grazing in the Prater, her love for the Gothic inspires a brilliant page on St Stephen's Cathedral, and she speaks with affection of the happy, lovable population of Vienna, which offers a perfect picture of concord and peace. 'One never meets a single beggar,' she asserts, 'for everyone takes such care of his fellows that no citizen of Vienna is lacking in the necessities of life.' Everything astonishes and delights her, working-class districts and aristocratic salons, the old towns and the surrounding forest, the kindly behaviour of the great towards the humble, of the rich towards the poor.

The Return of the French

Although the Treaty of Pressburg deprived Austria of Venetia, Tyrol and Swabia, although the Rhenish League put almost the whole of Germany at Napoleon's disposal, although Russia, in 1808, went over to the side of France in order to paralyze Austria in her eastward ambitions, although Austria was left practically isolated – Britain was officially her ally but one never knew what Britain would do for or against her allies – the country resisted Napoleon and became, in the eyes of anti-revolutionary Europe, the very symbol of 'legitimacy'. It had, fortunately, a great statesman at its head, Stadion, who strove to mobilize the whole nation, body and soul, in the struggle against 'the usurper'.

Although so unwarlike by nature, the people of Vienna prepared with unwavering courage and occasional enthusiasm to face the fortunes of war. In order to avoid being taken unawares as in 1805, they reinforced the bastions, and a special army was formed, the Landwehr, devoted as its name implies to the country's defence, in which all who were willing could enrol without distinction of class or profession. Even the timid felt their confidence heightened by the example of the Tyrolese, who remained faithful to Austria although the Treaty of Pressburg had handed them over to Bavaria, and the proud attitude of their leader, Andreas Hofer, who with his long beard, martial bearing and strange mountaineer's dress was much admired by the people of Vienna. 'It was a national war in the highest degree. Everyone was as deeply concerned about the affairs of the state as about his personal affairs. The nation had become an army, the army had become the nation in arms. All the citizens were inspired with love for their country, with enthusiasm for their independence, hatred for foreign tyranny, and a keen uplifting sense of their own valour and strength.'[6]

After this powerful and unanimous impulse of devotion to their country of faith in its glorious destiny and confident expectation of victory, the sudden arrival of the French, who reached the outskirts of Vienna on May 9, 1809, plunged the population into a state of despair that can well be imagined. It had been hoped that the Germans would stop or at least delay the advance of Napoleon, and the Germans, betraying their blood-brothers, had let the invader pass and, for the most part, had rallied to his standards. The efforts made by the whole population to consolidate the fortifications, to arm the bastions with massed cannon and to cut off the enemy's route had been vain. Vainly, indeed, had they tried to check the torrent with makeshift methods, ineffectual and sometimes ridiculous; they cut down the trees in the Prater, those trees planted by Joseph II to provide shady walks, and made absurd barricades with them, inadequate fences; they burned the bridge, which the French bridge-builders, picked men who were to distinguish themselves by their self-sacrifice during the retreat from Russia, promptly replaced by bridges of boats. It had been hoped that these desperate measures would enable the Archduke Charles to arrive from Bohemia with his army in time to bar the enemy's road.

Although the French had reached the outskirts, it was still hoped to defend the part of the town enclosed within the 'belt' (*Gürtel*) and protected by the Linienwall, but it was already too late. The couriers sent by Napoleon ordered the 'Emperor's apartment' in the castle of Schönbrunn, which the conqueror had occupied four years before, to be got ready for him, and soon after this his staff took possession of Maria Theresa's splendid castle, whose park served once again for their soldiers' manoeuvres, reviews and shooting practice, watched by the Emperor from an upper balcony.

All was not lost however; Archduke Charles might arrive at any moment, and the fate of battle would then change in the Austrians' favour: they must hold out until then. So Vienna fought on, with a noble courage and stubbornness that deserved a happier fate.

'Meanwhile the French army had succeeded in investing the town; the French lines, describing a huge circle, went on the one hand from Schönbrunn to the Danube through the western suburbs, Ottakring, Waehring and Doebbing; on the other, from Schönbrunn to the Wienerberg and the Danube. On the other side of the river lay the Austrian army corps under Hiller, but it was not strong enough to attack. The Archduke Charles and his army were expected from Bohemia. The Viennese rejected a summons to surrender the town, and on May 11 the French opened the attack on two sides. On the south, Napoleon had a bridge of boats laid over the

Danube canal, over which his troops reached the Prater. On the Prater were a number of Austrian grenadiers, ensuring communication between the city and the opposite bank of the Danube. While they were valiantly resisting the attack of the French troops, Vienna's attention was concentrated on the enemy's second operation. General Bertrand had had batteries set up behind the Imperial stables; they began firing as soon as it grew dark. Several fires broke out in the city.'[7]

This disquieting situation was worsened by the fact that the batteries on the bastions must inevitably be defeated in an artillery duel and that, since the grenadiers in the Prater had all been massacred, communication on that side had been cut off. This laid a heavy responsibility on Archduke Maximilian, who was in charge of operations and in command of the troops. To persist in standing out against an enemy far stronger than the town's garrison exposed the latter to a long siege or, worse still, to a bombardment so merciless that it seemed useless to save Vienna if Vienna were to become only a heap of smoking ruins. The Archduke therefore proposed to surrender the city, and it is much to the honour of the Viennese that they protested indignantly at what they thought a shameful capitulation.

Maximilian's attitude was less noble, but wiser; in any case, Archduke Charles could not possibly arrive in time to save the situation now. Cut off from all communication with Olmütz, where the Emperor was, he could not inform him of the disaster or ask for orders. When Francis, warned by a courier who had managed to get through the besieging lines, ordered the archduke to hold out at least two days longer, the message arrived too late; Maximilian had already informed Napoleon of the city's surrender. He had ordered the troops to retreat and the gates to be opened; the cannon on the fortifications had ceased fire. The white flag was floating over the Burgtor.

On May 13 at dawn, a delegation led by Burgomaster Wohlleben, Archbishop Hohenwart and Count Dietrichstein left for Schönbrunn amidst general consternation. At the same moment the French troops from the Prater marched down the Jaegerzeile towards the centre of the town. The

Vienna in 1770

A perspective view of the centre of Vienna in 1770 showing (*top left*) the
Hofburg, (*centre left*) the Graben and St. Stephen's Cathedral and (*right*) the city
ramparts and the Danube

Maria Theresa

2

Maria Theresa, Empress of Austria from 1740 to 1780, whose taste for luxury and display was more to Viennese liking than her son's attempted austerity

3

The Gloriette, built in 1775 in the gardens of the Schönbrun palace, Maria Theresa's favourite residence

Joseph II

4
Joseph II (1780–90), the 'revolutionary' Emperor

5
Joseph II taking the plough. One of his many reforms was
the abolition of serfdom in 1783

Pomp and Circumstance

6

The Belvedere with its gardens, generally considered the
masterpiece of Lukas von Hildebrandt, was built in 1714–
1723 for Prince Eugene of Savoy

7

Tightly-laced stays and high panniers, fashions banned by
Joseph II: a satirical engraving of 1784

8
Joseph II driving in the Prater, with the Lusthaus in the background

9
Pope Pius VI, disturbed by Joseph II's anticlericalism, visits Vienna in 1782

The Life of the People

10

A market scene in the Am Hof Square, typical of the lively Viennese streets

11

The Prater was the favourite resort of the people; this picture shows the *Funfkreuzerdanz*

12

The famous St. Bridget's Day celebrations in the Prater were attended by large crowds from all classes

13
The first railways, built in 1823, were regarded by the
Viennese as a new form of entertainment

14
This picture of the Archduchess Sophie with her four eldest
children reflects the sentimental taste of the biedermeier
period

15 and 16

The writings of Adalbert Stifter (1805–1868) (*right*), the romantic poet and novelist, and Franz Grillparzer (1791–1872) (*below right*) are a valuable source of information about daily life at this time

Music

17

Wolfgang Amadeus Mozart (1756–1791), who was taken up by Maria Theresa as a child prodigy, but neglected by the Viennese in later life

18

A view of the Graben, where Mozart lived in 1781 and again from 1783–4

19

Ludwig van Beethoven (1770–1827) composed some of his greatest works in Vienna from 1792 onwards

20

The Burg-Kapelle in the Hofburg, one of the centres of the great Viennese musical tradition. A Te Deum is being sung and the orchestra can be seen up in the boxes

21

Franz Schubert (1797–1828) and his friends at one of their
celebrated musical parties. Schubert's spontaneous and
lyrical gifts made him a far more popular composer with the
Viennese than were Mozart and Beethoven

Opera and Theatre

22

(*right*) Emmanuel Schikaneder (1751–1812), who wrote the libretto of *The Magic Flute*, in the rôle of Papageno

23

(*below*) The famous *Theater an der Wien* where *The Magic Flute, Fidelio* and *Die Fledermaus* were first performed

24

(*left*) An engraved title-pag
The Magic Flute, shov
masonic symbols

25

A scene from *Der Diaman*
des Geisterkonigs, one o
Ferdinand Raimund'
famous magic plays

26
Johann Nestroy (1801–62) (*right*), Raimund's successful rival on the
stage, with two actor friends

27
The *Silbernen Kaffeehaus* was the scene of many literary and musical
gatherings. On the right of the cashier are Lanner and the elder
Strauss, while in front of them with raised arm is Ferdinand Raimund

28
The old Burgtheater, founded by Joseph II in 1776 as a national theatre

The Napoleonic Wars and after

29
The gaiety of Vienna was disturbed by the Napoleonic Wars.
In 1809 French troops besieged the city and captured it for
the second time

30
At the Congress of Vienna in 1815 the future of Europe was
decided. This contemporary engraving shows assembled
rulers and delegates to the Congress

31
During the Congress Vienna was a hotbed of rumour and espionage, and meeting-places like Junglings Coffee House were centres of gossip and intrigue

32
Josef Lanner (1801–1843), the famous composer of waltzes
and rival of the elder Strauss, in his uniform of Kapellmeister
of the 2nd Vienna City Regiment

33
Johann Strauss the younger (1825–99)

34
The *Goldenen Birne*, one of the many ballrooms in early nineteenth-century Vienna

35
This contemporary engraving illustrates the passion for dancing among all classes of society. Places of enjoyment included (*top to bottom*) a masked ball, the Sofienbadsaal, Dommayers Casino, the Elysium, a barracks, and a private house

36
The Elysium, in the Annagasse, had two ballrooms, the
Gemütliche (or homely) *Europa* (*above*), and the *Elegante
Europa* (*below*) for the higher ranks of society

1848

37

The students' watchguard played an important part in the rising of 1848

38

Fighting outside St. Stephen's Cathedral in October 1848

garrison had been summoned to lay down its arms and hand them over to the victors; soldiers would be treated as prisoners of war and taken off; the militiamen of the Land-wehr, whose military status France did not recognize as legal, could have been treated as irregular snipers and shot; but Napoleon proved generous, and merely ordered these regiments to be dissolved. He issued warning, however, that any citizens rash enough still to belong to such paramilitary organizations would be executed, that their homes would be burned and their property confiscated.

Had the surrender been premature? Had Archduke Maximilian capitulated too hurriedly? Could the two days' resistance ordered by the Emperor have saved Austria from disaster? Probably not. When the French troops piled their arms in the squares of Vienna and installed themselves in its public buildings, Charles and his troops had only reached Bisamberg on the Danube, and had there come into conflict with Napoleon, who had advanced to meet them. On May 21 the two armies joined battle at Aspern and at Essling; the fighting went on until July 12, when an armistice was signed which both sides desired equally, Charles to allow his troops a breathing-space, Napoleon to avoid a battle whose issue was uncertain. Charles had acquired glory at Essling, where he had faced the Grande Armée and its allies alone. This won him the fine title of 'conqueror of the Uncon-querable One', first bestowed on him by Von Kleist.

For many Viennese the armistice came as a relief; they could hope, indeed, that once peace was concluded the French would depart. The latter's presence was resented by many people as humiliating and deeply distressing. Old Haydn died of grief. Salieri had given his oratorio, *The Creation*, before the capture of the city, on March 28, in the *Aula Magna* of the University, and on this occasion a touching scene had been witnessed: Beethoven kissing the old master's head and hands, with affectionate fervour. The sight of French uniforms in the streets of his beloved Vienna was so rude a shock to the veteran musician that he took to his bed, leaving it only to go to his piano and play the national hymn which he had composed three years earlier; the effort and the emotion exhausted him, but he was resolved to share in his country's sufferings. By a supreme irony, when he died on May 31, French uniforms surrounded his coffin. Napoleon, showing himself a magnanimous victor, aware of a great man's worth and also of the way such a gesture would be appreciated throughout Europe, had provided a guard of honour for the former Kapellmeister of the Esterhazy princes.

The city meanwhile was gradually growing used to the presence of the French. Napoleon's birthday was celebrated on August 15 with the same ceremonial and the same rejoicings as that of Emperor Francis, without provoking untoward incidents. Vienna had ceased to regard the great emperor as the 'Corsican Ogre'; his officers were welcomed in aristocratic drawing-rooms, waltzed and no doubt flirted with Viennese girls.

The liberals were grateful to the French for certain measures these had taken, particularly the abolition of censorship. This was cunningly done, for the Emperor retained the right to seize any book or newspaper whose tone displeased him; he kept personal watch over them. On the other hand, as a former Jacobin, he noted with satisfaction the ferment of subversive ideas which this freedom would encourage; whatever favoured anti-Hapsburg propaganda in any degree served his own policy at the same time, and he knew that nothing would more certainly weaken Austria than the diffusion of revolutionary ideas.

A section of the population was won over to the French by means of this cunning tolerance. The 'resistance movement' diminished gradually as the Viennese came to realize with relief that the French were not such terrorists as they had been made out. Great as had been their former loathing for Napoleon, they did not approve of the attempt made on his life by Staps, son of a German pastor, who had come from Naumburg to Vienna to stab him. Vienna had now accepted Napoleon as 'the man of destiny', and with its usual fatalism was ready to endure his triumph, though hoping this would not last too long. The attempted assassination, nevertheless, was highly detrimental to the Emperor's prestige. Napoleon wanted the Council of War that tried the young man to declare him insane; Europe must be made to think that only a madman was capable of an attempt on the life of the Unconquerable One. This would have allowed him to display generosity towards this impulsive and demented student by granting him his life. Staps, with great resolution, declared himself fully responsible for his act, and, proud as an antique Roman, replied to the judges who urged him to express regret for his behaviour in these simple words: 'I regret nothing, save having failed in my object.' He spoke with such noble simplicity, courage and wisdom that the military tribunal had no other course but to condemn him to death and send him to the firing squad as soon as sentence had been pronounced.

The feelings of the Viennese had been stirred on the unfortunate young hero's behalf; they did not like Napoleon's attempt to diminish the greatness of the youth's action by attributing it to the aberration of a madman. This seemed to them a petty-minded gesture unworthy of such a man. They also wished that, having been obliged to condemn him, Napoleon had then reprieved him. By so doing he might have won their hearts and ensured his popularity amongst them. By executing young Staps he had increased the latter's stature: the poor boy became a national hero, a glorious figure worthy of popular remembrance, the symbol of Liberty rising up against Tyranny as though in some great allegorical fresco. The Treaty of Vienna, which was signed three days after the death of Staps in the moats around the city, appeared all the more cruel and unjust to the Austrians, whom it deprived of many splendid provinces. The Ogre was showing his true nature again, they said, and it was with very mixed feelings that they learned, a year and a half later, that the Emperor Francis had consented to give his daughter Marie Louise in marriage to this 'crowned adventurer'.

The Sacrifice

The arrival of Marshal Berthier bringing this 'proposal' to the Hofburg did not arouse the violent reactions that Bernadotte and his flag had provoked, but an incredulous stupefaction. People could not believe that a Hapsburg would consent to the marriage of an Austrian princess with a former soldier of fortune, who had forced his way on to the throne. They recalled despairingly Marie-Antoinette's departure for Paris; and after all her bridegroom had been a Bourbon!

A marriage concluded under such circumstances could not have any favourable consequences; so thought the Viennese, incapable of discerning the political background to this diplomatic move, which they considered monstrous. And the people's judgment was correct, on the whole, since the political considerations that had moved the two rulers did not have the results they anticipated. Napoleon was soon to discover that a marriage does not necessarily mean an enduring alliance. This union, which brought Napoleon into the 'family' of crowned heads, was an illusory pledge of peace, valid only so long as Francis judged it to his country's advantage.

The day the marriage was celebrated in Vienna, March 11, 1810, Napoleon did not attend; people took note of this with a superstitious mistrust of marriages by proxy. They might have pointed out, too, to the simple souls who expected endless benefits from this ceremony, that Napoleon's representative at the altar was not one of his brothers nor one of his marshals, but Archduke Charles himself, the hero of Essling and Aspern, the 'conqueror of the Unconquerable One'. How could Vienna fail to see in this circumstance an omen of future misfortunes, fresh campaigns: the proof that the era of lasting peace had not yet come for the capital of the Empire?

CHAPTER SEVEN

CONGRESS DANCES . . .

Pageantry and Scandal—Memoirs and Plice Archives—
Vienna's Hundred Thousand Foreigners—Pamphlets and
Satires—The Leading Rôles—Castlereagh—Prince de Ligne—
Talleyrand—Alexander I—Metternich

There are various ways of writing the history of the Congress
of Vienna. One can treat it as did the Comte de la Garde-
Chambonas, obsessed with social gossip and immensely
proud of attending every reception, merely as a chronicle of
the intrigues and pleasures in which princes and princelings
indulged, as between balls and supper-parties they tore
France to pieces and played fast and loose with the rights of
national minorities.

One can consider it with the critical eyes of a Byron, as a
vile spectacle, arousing the disgust of any generous-minded
man. Or one can follow one of the most fascinating diplomatic games of chess in which European statesmen ever
indulged, and disentangle the threads of one of the most
complicated attempts ever made to ensure enduring peace to
a continent which Napoleonic wars had exhausted and bled
white.

Or finally, and this angle is the only one befitting the theme
and plan of the present work, one can watch the actors of this
play, which was alternately tragic and comic, and most
frequently both at once, with the eyes of a middle-class
citizen of Vienna, bewildered at seeing his dear city suddenly
made the centre of European activity, the stage on which a
new world was being created, or attempted, according to the
hopes of idealists.

The spectacle of these sovereigns threatening small States
in order to win them over, or securing their support through

dubious bargaining, was undoubtedly a vile one; but it was none the less a spectacle, and that was what mattered to the Viennese. To the man-in-the-street in Vienna, ill-informed of the political problems at stake, and barely acquainted with the private lives of these men who were making history, the Congress was just a long series of festivities which he witnessed from a distance, a pageant which went on for months and which was the more impressive because the actors bore illustrious names and wore magnificent clothes.

Pageantry and Scandal

But, throughout the Congress, the average gossip-loving Viennese was even more keenly interested in the scandals which were seething behind the scenes, the news, true or false, that each morning brought about the private lives of eminent personalities. This unwritten history was passed from mouth to mouth, transmitted by lackeys, chambermaids, footmen and grooms. Whoever picked up an exciting rumour hastily passed it on to his neighbours, and in a few hours it had gone all round the town and reached the suburbs.

Instead of its usual passionate concern with real or apocryphal incidents in the private lives of actors who had been its idols, Vienna now developed an interest in the clandestine liaisons of various sovereigns, in the shifting patterns caused by their continual change of partners as though in a quadrille. Nothing else was talked about in aristocratic or bourgeois drawing-rooms; rumours, often started in antechambers, spread to the courtyards of humble houses and ran through the streets, and the inextricable police network with which Hager, the Minister, had covered the whole city retained whatever bits of gossip might interest the Hofpolizei, adding fresh details and noting down the most insignificant tittle-tattle, all grist to the policeman's mill.

To the interest taken by the Austrian police in scandalous tales must be added the inquiries of the countless secret agents that each delegation had brought with it, disguised as secretaries or servants, who also listened with all their ears, searched the wastepaper baskets and the piles of rubbish that were swept away each morning, sure that they would happen some day upon an important document which would immediately be transmitted in cipher to the legation concerned. As the ingenuity of these spies had broken the most impenetrable codes, as letters were unsealed at the post office and read in a dark room before being sealed up again and sent to their addressees, as it was in everyone's interest to intercept everyone else's mail and find out what was in it, it happened that the population of Vienna knew all about what had been discussed in the Congress, or decided in some corner of a drawing-room between a group of diplomats, before the Governments concerned, in their far-off capitals, were informed of it.

All this was wildly exciting for gossip-mongers and formed the main topic of conversation between idlers at cafés, during the intervals of plays, or on expeditions into the Viennese forest, and every citizen of the capital thus had the flattering illusion of taking part in the Congress in a modest way, and of living through the exciting vicissitudes of this vast international comedy. Even more than the material benefits to be drawn from this influx of rich, idle foreigners, which was 'so good for trade', the Viennese appreciated the signal honour enjoyed by their city of harbouring so many visiting monarchs with their courtiers and attendants.

The benefits were real, in fact, only for those who profited directly from trade, for the considerable increase in demand, while supply remained roughly stationary, produced a scarcity of goods and a rise in the cost of living; the economic consequences of the Congress were thus the enrichment of a large number but, on the other hand, great inequality of wealth, causing disquiet in social relations; the eventual results of this were to be seen in the Revolution of 1848, which in certain respects sprang from the Congress.

A notable deterioration in morals was also an effect of this spectacular gathering, which, while it gave the Viennese so much to marvel at, also set some very bad examples. The dissipations of great men of every nation in this decent, well-behaved city, which delighted in innocent and almost childish amusements and whose very frivolity was incompatible with corruption, seemed to justify an immorality

157

which the subjects of Maria Theresa, Joseph II and Francis I had always considered reprehensible, and in any case had never met with in their own rulers; the licentious conduct of men as highly placed as the Tsar Alexander, the Grand Duke of Baden or the King of Würtemberg, to name only the most illustrious, might seem excusable or at least outside the range of criticism.

An undoubted lowering of moral standards also resulted from the fact that the Hofpolizei recruited so many ill-paid supernumeraries in addition to its regular personnel – a great many were needed, for there were so many people to be watched – and these amateur detectives, including society women as well as hotel chambermaids, developed a taste for this exciting profession, and prided themselves on playing a part, albeit a very minor one, in the vast comedy of which Metternich was director.

It was impossible to know who did or did not belong to these squads of voluntary spies, some of whom, the most highly-placed no doubt, had the enviable privilege of sending their reports direct to Hager, signed with their own names, or a pseudonym, or an identifying sign. The others communicated with the Ministry through the medium of various agents interposed between themselves and their supreme chief, and so had neither the chance of being rewarded for their successes nor, on the other hand, the misfortune of being blamed for their blunders or for an excess of zeal.

Memoirs and Police Archives

Our knowledge of the private history of the Congress comes to us through the memoirs of the time, which are innumerable, for almost everyone who took part in it wished to immortalize that honour by writing and publishing his or her recollections. The Memoirs of La Garde-Chambonas, those of the Baron de Vitrolles, those of Caulaincourt, Mme d'Arblay's Journal, that of the Duchess of Dino, Lady Holland's, and the monumental diary of Mme Junot, the letters of the turbulent Princess Lieven, the Creevey Papers and the Croker Papers, the correspondence of Lady Burghersh,

the Memoirs of Bourrienne and those of the Comtesse de
Boigne, and the precious Journal of Bertuchy give a slight
indication of all that was written by the protagonists and
witnesses of this troubled period.

And I have not mentioned the secrets revealed by the
leading actors, Castlereagh, Talleyrand, Metternich, Welling-
ton, Gentz and so many others.

The most picturesque and valuable documents are those
provided by the Hofpolizei itself, if we take the trouble to
scan its archives. The background of the Congress is disclosed
with as much indiscretion as shrewdness; few secrets escaped
the eyes of Hager's myrmidons. The Emperor Francis had
the reports of the day before brought to him each morning,
and he devoured them with childish curiosity; it amused him
enormously to discover what foreign rulers had been doing,
even when their actions were perfectly insignificant and quite
devoid of political purport. When we look through these files
we learn that on such a day, at such an hour, the King of
Prussia went out in civilian clothes with a round hat pulled
down over his eyes, and that at ten in the evening he had not
yet come back; that the Emperor of Russia had a big block of
ice brought to him each morning to wash his hands and face;
that the Grand Duke of Baden had spent the night in a
brothel . . .

Spies were recruited everywhere. Baron Hager urged his
agent Siber and State Councillor La Roze to make frequent
use of the Jews. 'On account of the influence you have in the
leading Jewish houses, you will easily find among the heads
of these houses or the more intelligent of their sons, individuals capable of procuring information likely to be of interest
to the political police.'[1]

Similar instructions were given to people well-known in
society who were not averse to procuring information, such as
a certain Baron von Leurs, to whom Hager wrote as follows:[2]

'I have the honour to request you not only to take pains to draw
every possible advantage from your connections and your
sources of information, so as to provide me every day with an
ample store of news, for which I shall not fail to compensate
you by taking into account the additional expenses which you

may incur, but furthermore to be kind enough to indicate to me the names of persons whom you may think suitable for similar employment under present circumstances and for the duration of the Congress, and who might be persuaded to come to an understanding with me about this.'

The cynicism with which the Chief of Police invites a man of title to become an auxiliary agent of his and, more piquant still, to recruit others for that purpose, also inspires a note to Councillor Siber, Chief Director of the Vienna Police (Hager was director of the State Police). The Councillor is urged to take pressing measures in view of the expected influx of foreign guests:[3]

'The imminent arrival of these princes obliges us to make special arrangements, to strengthen our surveillance so that we are able to know every day, and in every detail, whatever concerns their august persons, their immediate entourage, and any individuals seeking to approach them, together with all plans, projects and undertakings connected with the presence of these illustrious guests . . .'

The danger was that the considerable number of persons who had to be watched and agents responsible for watching them might cause such an accumulation of reports of all kinds that the Chief of Police would be incapable of distinguishing the significant from the trivial. Sifting must have been a problem; each day brought fresh sackfuls of confidential missives to Hager's desk. The trivial predominated, no doubt, for the foreign guests, knowing themselves watched and also watching one another, took care not to let compromising conversations be overheard, and put important papers under lock and key. For such messages they would certainly avoid using the 'secretarial offices' from which Hager expected such wonderful results. These were an ingenious invention of Siber's, making use of public scribes as police informers. 'In order to pick out, amongst this great throng of foreigners, those who have come here without authorization, we should set up under police surveillance secretarial offices for the convenience of foreigners, such as exist in Paris, with booths close to the public squares. Only such offices as are directed by our agents will be authorized, and these must only employ scribes approved by the police.'[4] Siber proposed as chief of one of these bureaux a Russian named Leimann, who spoke and wrote German and French very well, English and Italian fairly well, and he gave further details as to the personnel to be engaged for these offices, which were to provide valuable information.

It seems that Siber, though a high-ranking official, must have retained considerable naïvety, in spite of his functions, since he imagined that diplomats' secretaries would be rash enough to dictate their letters to public scribes; but experience had taught him that diplomats themselves were often guilty of incredible carelessness, of which one must always be ready to take advantage. Thus the Duke of Dalberg, attached to the French mission, had thrown into the waste-paper basket, without more precaution, a letter proposing to the French Minister at Leghorn to kidnap Napoleon, with the connivance of the captain of the ship in which he sometimes spent the night. This letter, brought to Hager and submitted to the Emperor Francis, aroused a certain anxiety among the members of the Congress.

Vienna's Hundred Thousand Foreigners

Six sovereigns, more than seven hundred diplomats, their secretariats, their domestic staff, their courtiers – namely a hundred thousand foreigners, men and women, living in Vienna at the time of the Congress – caused a considerable upheaval in the city's daily life. A good many adventurers mingled with the official guests, as well as a good many swindlers and professional cardsharpers, and the demi-monde had delegated a profusion of pretty young women whose job was to seduce the rulers; they were accompanied by their lovers and protectors, and watched over by the police, who encouraged them to have sharp ears and nimble hands.

An anonymous note to Hager, dated October 9, 1814, and signed with two rings with a cross over them, the author of which is undoubtedly a man or woman having access to all the salons and on confidential terms with all the Highnesses, makes a striking criticism of the 'mobilization' of society people by Hager's police. This letter is worth transcribing in its entirety, for it throws a remarkable light on social conduct in Vienna during the Congress. It bears the number F.2.4188 and 3565 in the archives of the Hofpolizei, and has been reproduced in Weil's fascinating collection of documents, published as *Les Dessous du Congrès de Vienne* (The Underside of the Congress of Vienna).[5]

'I have heard much talk from Prince Starhemberg about the spying that goes on between courts and missions and in society. It is said that "courts and missions are very busy spying on one another". This is very natural and easily explained. It is certain that when they leave us these foreign rulers will have a thorough knowledge of our own Court; but society espionage amongst the Viennese themselves, espionage within Society has become intolerable. Ferdinand Palffy belongs to the secret police, Countess Esterhazy-Roisin and Mlle Chapuis are spies for old Princess Metternich, who instructs and inspires them. Prince Kaunitz, Franz Palffy, Friedrich Fürstenberg, Ferdinand Palffy offered their services to the rulers present in Vienna; these were declined. There has never before been such an espionage service in Vienna. Prince Metternich has already questioned me on this subject and told me that all my conversations were known. I replied that the prince ought to help me by finding me a position and that I would sing his praises unreservedly. I am in fact under obligation to him on account of my lottery, but what I cannot forgive him for, what I cannot accept, are these Binders, Paul Esterhazys and such like with whom he closets himself and who are his confidants. This is what Prince Starhemberg said to me.'

The unknown agent to whom such confidences were freely made by one of the highest nobles of the Empire, since he had been Austrian Ambassador to London, also frequented the German legations. He reports that Baron Spat repeated to him one day this despondent remark by the King of Saxony: 'Prince Anton of Saxony and the Archduchess his wife told me at Schönbrunn: Saxony is lost, as far as we are concerned. We shall never go back there.'

He was clever enough, or highly-placed enough, to penetrate into the French Embassy. 'The Comte de la Tour du Pin took me yesterday to Talleyrand's. This is perhaps the most interesting house of any for an observer. But it is also the *refugium peccatorum*. Here the two Princes of Coburg, Cardinal Consalvi and the Papal Nuncio Severoli pay assiduous court to the master of the house, who scarcely deigns to look at them. Schulenberg, Saint-Marsan, Castelalfer, Salmour, Count Marshall, Commander Ruffo, Baron Vrintz all the émigrés come here to report whatever they know, whatever they have seen or been able to find out.'

Prudent diplomats, it is true, took care not to leave letters lying about, to the great annoyance of the domestic spies attached to their service. The agent Schmidt complains to Hager that nothing can be found at Talleyrand's.

'The house is nothing but a kind of fortress, in which he keeps garrison with those few individuals on whom he can rely. In spite of these precautions, however, we have succeeded in intercepting a few documents sent from his offices. We have furthermore been able to win over an old servant who has already been in the service of three French Ambassadors, as well as a caretaker or attendant from the Chancellery, thanks to whom we have managed to secure a few torn papers found in Talleyrand's own office. There is nothing promising for the police as regards the Prince's visitors or guests. These are either foreign diplomats preoccupied only with their own interests, or else functionaries or diplomats from here, who have already been engaged by other high-ranking personalities and are completely at their disposal ... Dalberg's establishment presents the same problems as Talleyrand's. He lives in the same house, and moreover he is a German and very well acquainted with the city and the field in which he has to operate.'[6]

The legations defended themselves as best they could against the investigations of professional or amateur spies. The English were best at keeping their secrets. Their mail was sent to London by diplomatic bag and thus escaped the probings of Hager's 'dark room'. 'It is quite impossible to intercept anything,' an anonymous agent wrote to the head of the Hofpolizei on October 4, 1814. 'The lord sends everything by his own couriers, and his secretaries collect and burn all papers. On the 2nd, couriers were sent to Munich,

Brussels and Naples, and during the night papers were burnt till two in the morning.'[7] One of the agents in charge of exploring the British Embassy warns his chief that it is useless trying to find out what is in the safe that Lord Castlereagh keeps in his office, for it contains only private letters and 'would not justify the time spent or the risk of such operations' (Hager's report to the Emperor, October 8, 1814). The English had brought chambermaids from England, so that no Viennese could find an excuse to get into the house. Fearing there might be leakages from the building where he lived, *Im Auge Gottes*, 'In God's eye', the Ambassador had moved to the first floor of No. 30, in the Minoritenplatz, but it is interesting to note that the police did not completely give up procuring torn papers and the contents of waste paper baskets, which the Englishwomen probably considered of no importance and sold, without more ado, to ragmen who promptly took them along to Hager's desk.

Attempts were also made to get Castlereagh's secretaries drunk and have them questioned by the agreeable young women they picked up. One agent of the Hofpolizei informs his chief that the Englishman Parr, asked about the way his compatriots spent their leisure, had told him: 'As they are on holiday, they spend the day sightseeing in the capital and the country round. In the evening they visit young Countess Rzewuska, who gives them a friendly reception, and then they go off to some wench and get drunk on Bude wine.'[8]

Pamphlets and Satires

The Emperor also took an interest in popular comments on foreign rulers; he was kept regularly informed about the nicknames conferred on them by the mischievous Viennese. These made fun of Bernadotte, Prince Royal of Sweden, recalling his misadventures while Ambassador in Vienna after Campo-Formio, and the incident he had provoked by flying the tricolour flag from the balcony of Geymüller's house at a time when the Revolutionary standard was an object of particular loathing.

These nicknames played on the names of the streets in

Vienna which popular malice allotted to the various kings, according to their peculiarities. The King of Würtemberg, who was huge and debauched, was given the Fleischmarkt – the meat market; the King of Denmark, who was reputed to be poverty-stricken, *im Elend* (in misery); today it is impossible to guess what scandal or what comical peculiarity entitled the Grand Duke Constantine of Russia to be sent to Nail Street, or the King of Prussia to the Windmill, but the frequent visits paid by Tsar Alexander to the beauties of the court, who were far from coy towards the ruler of All the Russias, earned him a fictitious residence in that corner of the town known as *im süssen Loch*, 'the nice little hole'.

It was perhaps on account of the licentious adventures in which some members of the Congress indulged so freely that a certain Mayer, who for that matter was *persona grata* with Prince Kaunitz and Baron Hacke, made his living by selling remedies against venereal disease to princes and nobles, as we learn from a report of Hager's to the Emperor dated October 23, 1814.[9]

The people of Vienna did not for long remain in awe of the horde of eminent personalities, but openly mocked their vices and foibles. The Russian Emperor had become 'He likes anything' or 'He makes love for everybody'; the King of Prussia, 'He thinks for everybody'; the King of Denmark 'He drinks for everybody'; the Grand Duchess of Oldenburg 'She loves everything'. As for the Emperor Francis, who had to shoulder the costs of the copious hospitality offered to sovereigns, diplomats and the crowd of people who accompanied them – the Viennese, who paid the taxes, knew what they were talking about – his nickname was: 'He who pays for everybody'.

Satire was freely dispensed, too, in pamphlets imitating theatre posters. One of these announced a play entitled: *Le Trône ébranlé par un mur abattu* (The throne shaken by a fallen wall). Second performance of *Napoléon détrôné. Murat battu* (Napoleon dethroned. Murat beaten), for the benefit of the Allies. And the price of seats was listed as follows: 'Circle seats, one louis. Pit: one napoleon.'

A famous vinegar of the time being called '*des quatre*

voleurs', Napoleon's marshals were incorporated in the following cookery recipe:

> *Dans un beau chaudron, sur un feu bien ardent*
> *Mettez Davout, Ney et le beau Bertrand*
> *Et joignez-y sans artifice*
> *Savary, chef de la police.*
> *Faites bouillir, levez-en les fleurs*
> *Vous aurez du vinaigre aux Quatre Voleurs.*

The Leading Rôles

Lord and Lady Castlereagh caused much amusement by their typically English indifference to the impression they might make on the Viennese. They strolled about the street, dressed in the London fashion which was not that of Vienna, arm in arm and laughing at everything. They went into all the shops, had everything shown them and finally went off without buying anything. Lady Castlereagh was much criticized for lack of decorum when, at a masked ball at Prince Metternich's, she wore her husband's Garter ribbon as an ornament in her hair.

Castlereagh

Lord Castlereagh was one of the most singular and inscrutable figures at the Congress. His coldness, his stiffness, his secretiveness made him unpopular. An Irishman by origin, he had been one of those responsible for the pact giving Ireland up to England. Tom Moore and O'Connell called him 'the assassin of his country' and Shelley stigmatized him in two famous and splendid lines:

> 'I met Murder on the way,
>   He had a mask like Castlereagh.'

Very proud and very shy, he hated having to speak in public; incapable of real communication with those around him, he was naturally very lonely, and this explains the growing melancholy which possessed him at the end of his life and led him to cut his throat with a razor.

Byron applies the most insulting epithets to him; he calls him a 'tinkering slave-maker' because of his lack of enthusiasm for the abolition of the slave trade, 'a bungler even in his disgusting trade', an 'intellectual eunuch', a 'cold-blooded, smooth-faced, placid miscreant'. Castlereagh shared with Metternich, in the eyes of liberal poets, the opprobrium of belonging to the 'tools of reaction'; while Romantic lyricism could not fail to condemn his drab, stilted way of speaking – in Byron's words again, 'that long spout of blood and water'.

This haughty diplomat, whose very silences seemed disquieting and ominous, professed indifference to the dislike of those who came in contact with him. 'Unpopularity,' he said, 'is more convenient and gentlemanlike.'

Sir Harold Nicolson, in his book on *The Congress of Vienna*,[10] gives an admirable and unbiassed description of this strange personality, 'odd even for an Englishman', as the Viennese said.

'Castlereagh possessed a solitary soul and derived but little pleasure from the amenities of society. He had little gift for intimacy and the only two people whom he really loved, his wife and his half-brother Charles Stewart, never shared with him the lonelier recesses of his mind. The former, with her blousy sprightliness, with her wide-eyed uncomprehending self-satisfaction, was too unintelligent to understand the inner mysteries of Castlereagh's nature. The latter, being a conceited man, was too insensitive. The social shyness which had tormented Castlereagh since his boyhood in County Down had induced him to hide himself behind a screen of glacial good manners. Handsome and seemingly imperturbable, his sober apparel contrasting with the gold lace and decorations of the foreign potentates and plenipotentiaries, he would in his uncertain French exchange conventional but icy compliments with those who addressed him. Even to his own compatriots he appeared incomprehensibly aloof. "He can neither feel nor feign," said Canning. "So opposed," wrote the Duke of Buckingham, "was his nature to display." Only those who watched him fingering tenderly the flowers in the North Cray garden or playing with children realized the gentler delicacies of his temperament. To the foreigners who flocked to Vienna he was an enigmatic figure. They were impressed by the patrician dignity of his demeanour; they were amused by his almost bourgeois domesticity. They would recount to each other how on Sunday mornings Lord Castlereagh, his wife and sister-in-law, his colleagues, his staff and his domestics, would all gather in the drawing-room at the Minoritenplatz and sing Church of England hymns to the harmonium.'

He was laughed at for taking secret dancing lessons with his wife; they were very bad at it, and would waltz round their drawing-room alone till they were out of breath in order to cut a better figure at official balls. Castlereagh had the misfortune to be married to a stupid woman, who had been pretty in her youth but had soon coarsened, and who was as dull in mind as she was ungainly in body. She was shrewdly described by Lady Bessborough, who wrote of her: 'No one was ever so invariably good-humoured yet she sometimes provokes me; there is a look of contented disregard of the cares of life in her round grey eyes that makes me wonder if she ever felt any crosses or knows the meaning of the word anxiety. She talks with equal indifference of Bombardments and Assemblies, the Baby and the Furniture, the emptiness of London and the massacre of Buenos Aires, Lord Castlereagh's increasing debility and the doubtful success of Mr Greville's new opera – all these succeed each other so quick and with so exactly the same expression of voice and countenance that they probably hold a pretty equal value in her estimation.'[11]

The eccentric notion she had had of wearing the Garter ribbon in her hair at a masked ball was only one of the tactless blunders which spiteful gossips delighted in retailing.

The other members of the English delegation had neither Castlereagh's impressive bearing nor his discretion. His half-brother, Sir Charles Stewart, the future Marquess of Londonderry, was a fairly good diplomat, but he was vain and ostentatious and on that account frankly unpopular. Castlereagh's unpopularity was due to qualities which were, on the whole, worthy of respect; if Stewart was disliked, it was on account of the faults which he displayed blatantly and which made him ridiculous, for he was too full of himself to be aware of them. He was 'an insolent ill-behaved fellow', according to the German publisher Bertuch, Goethe's friend, and the Viennese had nicknamed him 'Lord Pumpernickel'. This did not prevent him from having a certain wit, which he displayed at the expense of others. It was he who said of Lord Cathcart, the British Ambassador to St. Petersburg, who was slow of speech and thought: 'he never begins to think until other people have finished.'

Another Englishman, Sir Sidney Smith, was not a member of the British delegation; he represented Swedish interests in Vienna*. He owed his nickname 'the sea-god', which greatly amused the Viennese, to the fact that as admiral of the British fleet he had taken St John of Acre. Nevertheless he was described as 'that mere vaporizer' by Croker, who spared neither foreigners nor his compatriots.

The only problem that interested Sidney Smith was the suppression of the Barbary corsairs; he thought the Congress could have no object more urgent and important than this. Extremely self-satisfied into the bargain, dressing with loud and extravagant luxury, he gave sumptuous parties to which nobody went, so tiresome and grotesque was he considered. The eccentricities of these Englishmen caused the Viennese much amusement. Some of them are noted in police reports, for instance: 'Lord Stewart has been up to his tricks again. He went home by way of the Graben and the Kohlmarkt. His horse's head was decked with lilies of the valley; he himself carried a huge bunch of these flowers, roared with laughter and seemed to have drunk rather too much. Everybody stopped in the street to stare at him and make fun of him.'[12]

* * * *

The concern of Sidney Smith, 'Swedish' though he was, about piracy in the Mediterranean, a long way from Stockholm, gives one a glimpse of the innumerable questions which the Congress had to settle. The problem of Europe, which the great powers intended to decide amongst themselves, had already arisen; there was also the question of small States and the various nationalities. And besides the representatives of States there were innumerable delegations of every sort, come to defend the most varied interests: those of the Order of Malta, whose Grand Master, Carraciolo, wanted to be officially recognized by the Congress; those of German

---

* Those of the Vasa dynasty.

publishers, introduced by the distinguished bookseller Cotta, who published the complete works of Goethe, and his colleague from Weimar, Bertuch, who related the events of the Congress in his exciting Journal. It is from Bertuch that we learn about Metternich's great masked ball on November 8, 1814, where Lady Castlereagh made herself conspicuous in the manner already mentioned, and the success of the concerts conducted by Beethoven.

There was the Turkish delegation, led by Mavrojeni Pasha, which put before Congress the vexed question of Greece and the Balkans. Representing the Pope there was Cardinal Consalvi, who left so amusing a description of a ball at Sidney Smith's, and there were grotesque figures like Don Pedro Gomez Labrador, who with typically Castilian arrogance vetoed every resolution which did not seem to satisfy the honour of Spain.

There were two delegations from the kingdom of Naples, one sent by Murat, the other by the Bourbons, and both would stand up together when the question of Southern Italy arose. The Jewish community of Germany, represented by Jews from Frankfurt, demanded a more liberal status. Nathan Rothschild had freely bribed certain plenipotentiaries to consider this request, which was to be put by Gentz, the German ambassador.

Prince de Ligne

The question of the slave trade was also on the order of the day, but the slaves had sent no delegates, which was considerably to their disadvantage. Under these conditions it is easy to understand how the Prince de Ligne, who was not entirely obsessed with balls and waltzing, replied to someone who asked him how the Congress was going: 'The Congress isn't going, it's dancing!' This Prince de Ligne was a strange man whose witticisms were repeated in salons and streets, and who was lively enough, at eighty years of age, to make rendezvous with the girls that took his fancy in the street on winter nights. It was in this fashion that he caught the chill of which he died on December 13, 1814, in his house in the Mölkerbastei. The whole of Vienna mourned him. We catch an echo of the grief caused by his death in the report of an anonymous agent, certainly a member of Society, to Baron Hager, dated December 14: 'The death of the Prince de Ligne has made a profound impression in Vienna and will be felt throughout Europe, where he was well-known, respected and loved. He was fundamentally a good man, and if he had undoubted weaknesses and even faults, he had charm, amiability, dignity and wit, such as no one else possesses or ever will possess.'[13]

His mischief was never spiteful; he rarely hurt people. He called General Uvarov, who accompanied Tsar Alexander everywhere, the Strangler, on account of the part he had taken in the murder of Paul I. The following fragment of conversation with Talleyrand is characteristic of his turn of wit, his frankness and daring. Having said to the Prince of Benevento: 'You are playing an important rôle now, you are King of France, and Louis XVIII will have to dance to your tune or it'll be the worse for him,' Talleyrand replied: 'Prince, for seven years Bonaparte was suspicious of me.' On which the Prince de Ligne threw up his arms: 'What, only seven years? I've been suspicious of you for twenty.' The strangest funeral oration uttered after the death of this witty nobleman was that of the Papal Nuncio, who disapproved of him: 'The Freemasons of Vienna have lost in him their greatest support, their most zealous protector.' At all events this was the comment reported by the agent Freddi, who had his entrée to the Nuncio's residence and knew how to take advantage of it.

Talleyrand

When Talleyrand made his historic reply to someone who asked him what he had done during the Congress: 'I limped,' he was referring not to the natural infirmity which had destined him to holy orders from childhood, but far more to that sort of 'moral lopsidedness' which was the essential character of his policy throughout his career, under the various régimes he served. His attitude was an equivocal one, and it could not be otherwise in the circumstances of France in his day. The unfavourable picture of him which we get from the newspapers and correspondence of this troubled period is that of a disturbing and baffling man, whose face revealed that great moral and physical corruption of which Miss Berry speaks.[14]

Another Englishman, Croker, had a similar impression of him. 'Talleyrand is fattish for a Frenchman; his ankles are weak and his feet deformed, and he totters about in a strange way. His face is not at all expressive, except it be of a kind of drunken stupor; in fact he looks altogether like an old, fuddled, lame, village schoolmaster, and his voice is deep and hoarse.'[15] In fact this inexpressive countenance concealed the reflections and projects of a statesman, who believed in the necessity of the Restoration but knew that a return of the Empire was still possible – the near future was to prove him right – and intended to save his stakes and those of France, whatever turn events might take. We see thus in the portrait painted by Ary Scheffer, secretive, taciturn, inscrutable, his thin lips hermetically sealed, his eyelids half closed. Not a fuddled schoolmaster, as the Englishman spitefully suggested, but a shrewd and prudent statesman, made even more circumspect by his experience of the instability of human affairs and the crushing responsibility incumbent on France's spokesman during these tragic months.

Talleyrand lived in the Kaunitz palace on the Johannesgasse, not far from St Stephen's Cathedral. He had brought with him a number of career diplomats, La Tour du Pin, Dalberg, La Besnardière, Alexis de Noailles, and his favourite musician, Neukamm, an Austrian by origin, who still had relatives at Salzburg. Talleyrand's passion for music endeared him to the Viennese, who retailed with satisfaction, as being greatly to his credit, that he liked having the piano played to him even while he was working. Whereas he sometimes spent whole days without speaking to anyone, Talleyrand would keep Neukamm by his side, demanding that 'background of sound' which he needed, perhaps, the better to collect and concentrate his thoughts. Neukamm used to tell his friends that, when he played thus beside the Minister's work-table (sometimes for hours at a time, for his silent companion urged him to go on whenever weariness obliged him to leave his instrument for a moment) he wondered whether Talleyrand was really listening to him or pursuing his own train of thought without paying attention to what was going on beside him.

Talleyrand considered that everyone must accept sacrifices in order to ensure lasting peace for Europe. To those who asserted that any solution adopted before the completion of the work of the Congress would satisfy nobody, he replied: 'That is what is needed. That is how it must end. For things to go right, everybody must go away dissatisfied, and having made some sacrifice. From such partial sacrifices the agreement of all, the general good, will spring.' The only foreign ruler who understood and esteemed him was the Emperor Francis. As the Marquis de Bonnay tells him, in a letter which has come down to us because the Austrian police intercepted it and kept a copy in its archives before forwarding it: 'I don't know how the devil you've managed, but you may rest assured that he sings your praises incessantly and has even done so, perhaps even with malicious intent, to more than one sovereign and more than one principal Minister.'

Alexander I

The Tsar of Russia was probably the most popular of all the rulers present in Vienna between the spring of 1814 and May 28, 1815, when he left. Because of this popularity and also perhaps because of the majestic regularity of his features, his bust was frequently used as a shop sign by Viennese wig-makers; there was one on the Cathedral square, another in the Schwertgasse. They were placed in the shop front and used to display wigs. Some Russian officers, who considered this a serious insult to the Imperial person, tried to persuade a wigmaker to use some other dummy. When he refused, they tried to bring in the police, but were told that the wig-maker's action was a mark of sympathy, not of disrespect, and that the Tsar himself had certainly not been offended by it.

Alexander, in fact, had other preoccupations than watching hairdressers' windows. Autocratic and mystical, imaginative and subject to depression, he was to end his life in a

mysterious fashion, perhaps under the borrowed identity of
a peasant pilgrim, a sort of hermit or *staretz*, in order to
expiate his sins. All his life he remained obsessed
by the tragic event which had darkened his adolescence and
brought him to the throne: the murder of the Tsar Paul I
by his wife, Empress Maria, Alexander's mother. (Catherine
II was the grandmother of Alexander I; his mother was
Maria Fedorovna, princess of Würtemberg. Catherine II
had had her husband Peter III assassinated.) The essential
features of this complex character have been clearly brought
out by Sir Harold Nicolson, whose admirable book we must
quote once more:[16]

> 'Alexander was certainly incalculable; but he was not in-
> scrutable. "It would be difficult," said Napoleon to Metter-
> nich, "to have more intelligence than the Emperor Alexander;
> but there is a piece missing; I have never managed to discover
> what it is." A modern psychiatrist would experience no
> difficulty in deciding what, among the Tsar's great gifts and
> qualities, was the missing component; it was the faculty of co-
> ordination. Tainted as he was with his father's insanity, the
> Emperor Alexander was afflicted with split personality, or
> schizophrenia, which in his later years degenerated into de-
> pressive mania.'

He would seek predictions in the Bible to guide his
actions. He was happy only when amongst soldiers; distant
and gloomy at the gayest festivities, he preferred military
reviews to balls. 'I hate civilians,' he told his Ministers one
day, 'I am a soldier, I only like soldiers.' One evening at a
ball given by Prince Metternich, he told Princess Esterhazy
that he preferred the grand parade which he had witnessed
that morning. 'This is a fine entertainment, but after this
morning's no other should have been given. The ball is
splendid, the ballroom is large and handsome, but there's
always something diplomatic about such things and I don't
like falseness.'

Having made the same remark to his Ambassador Razumovsky, who was a wit and a patron of the arts – a great
deal of music was played at his home, and Beethoven, who
was one of his intimate friends, dedicated some of his finest

works to him – the Ambassador replied to the Tsar's criticism: 'I'm glad to know that. I shall invite to my ball, to please Your Majesty, a company of his regiment.'

He showed his instability in private life; his countless liaisons were legendary in Vienna throughout the Congress. He was cruelly wounding to the Empress, reproaching her constantly for being less beautiful and less intelligent than her sister, and forcing her to receive the women who were, or were supposed to be, his mistresses. The Duchess of Sagan, Princess Bagration, Countess Narishkin, Countess Esterhazy were much admired and courted by him. Julie Zichy and other women of the nobility, the bourgeois world or merely the demi-monde were honoured with his favours. He had brought along with him from St Petersburg the banker Schwarz, so as not to be parted from the latter's wife, with whom he had for some time been on very intimate terms. This, however, did not prevent the fair Mme Schwarz from also receiving visits from Von Scholten, the Danish King's little aide-de-camp, who extracted precious secrets, in confidential moments, which he probably passed on to the Hofpolizei.

Everybody in Vienna knew about the parlour games played by the Tsar with his lady friends. At a supper given by Count Zichy, Alexander and Countess Wrbna-Kageneck had an argument as to whether men or women spent longer over their toilette. To settle the question, they withdrew together to undress and dress again; apparently the Countess won the wager. Such pastimes may have been innocent, but they set tongues wagging all over the city, and some Viennese summed up the general opinion of Alexander by saying that he had been admired at first for his fine presence, his good looks, his majesty, but that these had soon palled, and now he was just a man like any other, in the hands of women; adding that his departure would be mourned chiefly by prostitutes.

In this, however, Vienna was doing him an injustice: Alexander chose his mistresses chiefly among society women, who were very ready to oblige him, whereas other sovereigns, such as the Grand Duke of Baden, spent all their evenings in brothels. The Papal Nuncio denounced the undressing episode, in the presence of the agent Freddi (who repeated his words to the police): 'This is the kind of man by whom the world is governed! The gossip-mongers of the Congress will add this choice incident to the other shameful and shocking stories about this prince of coxcombs, and posterity will learn one day how the palace of the Emperors served as a brothel for the Tsar of Russia.'

Let us not be so severe as the worthy prelate. To be sure, there was much self-indulgence during the Congress, a great deal of dancing and love-making; this was inevitable. This society needed entertainment, and if it preferred frivolous entertainments, if on the whole it chose to listen to Johann Strauss and his 'diabolical violin' rather than to Beethoven, was it not because in this lingering twilight of the old régime a whole social set which still retained the insouciance of the eighteenth century displayed its graces, its elegance and luxury? For these were exquisite women, whose kisses doubtless meant more to their exalted lovers than the destiny of Europe, and the fashions of the time lent unfamiliar piquancy to their beauty. The Duchess of Sagan, Princess Bagration, Aurore de Marasse, Julie Zichy, Princess Galitzine assuredly had considerable influence on the Congress; they set it dancing, for one thing. There were bourgeois beauties, too, such as Mme Schwarz, Mme Bigottini and Mme Fischer, who sold her lovely daughter to the highest bidder, not to the highest title.

All Vienna knew, or believed, that the Duchess of Sagan had had an illegitimate daughter, although nobody knew the father, and the men who flocked round all these great ladies included not merely Highnesses but noblemen of high or low degree, whose names were on the Hofpolizei list, and adventurers of every country, fishers in the troubled waters of this international carnival, which had been going on for almost a year.

The Viennese could not fail to be affected by the spectacle of this demoralization, which was constantly before their eyes. The long delays of the Congress, which caused Humboldt to reply to those who asked when it would finish: 'Tell me rather when it will begin', obliged Metternich to expend much money and imagination on entertaining the capital's illustrious guests. Expert as he was at staging pleasures as well as diplomatic sessions, Metternich had constantly to contend against the economy, almost amounting to stinginess, of his master the Emperor Francis, who was rightly disturbed by the enormous drain on the finances of the Empire involved by this host of foreigners. Each dinner, it has been reckoned, cost fifty thousand florins.

On the other hand, these guests made sparing purchases, even if they did not go so far as Lord and Lady Castlereagh, who visited every shop without buying anything. People complained about it, as the Danish diplomat Hedart observed:

'The population of Vienna, much as they delight in pageantry and entertainments, have nevertheless begun to weary of continual festivities, and they would doubtless be glad to see the last of these august foreigners, particularly as the rising cost of living is attributed to their protracted stay in the capital, and it is feared that the enormous expense of entertaining the Emperor's guests will be paid for by his subjects by means of taxes ironically known as *Burgeinquartierungs Steuer* (tax on billets in the town). It may be supposed that the Emperor himself would be glad to see the departure of all these rulers who, with their families and large trains of followers, live here at his expense, and are moreover an embarrassment to him, through the trouble that entertaining them entails, and the unaccustomed way of life he is himself obliged to follow.'

The Danish councillor was right: Francis was growing impatient of these endless delays, he knew that the people were discontented, that ladies of the upper middle classes complained if they were not invited to the festivities and, when they were, grumbled about the continual outlay they were forced to make on dresses and jewellery in order to look their best. Their husbands, for their part, were horrified at the inroads made in their exchequer by the constant purchase of jewels, shawls, scarves and other adornments; many of them moreover longed for the prompt departure of the sprightly aides de camp and gallant Embassy officials who clasped their wives somewhat too closely in the waltz.

People were getting tired of it all, even of jokes about the obesity of the King of Würtemberg, known as the 'Würtem-bergish monster'. A caricature was going the rounds which showed him raising his hands to heaven in despair because his huge paunch prevented him from seeing the trouser-button on which his kingdom was drawn. The caption ran: 'How wretched I am, I cannot even see my State!' The entertainment provided by the Tsar's illicit amours was thought hardly worth the million florins spent on organizing his stay in Vienna, and in any case had soon palled. The good citizens of Vienna no longer cared with which of his lady friends he spent the night, and were only amused when copies of one of his love-letters, intercepted by the police,[17] finally circulated in the town; it was addressed to a beautiful Dutch woman, Louise-Frederika Boode, wife of Simon-Maurice de Bethmann.

We may take advantage of this indiscretion on the part of the police to read, over the shoulder of Baron Hager, this effusion from the Tsar of all the Russias. It was sent via one Mlle Idzstein of Frankfurt, who served as confidant and 'letterbox' to the lovers when they were separated:

'At last I have news of you, my beloved. My eyes, so long deprived of your letters, have had the joy of beholding your precious writing, the mere sight of which proves to me how dear you are to me, how everything in the whole world fades away when something from you comes to my sight. And what sets the seal on my happiness is the conviction that you are well, that the only little creature of whom you so ingeniously assert that you might be jealous, in a word the object of your tender affection......well. And so how, after such news, can I express to you all that has gone on in the depths of my heart? It takes all my sense of duty, all......the imprudence I should commit if I were to precipitate things, to stop me flying to your arms to die of happiness there. I risked writing to you twice, even before receiving news of you. I addressed my letters, as always in the past, under cover of our kind friend, and you have said no word about them, which makes me fear lest they have gone astray. The way in which you have sent yours is a good one and very safe. I implore you on my bended knees to write me again. Farewell, my only love.'*

* Passages marked with a dotted line are illegible in the manuscript.

He may have been sincere; the versatility of his character led him no doubt to live entirely and exclusively in the moment, in politics as in love. And even if he had just left the arms of Mme Schwarz, and was about to hasten to those of the Duchess of Sagan, when he wrote to a 'far-off beloved' with such touching simplicity, such schoolboy naïvety, that would not prove that he was not expressing his most genuine thoughts and feelings.

Metternich

Amidst the whirling round of intrigues and pleasures which he stage-managed with a calm and lucid political genius, Metternich unswervingly pursued the object of his plan: a return to absolutism. Certain princes in the Congress hated him and called him the 'Scapin' of diplomacy, but those who called him the Rock of Order saw things more justly. It was also said of him that by setting up as champion of legitimacy he was trying to stop the course of history. Inflexible, unshakable in what he thought to be right, just and good, Metternich was the exact opposite of Talleyrand, who judged him severely by the very fact of the opposition between their two natures. After a particularly stormy session – it was principally the Tsar who opposed him with extreme violence – the Prince of Benevento wrote: 'Prince Metternich displayed at this meeting the full extent of his mediocrity, his taste for mean intrigues and devious methods, as well as his virtuosity in the use of vague and empty language.' He was admired on the other hand, by small sovereigns like the King of Würtemberg and the Bourbons of Naples, whose interests he defended not out of consideration for themselves but solely because they represented the principle of legitimism to which he was ready to sacrifice everything.

This absolutist, who dreamed of maintaining anachronistic ways of ruling and of thinking, considered himself a progressive. 'I should have been born in 1900,' he once said, 'and have had the whole of the twentieth century in front of me.' Hostile to constitutions, to parliamentarianism, to whatever savoured of liberalism or jacobinism, he was a reactionary in this respect, but in foreign politics he professed opinions far in advance of those of his contemporaries. Harold Nicolson, who has correctly analyzed his character and his 'system',[18] rightly says that Metternich believed firmly and sincerely in the 'concert of Europe' as in something superior to the particular interests of each State. And he spoke prophetically when he wrote:

> 'Politics is the science of the vital interest of States, in the widest sense. Since the isolated State no longer exists and is to be found only in the annals of the pagan world . . . we must always consider the *society* of States as the essential condition of the modern world. The great axioms of political science proceed from the knowledge of the true political interests of *all* States; it is on these general interests that the guarantee of their existence is based. The establishment of international relations on a basis of reciprocity and under the pledge of respect of acquired rights . . . constitutes, at the present time, the very essence of politics, of which diplomacy is only the day-to-day application. Between the two, in my opinion, there is the same difference as between science and art.'

The libertarians of 1848 who were to expel him from the capital and rejoice at the collapse of his 'system', which had prevailed at the Congress, were in fact to be far less 'modern' than this statesman who is called retrograde by those who fail to understand him, and who may be considered a precursor of the League of Nations and the United Nations Organization. He had understood, too, that the working sessions of the Congress must alternate with festivities, because pleasure and entertainment provided the necessary lubricant.

Moreover, by organizing and directing the amusements of his foreign guests he was able to maintain his control over them. He thought by means of lavish display to serve the cause of the house of Hapsburg by testifying to the soundness of Austrian finances. The idea that one must spend freely in order to gain credit, at least morally, was well-founded; the Viennese did not always understand it, and the unpopularity of Metternich increased in proportion with the rise in the cost of living, which always affects 'average incomes' so unfavourably.

If we try to draw up a balance-sheet of the profits and losses which the Viennese incurred from the Congress, we are left with a notable deficit. The luxury trades gained by the presence of several tens of thousands of foreigners, but not excessively; those who got most profit therefrom were the purveyors of pleasure, the keepers of fashionable restaurants and ballrooms, and those who supplied fresh foods to these aristocratic gourmets. The majority of the inhabitants observed, with their usual sagacity, the extravagant behaviour of these illustrious guests, but did not imitate it, well aware that it was like a stage show at which one could gape and laugh and applaud, but that one must not take seriously an entertainment which had gone on so long that it had become wearisome. Those whose heads had been turned by this mad round of festivities quickly regained their equilibrium as soon as Vienna was rid of those it had come to regard as intruders, no longer interesting once they had ceased to amuse.

Thus, after the chandeliers had gone out in the ballrooms and the 'rain of Sires', in the mocking words of the Prince de Ligne, had scattered to the four corners of Europe, Vienna resumed its old appearance. The Napoleonic wars, nevertheless, and the Congress which was the closing act of these, left recognizable imprints on social life; they had, in Austria as in other countries, favoured the advent and accession to power of a new class: the bourgeoisie.

CHAPTER EIGHT

IN THE LAND OF THE WALTZ

Dangers and Delights of the Waltz—Dance Halls—Inauguration of the Apollo Palace—Picturesque Types—Great Purveyors of Entertainment—The Strauss Family

---

Their passion for dancing was one of the characteristics of the Viennese which struck foreigners most forcibly: when the Irish tenor O'Kelly, who was Mozart's constant friend and sometimes sang in his operas, wrote down his recollections of Vienna in 1787, he devoted considerable space to what he described as its mania for dancing.

> 'When carnival time drew near,' (he writes) 'merriment broke out everywhere; with the advent of the festival period proper its manifestations exceeded all bounds. The *Redoutensaale* in which the masked balls were held were in the Kaiserburg; though they were of vast extent, they seemed like a bottle-neck, so tightly packed were they with masked figures. The passion for dancing and masquerades was so pronounced among Viennese ladies that nothing could make them curtail their favourite amusement. This went so far that for expectant mothers who could not be induced to stay at home separate rooms were provided with all conveniences; rooms indeed in which the child could be brought into the world if unhappily this should prove necessary. The arrangement was discussed in all seriousness in my presence, and I am almost convinced that cases really arose which demonstrated the utility of this arrangement.'[1]

Dangers and Delights of the Waltz

If the sight of Viennese women nine months pregnant whirling round wildly in the waltz seemed fantastic to the Irishman, he noted none the less that 'the ladies of Vienna are particularly famous for their grace and their movements in rotating, an exercise of which they never tire'. They had adopted the new dance with such enthusiasm that they did not realize how detrimental, according to critics of the waltz, this exercise was to their health. 'I for my part considered that waltzing from ten o'clock at night till seven o'clock in the morning was a form of continuous frenzy, tiring for both eyes and ears, not to speak of other and worse consequences . . .'[2] In order to divert society from this perilous amusement, critics laid stress on the 'mortal' dangers entailed by the waltz, particularly when danced as Adolf Bauerle describes it, in rooms of prodigious length, down which couples sped as fast as possible. They went seven or eight times round these rooms at top speed, each couple trying to pass the rest, and it was not unusual, apparently, for a fatal accident to bring this mad race to an abrupt close.

In spite of this, the Viennese seemed to have no other thought than to live for dancing, to die dancing. What did this dance mean to the Viennese, as H. E. Jacob asks in his delightful book on Johann Strauss?[3] 'A narcotic? Or its opposite – something regenerative? We do not know. A strange concoction, heavy with sweetness, demoniac frenzy and follies, and yet leavened by a certain nobility.'

How far does this passion for dancing go back? Historians have not attempted to tell us, and since a collective taste as general and as strongly marked as this cannot be of recent development, one must suppose that, like their love for music, it has long been deep-rooted in the character and habits of the Viennese. No doubt it was fostered by all the strange and beautiful dances peculiar to the different peoples of the empire: Tyrolean ländler, Hungarian czardas, the mazurkas and polkas which originated in Poland, even the kolo from the Balkan highlands. All these were superimposed on the dances generally practised in the eighteenth century: the gavotte, the minuet, and so many other national and provincial dances which vanished almost entirely when the waltz appeared. At the time of the Congress, the minuet, so famous in the preceding century both as a musical form and as a ballroom dance, was so completely forgotten that when it was asked for one day at some princely function, only one member of the Congress could be found who knew how to perform its figures: the amusing Comte de la Garde-Chambonas, who won great admiration from the spectators, or so he tells us in his *Souvenirs*, where he complacently enumerates his personal successes during the Congress.

The Viennese had always loved dancing, there can be no doubt of that, but with the advent of the waltz this love became an overwhelming passion, which we have seen described by Bauerle and O'Kelly, and which attained, under the Strausses, the dimensions of a real social pheno-menon. This dizzy, whirling dance was an intoxication, bringing for a few hours escape from the dreary round of daily life. Jacob wondered whether it was a narcotic or a stimulant: the answer is, it was both at once. The success of the waltz was due to its frenzied rhythm, which swept the dancers away, its whirling movement which made them dizzy, and (let us not forget this) the close contact with one's partner's body, in contrast with old-fashioned dances where one 'kept one's distance'.

To use the vocabulary of art historians, one might say that dancing is a 'symbolic form' reflecting the spirit of a nation and an epoch. The advent of the waltz would thus be the sign of the profound transformations that took place in society at the end of the eighteenth century, bringing an apparently rustic dance into the drawing-room. But if we study the development of the waltz throughout the nine-teenth century up to the 'hesitation waltz' of 1910, we see that it moves constantly further from its popular origins, without thereby ceasing to be the favourite dance of the people of Vienna. We may also note that nineteenth century composers wrote waltzes as assiduously as their predecessors had written minuets. In the course of these transformations the waltz-for-dancing of the elder Strauss becomes, in the son's hands, a symphonic form to be heard in the concert hall, and more delightful to listen to than to dance to: *The Emperor's Waltz*, for instance.

The history of the waltz as a form of musical expression does not form part of our theme here; it would need a volume to itself. We are concerned, rather, with the repercussions it had on the life of the Viennese and the changes it brought about in the very aspect of the city. Socially, we may note, the advent of the waltz coincides with the twilight of the old régime, whose symbolic form is essentially the minuet. The waltz may be considered as a 'revolutionary' dance. Philologists seek its etymology in the latin *volvere*; the fact of *revolving* is its essential characteristic; to revolve on oneself while sharing in a collective revolution, as in certain religious dances of the East, such as Tibet. The speed with which the dancers revolved, and the freedom with which they clasped their partners close, caused it to be considered licentious and as such to be banned from aristocratic drawing-rooms.

It was in 1780, during the reign of Joseph II, that the term 'waltz' was used for the first time and that the dance itself appeared on the stage, in the opera *Cosa Rara* by Martin y Soler. H. E. Jacob points out, in the book already quoted, that this substitution of the waltz for the traditional minuet on the stage of the Emperor's theatre surprised no one; the waltz had become accepted. Vienna, Austria, the whole of Europe adopted this captivating, bewitching dance, despite the 'dangers' it entailed, probably because European society at the beginning of the nineteenth century recognized therein its own aspirations, its appetites, its dynamism, and also its desire for intoxication. The epithet 'Viennese' was added to the word 'waltz' from the moment when Johann Strauss and his demoniac violin set Europe afire, and the 'Viennese waltz', the radiant centre of the 'Viennese operetta', enjoyed uncontested triumph until the eve of the first world war.

The waltz modified the aspect of Vienna because it became necessary to satisfy this 'dancing mania' which possessed the entire population, from proletariat to aristocracy. The horde of dancers and the space the dance required obliged dance-hall proprietors to build enormous rooms, including annexes where dancers could retire to rest and renew their strength by eating and drinking. The minuet was an almost stationary dance, performed with a grave elegance and restraint which did not exhaust the participants. The wild rapidity of the

waltz, as danced in Vienna at the beginning of the nineteenth
century, left dancers exhausted and panting as after a race.
I know of course that the tempo of the waltz must have
differed according to whether it was danced in suburban
pleasure-gardens or Imperial drawing-rooms, but the principle was the same. To arouse the required frenzy in the
dancers a large band was required, dominated by the violin,
that essentially romantic instrument, which had attained an
exceptional eminence, perhaps because of the important part
played in Viennese life by Hungarian musicians, those gipsy
fiddlers who are born, as the saying goes, with a violin in
their hands. Not only was the first violin the leader of the
dance orchestra, he was also its conductor; maestros like
Lanner and the Strausses conducted with their violins; in
the preceding century the conductor had sat at the harpsichord.

Dance Halls

The men who were clever enough to understand what was
needed by this new epoch, this new society, were not only
concerned with offering the thousands of dancers who
thronged into their establishments the space required for
their movements; they knew that their patrons, among whom
presumably the lower-middle-class predominated – petty
officials, employees and clerks – yearned to see themselves
surrounded by a luxury equal to – and why not surpassing? –
that of aristocratic drawing-rooms.

They therefore used all their ingenuity to add to the dance-
hall proper, with its shimmering lights, its crystal chandeliers
reflected in enormous mirrors, all the 'attractions' which
would turn it into an earthly paradise. This luxury was
ostentatious perhaps, but by no means vulgar, for the spirit
of the age was not vulgar, and Vienna has never been so;
it was a luxury characteristic of the advent of the bourgeoisie
and the 'moneyed powers', an authentic luxury, displayed
for instance in the amazing silver plate, princely in its
splendour, the profusion of flowers (the balls given at Sperl's
were advertised as *Sperl in floribus*),[4] the elegance of curtains
and furnishings. In the restaurants attached to the ballroom

were served an abundance of different dishes, at moderate prices, for great as was the sumptuousness of these establishments, everything was cheap there so that all could freely enjoy this splendour. And there was one precious innovation, unknown to taverns and rustic dance-halls, which deeply impressed those unfamiliar with such luxury: wonderfully polished floors over which one could glide effortlessly and where one felt carried away, swept along by the demon of the waltz.

These establishments increased in number, and yet all of them were crowded. A German journalist noted with wonder that every evening fifty thousand people thronged thither, and calculated that one in four of the Viennese must spend their evenings waltzing. This was in 1809, at a time when the vogue for gigantic dance palaces had not yet reached its peak. The rivalry between these establishments became so acute that audacious directors spent considerable sums on satisfying the taste for luxury which they themselves had rashly aroused in their patrons. Clever speculators, knowing what profit could be got from the craze for dancing which possessed the Viennese, determined that these popular halls should be as richly and splendidly decorated as the drawing-rooms of the nobility, and their lavish expenditure was often matched by exquisite taste; the sight was truly magical.

It was at this point that certain extraordinary personalities made their mark: Pramer, Wolfsohn, Sperl, Schwender, Dommayer, whose lives read like some strange adventure story. In order to strike the imagination of their patrons, these directors inaugurated their ballrooms with dazzling festivities, becoming on such occasions lavish and generous hosts who displayed for their own delight and that of their guests all the refinements to be found in the drawing-rooms of the great Jewish bankers and the palaces of the Kinskys and Esterhazys.

Inauguration of the Apollo Palace

Here, for instance, is the inauguration of the Apollo Palace, built by Sigmund Wolfsohn, the date of which had been chosen so as to coincide with that of the Emperor's wedding:

historic dates both. 'More than four thousand persons,' writes H. E. Jacob, 'were present at the opening. As entrance fee the huge sum of 25 gulden was demanded, so that the first evening brought 100,000 gulden. But such enormous receipts were very necessary in order that the expenses of construction (the building had been carried out under the famous Moreau) and the wages of the employees might be gradually amortized.'

Wolfsohn did things on the grand scale, and yet he had not seemed destined for this profession. Born in London in 1765, he had studied medicine, and being particularly interested in surgical appliances had manufactured artificial limbs. The wars of the Revolution and the Empire had been favourable to his industry. He showed great skill in providing cripples with articulated arms and legs. He also invented rupture belts which were enormously successful and won him the fame of a philanthropist. This generous benefactor also knew how to turn to his own profit the caprices of his fellow-citizens; every Viennese beauty insisted on sleeping on the 'health bed' he had invented, a bed which ensured delightful and amorous dreams, although it was merely an inflated mattress made of reindeer skins.

Rewarded with copious honours by the Emperor, enriched by his trade in bandages, artificial limbs and 'health beds', Wolfsohn conceived the ambition of eclipsing all other dance-halls, the 'Sophia', the 'Flora', the 'Black Goat', the 'Bunch of Grapes', the 'Sheep', the 'Moonshine' and the 'New World'; he set up his establishment under the sign of Apollo, which, he thought, must ensure him the favour of the gods as well as that of the Viennese. Statues of Greek goddesses, of the Muses, of genii, alternated, along the walls of the huge hall, with green fir trees. Wolfsohn had aroused the curiosity of his patrons by publishing an advertisement asking for twenty-four kitchen and cellar staff, ten waiters and four carvers. Everybody was talking about the wonders accumulated by the director of the Apollo, and was impatient to behold them; an enormous crowd gathered in front of the doors, and a corps of mounted police had to be brought to keep order amongst pedestrians and carriages. On ordinary days the entry was to be five gulden, but the twenty-five demanded for the opening night deterred nobody; there was room for four thousand dancers; five thousand were admitted, but the crowd outside protested and tried to break in . . .

An anonymous pamphlet describes, in romantic terms, that memorable evening of which Vienna went on talking long after:

'Imagine, my dear Clio, a circular hall of harmonious proportions. At equal intervals Ionic pillars are placed against the blue background of the walls and between these are narrow mirrors with wall brackets. Below the cornice there are little niches all round the room which are covered by coloured glass and illuminated from within. Mythological pictures decorate the ceiling. Set about the room there are one hundred round tables, each with its own tasteful easy chairs. On each table there is a centre-piece, either a figure, a candelabra, or a basin from which springs a fountain . . .'[5]

Such was the dining-room. In the ballroom, the orchestra was invisible and the frenzied fiddling seemed to come down out of the sky. When the dancers were weary of whirling dizzily, billiard rooms were at their disposal. There were artificial grottoes, confectioners' booths painted with realistic mountain scenery, groves and arbours, and small rooms on the first floor where one could dine quietly without a thousand fellow guests. There was something for everyone's taste.

The inaugural soirée went perfectly. On the opening night of the following season, 1809, however, there was a fight in the cloakroom, several people lost their coats and the chaos of carriages was such that some had to go home on foot. Wolfsohn, like a good sportsman, published apologies for these mishaps in next day's papers, and promised to compensate for losses suffered by his guests. Long and enthusiastic descriptions of the Apollo may be read in the papers of the time and in such works as the *Alt-Wiener Wanderungen* of Adam Müller-Guttenbrungen, or the *Schilderungen des Apollosaales* of Baron von Efrimfeld, which was also made into an operetta by Conradin Kreutzer.

The period of the Congress was a fortunate one for the Apollo; crowned heads frequented it, and enjoyed simple pleasures in the company of middle-class folk. Wolfsohn made a great deal of money, but with his prodigality and his love of luxury he eventually spent even more. The devaluation of 1811 impoverished the Viennese and forced them to learn prudence; the florin having lost four-fifths of its value, everybody became economical. Wolfsohn prided himself on not lowering the style of his establishment, but he sank his whole fortune in it. In the middle of the Carnival season of 1819, the walls where, eleven years earlier, the splendid opening night of the Apollo had been advertised now bore placards proclaiming his bankruptcy. '*Licit*, a house at Oberneustift, called the Apollo Ballroom, and the whole of its contents, to pay the debts of the proprietor Sigmund Wolfsohn, amounting to forty thousand florins.'

Everybody wanted a souvenir of the Apollo, be it only a silver-gilt plate or a lacquered stool, so the furniture sold pretty well, but none the less the unfortunate Wolfsohn fell abruptly from the heights of his splendour and his fame into the darkest destitution, and this man, who had once bought six hundred thousand florins' worth of silver, did not possess a single kreutzer when he died at the age of eighty-five, having lived for the rest of his life on public charity.

Picturesque Types

These great purveyors of entertainment are highly characteristic Viennese figures; the period we are studying abounds in remarkable and picturesque types, such as the brewer Anton Bosch or the tailor Josef Gunkl, whom Vienna has never forgotten. Gunkl, the fabulous 'artist in dress', was immortalized by Nestroy in his play *Der Zerrissene* (The Torn Man). The hero of the comedy declares at one point: 'I own fourteen suits, some light and some dark. Coats and trousers, they all come from Gunkl's, and nobody who sees me can imagine that in spite of my wardrobe I am really a torn man.'

The tailor's success was due to his talent, true, but also to his ruthless treatment of his customers. In a letter to his mother, the youthful Moltke describes his first visit to the master's workshop. 'I went to Gunkl's,' he writes, 'to consult him about dress – *en fait de toilette*. After casting an inquisitorial eye on my outfit, he wanted to know who had made it for me. "Kley, of Berlin," I replied. "It's not bad," said the artist, "but it just doesn't come off." He advised me to wear dark green, warned me that white waistcoats looked idiotic and that there was only one sort of black cravat that was wearable.' His influence was immense, for all the dandies in Vienna obeyed his decrees, and he eventually influenced their minds as well as their outward appearance. 'He worked like a painter,' Leitich tells us, 'studied his customer, his movements, his habits, perhaps even his very soul, and then sketched the garment that suited him. As he was an intelligent man, his influence went far beyond problems of dress or the cut of a coat. He refined masculine society, within as without, as he considered necessary. It was impossible to be coarse or tipsy in a garment made by Gunkl, and he held it his duty to encourage lofty feelings.'[6]

The brewer Bosch is the embodiment of the spirit of large-scale enterprise that possessed Vienna in the 1820's. A German from Swabia, he had come to settle in Vienna while he was still penniless, and made an enormous fortune somewhat in the manner of the American prospectors, with the luck that favours some adventurers. He was so proud of his money and the rank he had won for himself in bourgeois society that when the Emperor offered him a title he refused it; he felt it would have been a come-down. In those days of economic rashness and insecurity, fortunes were often lost as suddenly as they had been acquired. Bosch was ruined by his son-in-law, the nephew of one of his colleagues, Franz Dengler, a Bavarian from Munich, who had begun as proprietor of a small tavern with a garden at Huttelsdorf.

This tavern became a huge brewery, which sold its products in luxuriously decorated halls and under the shade of fine trees outside. Dengler had a large staff of servants and a carriage. Artists and writers frequented his splendid home, where excellent music was to be heard. The only sorrow of this Napoleon of the beer trade – after all, Johann Strauss was known as the Napoleon of the violin – was that he had no son. His nephew, to whom he entrusted the direction of his affairs, chose instead to live like a lord, which at first greatly impressed his uncle and his father-in-law, the two German brewers who had come to Vienna ragged and bare-footed. The young man's extravagances soon swallowed up both fortunes, and after having known such astonishing abundance, Dengler and Bosch relapsed into poverty and obscurity, just as the unfortunate Wolfsohn had done.

Great Purveyors of Entertainment

Vienna is as capricious and flighty as a woman. Her passion-ate infatuations have been followed by abrupt desertions. Her idols cannot count on long survival, and Raimund's suicide is a warning to all those who think they can rely on the loyalty of the public. The luxury, fantasy and taste lavished on their establishments by the directors of dance-halls drove them to bid ever higher, for once their customers had grown accustomed to these sumptuous surroundings they became ever more demanding.

The sudden enrichment of the bourgeois class and of the trades and industries which were dependent on it, combined with financial instability, encouraged thousands of Viennese to seek intoxication in waltzing amidst the lights, perfumes and music of these magnificent palaces, where everything combined to enchant the senses and numb the reasoning faculty. They flocked to the Mondschein, the Tivoli, the Odeon, to Dommayer's Casino and Schwender's Coliseum, to enjoy the sensual delight of whirling round to the strains of a languorous or frenzied waltz, headier than the wines of Hungary or the Viennese hillside.

A pleasure-loving age is always more or less an age of anxiety, for the hectic pursuit of enjoyment corresponds, whether consciously or not, to a wish to deaden some throb-bing uneasiness. The waltz cast a spell over its dancers which was absent from innocent Sunday country-dances on the green. Sour critics compared these dance palaces to the scenes of orgies under Nero, Sardanapalus or Heliogabalus. In fact, they merely represented another side of that dream-world which the theatre provided. A man who was not poet enough to imagine exotic fairylands found them realized for him. The historian of the Vienna Congress, August de la Garde, writes:

'The interior of the Apollo Palace, which occupied immense space contained magnificent halls and living shrubberies as in a garden. From a Turkish pavilion in glaring colours you could wander into the hut of a Laplander. Avenues bordered by fresh lawns planted with numbers of standard roses provided variations in the view. And all this was indoors. In the centre of the dining-hall there towered an immense rock from which murmurous springs emerged in tumbling cascades, the waters then being collected in tanks full of live fish. All styles of architecture warred with each other in the decoration of these rooms; there was the capricious Moorish style, the pure Greek and the Gothic style with its rich carving.'[7]

The passion for exoticism, that essentially Romantic phenomenon, was manifest in these pleasure-grounds, where a hundred various attractions were grouped around the central ballroom, all showing good taste and refinement, free from the noise and vulgarity that disfigure our modern pleasure-grounds.

Each of these establishments had its individual character. At Sperl's the company was somewhat mixed, but then Johann Strauss was leading the band, and that was enough to draw crowds. Heinrich Laube, who frequented these rooms assiduously, bears witness to the extraordinary atmosphere that prevailed there.

'... It is a very mixed company, but its ingredients are not to be despised ... Under illuminated trees and in open arcades people are seated at innumerable tables eating and drinking, chattering, laughing and listening. In their midst is the orchestra, from which come the new waltzes, the bugbear of our learned musicians, the new waltzes that stir the blood like the bite of a tarantula. In the middle of the garden on the orchestra platform there stands the modern hero of Austria, *le Napoléon Autrichien*, the musical director, Johann Strauss. The Strauss waltzes are to the Viennese what the Napoleonic victories were to the French, and if only the Viennese possessed cannon, they would erect a Vendôme column to him at the "Sperl" ... The motley crowds jostle each other, the girls warm and laughing push their way among the lively youths, their hot breath tickles my nostrils like the perfume of tropical flowers, their arms drag me into the midst of the tumult. No one apologizes, at the "Sperl" no pardon is asked or given.'

The crowd, however, was always quiet and well behaved; no coarseness or licence. Elsewhere Laube notes that 'Austrian sensuality is neither vulgar nor sinful; it is that of mankind before the fall.' And if the Viennese, for all their greed, never grew heavy from a surfeit of food, neither did they allow drink to dull their minds. Let us quote once more honest Laube, that impartial German observer: 'I was never present at any excesses in that place; there was no brandy to bemuse the senses . . . and no one was drunk. The light Austrian wines do no more than make one aware of one's senses, and the Viennese have large stomachs but narrow throats.' And all this merry-making went on without any untoward incident or jarring note, in an atmosphere of general joy, where the crowd, carried away by the dance, seemed to possess one soul, one body. And the same thing happened every evening in the dozens of huge dance-palaces where Vienna thronged in search of delight.

The Tivoli presented a somewhat different scene. This was a great park on the hillside, at Obermeidling. Raimund, in his *Nightingale*, celebrated this paradoxical and be-witching Eden with its deep alleys under the terrace trees, its lovely vistas, its groves, its quaint devices as in a romantic garden, together with all the attractions of a fairground. There were even cock-fights, which won little favour, notes Groner,[8] for since Joseph II had forbidden such things the Viennese public had lost the habit of them and the taste for them. Only in a few suburban arenas was turkey-fighting still kept up, chiefly by timber merchants who brought these birds from Hungary along with their purchases of timber. There was nothing like that at the Tivoli, where the tone was set by civilized people who disliked such barbarous spectacles. Overlooking the park, set against the hillside, rose the ballroom, with its high flights of steps and its imposing colonnades, which gave it somewhat the look of a Greek temple, Classicism being fashionable at that time as well as the neo-Gothic dear to Romantic hearts.

The Mondschein stood near the Karlskirche; contrary to what one might expect, it had nothing to do with moonlight; the name merely recalls – following an old Viennese tradition, retained out of piety or perhaps just out of laziness – that a brick factory belonging to one Margarete Mondschein once stood on the spot. The name was attractive, and it stuck. 'The Mondschein,' Bauerle reports, 'won an immortal name for itself at the cost of a high mortality among the young people who visited it, and who danced nothing but waltzes . . .' It had not a very good reputation, for women of easy virtue frequented it, but they had to maintain decent behaviour, for the Viennese police would not tolerate soliciting.

Any woman caught accosting a passer-by, even if he raised no objection, was arrested, shorn and made to sweep the streets, with shackles on her feet. This however, provided an opportunity to tease respectable citizens by sweeping quantities of dust and mud over their shoes; consequently, this penalty was abolished, and they were sent to wash linen for the sick in the hospitals, which they liked far less. This decision certainly contributed to the respectability of the city.

Franz Morawetz had had the ingenious notion of calling his dance hall after the Archduchess Sophia. Born in the small Bohemian village of Radnitz, he had settled in Vienna as apprentice to a tailor. Soon he married his master's daughter, who brought him a dowry of forty thousand florins. What should he do with this money? Morawetz decided to open a steam-baths establishment in the Russian style, to which he added a swimming-bath; these prospered and enriched him, and at a cost of two hundred thousand florins he had a gigantic ballroom built by Van der Null and Siccardsburg, renowned architects who also built the Opera house. This dance-hall was so huge and so daring in design that the police tried to close it down for fear the ceiling might collapse on the dancers. Morawetz appealed to the Emperor against the Minister's decision, and won his case. The ceiling which had alarmed the authorities could open up and let fall showers of rose petals on to the astonished dancers.

Ferdinand Dommayer opened his famous Casino in June 1838, close to the castle of Schönbrunn. His name is linked with that of the famous conductor and composer of waltzes, Joseph Lanner, whose orchestra played at memorable balls at the Casino and who wrote his famous Schönbrunner Waltz in honour of Dommayer. Just as Lanner and Strauss, at first friends and collaborators, became rivals and adversaries in the 'war of the waltzes', so Sperl and Dommayer came into conflict in the 'ballroom war'. This quarrel threatened to ruin both parties; so they did what the two great brewers, Bosch and Dengler, had done – they arranged a marriage between their children. And in any case the fifty thousand Viennese who went dancing every evening provided enough patrons to fill several halls and enrich their proprietors, even if some of these halls were as extravagantly large as the Odeon, which held ten thousand dancers.

Twice as large as the Apollo, three times larger than the Sophia, the Odeon had one disadvantage: if there were only a thousand dancers there they felt as if they were dancing in a desert. There was no atmosphere about the place when it was not full. And how could one make sure of attracting ten thousand people night after night? The Odeon was famous for its acoustics, and male voice choirs, so popular in Vienna, sounded better there than elsewhere. Choral meetings, however, were unfortunately not enough to cover expenses, and so the Odeon was made available for gatherings of a more or less political character, to which its size and its acoustics made it eminently suitable. This was on the eve of 1848; the working class population in the suburbs was growing restive. Political brawls succeeded fancy dress dances and carnival fêtes. The Odeon had lost its character and its original purpose; it had become a battlefield. Furious conflicts broke out periodically when a religious sect, the 'German Catholics', started holding meetings and services there. The preacher, an excommunicated Silesian priest called Johannes Ronge, launched violent attacks on the Pope and on the cult of saints and the Virgin. The fate of the unfortunate Odeon was sealed; having rung with heretical imprecations, it was burnt down on October 28, 1848, when the troops of Windischgrätz won back Vienna from the rioters.

The last in date of the great dance palaces of the Biedermeier period was built by a German from Karlsruhe called Schwender, who had begun as marker in a billiard hall.

With his savings he opened a tavern in a cowshed attached
to the castle of the great banking family of Arnstein-Pereira,
beside which lay a huge meadow. He set out tables in the
shade of the trees and awaited customers. They came in
crowds, for the place was attractive. Schwender was able to
build a proper restaurant. Soon a theatre director, Alois
Pokorny, appreciating the advantages of the spot, built an
open-air stage where a number of popular plays were performed. This summer theatre, with its boxes and galleries,
became fashionable, and Schwender became a partner in the
enterprise. After the show patrons flocked to the ballrooms,
which bore such names as Hall of Love and Hall of Flora,
and where masked balls of lavish splendour took place.
Another room, the Hall of Harmony, was devoted to concerts,
and yet another to *tableaux vivants*, the craze of the moment.

Amongst the strangest of the masked balls which took
place at Karl Schwender's was the Beggars' Ball, where
aristocrats and wealthy bourgeois came dressed in rags,
wearing repulsive masks. On the eve of Ash Wednesday, to
celebrate the beginning of Lent, was held the Red Herrings'
Ball, where dried fish were served on precious dishes.
Schwender, who had had the ingenious notion of organizing
an omnibus service between Vienna and Schönbrunn, which
had never been done before, drew crowds of dancers and
gourmets to his Coliseum. Memorable meals were served
there, and on certain evenings his chefs vied with one another
in producing masterpieces. The newspapers of the time were
eloquent about these culinary contests, which must have been
remarkable if the flavour of the dishes equalled the originality
of their titles: 'Fresco of boiled lobsters', 'Trout minuet',
'Orpheus sailing on a giant salmon', and so on.

And all round this cluster of dance halls, restaurants and
theatres Schwender displayed the marvels of what he called
the 'New World', with its illuminated gardens, its Arabian
Nights' palaces, its immense hothouses, its fountains, its
fairground attractions: the whole an epitome of the character
of pleasure-seeking Vienna, which is to say a great majority
of the Viennese, for one would need to be singularly sour-
tempered or to have absolutely nothing left to pawn not to

yield to such temptations, or to the frenzied appeal of the violins which summoned the whole city to go dancing.

The Strauss Family

'Very characteristic is the beginning of each dance. Strauss intones his trembling preludes; panting for full expression they sound tragic, like the happiness felt in childbirth while pain still reigns. The Viennese male partner tucks his girl deep in his arm and in the strangest way they sway themselves into the measure. For a time we hear the prolonged chest notes with which the nightingale begins her song and enchants our nerves; then suddenly her resounding trill rings out, the actual dance begins with whirling rapidity, and the couple hurls itself into the maelstrom . . .'[9]

Laube has well described, too, that moment of suspense, that almost painful expectation, that impatience with which the crowd waited for the conductor to raise his baton. And when Johann Strauss was on the rostrum a sort of idolatrous passion rose towards him from the waiting throng.

'Every eye was turned towards him. All eyes were turned to him, it was a moment of worship. You will be asked, I said to myself, the generations of the future will ask: what did he look like, this Johann Strauss? If Napoleon's appearance was classically Roman and calmly antique, if Paganini's was romantic and arresting as moonlight, that of Maestro Strauss is African and hot-blooded, crazy from the sun, modern, bold, fidgety, restless, unbeautiful, passionate. These are adjectives from which the reader may make his selection.

'The man is black as a Moor; his hair is curly; his mouth is melodious, energetic, his lip curls, his nose is snub; if his face were not so white he would be the complete king of the Moors from Ethiopia, the complete Balthazar . . . Under Herod Balthazar came bearing incense with which to capture the senses – and it is the same with Strauss; he, too, exorcises the wicked devils from our bodies, and he does it with waltzes. That is the modern way in which he, too, sways our senses. Typically African, too, is the way he conducts his dances; his own limbs no longer belong to him when the desert-storm of his waltz is let loose; his fiddle-bow dances with his arms; the tempo animates his feet; . . . the devil is abroad.'[10]

The names of the conductors of dance bands at Viennese balls have vanished into oblivion with the generations they delighted; they are only to be traced in old faded newspapers or on posters promising sumptuous 'galas'. Only one of them has become immortal, as composer and conductor: Johann Strauss, the 'Napoleon of the waltz'. And also his three sons, musicians like himself: Johann Strauss II (the most illustrious of them, composer of *The Blue Danube*), Joseph and Edward. Beside the name of the first Johann Strauss we must remember that of his friend and rival, gentle Joseph Lanner, whose waltzes have a more languid and melancholy charm, with an occasional accent that recalls Schubert.

Johann Strauss was born in 1804, in the working-class district of Leopoldstadt, where his father kept a small tavern. From early childhood he was possessed by the demon of rhythm, which he tried to express by striking two sticks together. Rhythm is so much the new and essential element in his music, both in his compositions and in the way he performed them, that when Hector Berlioz heard him on his visit to Paris, the composer of the *Symphonie Fantastique* was greatly struck by the fact, and it is interesting to see how Berlioz assessed the Austrian's talent, in one of his articles in the *Journal des Débats* of 1837.

'Is it not strange to see that in a city like Paris, the meeting-ground for the great virtuosi and composers of Europe, the arrival of a German orchestra constitutes a musical event? An orchestra which actually only claims to play waltzes? Why did the first concert given by this group arouse such enthusiasm? ... The professional merits of the executants, although above the average, would scarcely suffice to explain the prodigious success of the ensemble. The true reason lies elsewhere. There is, in the world of music, a domain hitherto neglected by everyone, by performers as well as by composers – and which is none the less of capital importance ... Can you not guess to what I am referring? To rhythm! ... Strauss's musicians are far more skilled at overcoming the difficulties of changing rhythm than are our own artists. The waltzes they present to us, the measures of which race madly, carried head-long by their own impetus, these waltzes are hard to play.

O

The Viennese perform them with ease. It is thanks to this mastery that the capricious elegance of their rhythm yields its full charm. And that is why Strauss's success seems to me a happy omen for the development of music in Paris. For I am convinced that this success is due to the rhythmic accent of the waltzes rather than to their grace of melody or their brilliant orchestration. Strauss roams freely in a world whose gates were opened to us by Beethoven and Weber – the wonderful world of rhythm, an infinitely fertile soil which will bear rich harvests to those who till it . . .'

When he was five years old little Johann Strauss was given a cheap fiddle on which he played incessantly. The sound of it being sour, dry and thin, he had the notion of pouring beer inside it, which, it seems, had fortunate results. On this violin he repeated from memory what he had heard, and also improvized incessantly. A friend of his family's, having recognized his gifts, had him given lessons; the child thus took up the career of a musician and obtained a post under the conductor Pamer, at first in a tavern and then, glorious promotion, at Sperl's.

At fifteen, he joined up with a trio of adolescents who like himself played in pleasure-gardens: the brothers Drahanek and Joseph Lanner. They climbed the ladder of success together; from a quartet, Lanner's band grew to an ensemble of twelve players; their conductor was already adored by the people of Vienna, whose character he interpreted to perfection, with its carefree lightheartedness, its transient melancholy. Strauss has something of the gipsy; Lanner is pure Viennese.

'Unlike Strauss, he remained suburban the whole of his life, and the harmony of his waltz compositions frequently resembles that of popular songs. As a violinist Lanner was not sensual but sentimental, and that alone made him the idol of the Viennese . . . When later Ole Bull (the great Norwegian violinist) came to Vienna, the audience at his concert was struck by the similarity of his bowing to Lanner's . . . Bull had a different arrangement from the ordinary on his violin; its unique construction with a very low bridge favoured polyphonic playing, though this was to the detriment of the full volume and energy of the tone. The touching quality of Lanner's playing was attained by his soft polyphony, his art in manipulating the "sobbing third", while the greatness of Strauss as a violinist lay in his abrupt rubati, in the power of his sensual bowing, which commanded where Lanner only flattered. As in their external appearance the fair man and the black-haired man were complementary to each other, so also were their temperaments; one was soulful, the other hot-headed.'[11]

The compatriots of Ole Bull declared that the Norwegian, who was a friend of Schumann, Andersen and Grieg, had acquired his talent by a magic process; the nixy of the mountain stream, it was said – and nixies are great musicians – had taught him the secret of melody. In that case Lanner must have got his genius from a water-fairy of the Danube. Unfortunately there was not room in Vienna for two 'kings'. Dancers and music lovers were divided according to their preferences and affinities with one or the other, and thus broke out that famous 'war of the waltzes' from which Strauss emerged triumphant victor. This shift of allegiance corresponds, in the sphere of music, to Nestroy's victory over Raimund. After the two friends, whose characters were no longer in harmony, had parted, each to conduct his own orchestra henceforward, goodhearted Lanner expressed the grief he felt at this break in his romantic waltz entitled *The Farewell*.

Johann Strauss had brought a new element into Viennese pleasures: an unbridled Bacchanalian frenzy, a self-intoxicated emotionalism. A journalist who watched the celebration of St Bridget's Day at the Brigittenau and saw Strauss set the dancers madly whirling, calls this a 'Red Indian festival'. His description explains his impression. 'Under an enormous moon, chains of fairy lights connected immense tents of foliage. A vast rotating movement seemed to involve the entire landscape. The whirlpool did not confine itself to dance floors, tents and booths, it leapt over valleys and hills, drawing trees and bushes into its crazy waltz.'

Wagner, who visited Vienna in 1832, was particularly struck by the personality of the musician, and the ecstasy he aroused in his listeners, a real physical ecstasy caused by the magic charm of the man himself. 'This demon of Viennese popular music,' says Wagner, 'trembles at the beginning of a new waltz as if he were going into a trance. The whinnying moan uttered by the audience, intoxicated not with drink but with music, drives the virtuoso's passion to a pitch that is almost anguish.' Red Indian festival, bacchanale, sorcerer's revel . . . and the origin of it all was just the bewitching violin of the Jewish innkeeper's son from Leopoldstadt.

The personality of Johann Strauss was so closely identified with that of his native city that his death was mourned by all Vienna as a national bereavement. The maestro had died in the home of his mistress Emilie Trampbusch from scarlet fever, brought back from school by one of the five illegitimate children he had had by this woman (his legitimate children were to become famous musicians themselves). The successes he had won in Germany, in London and in Paris were nothing by the side of his compatriots' fanatical devotion. His funeral was as solemn, and aroused as deep an emotion, as the obsequies of royalty. It is thus described by H. E. Jacob:

'In the narrow Singerstrasse through which, led by the priests, the funeral procession wended its way, the people stood tightly wedged in their thousands. Silent weeping women looked down from open balconies. The long human serpent swept round the corner of the Stefansplatz, through the immense door into the Cathedral. Members of the orchestra carried the coffin. Behind it paced Amon, the leading violinist; on a black cushion he carried the dead master's violin, its torn strings hanging down.

'All the altars were illuminated, the consecration of the corpse took place by the soft flickering light of torches. The organ pealed and the choir sang. Then the coffin, covered with a cloth, was lifted on to a magnificent hearse drawn by four black horses. Down the Graben and the Schottengasse it went at a foot pace to the Schottentor, where the members of the orchestra once more took over the coffin, and carrying it on their shoulders in turns, brought it to its resting-place in Dobling. Behind the mourners paced the band of the infantry regiment Ceccopieri under conductor Reznicek, and behind them the band of the second artillery regiment under Reinisch . . . Side by side with Joseph Lanner, Johann Strauss was given to the earth. The Men's Choral Association sang in unison while the mound gradually began to rise over the grave. Darkness fell and the air grew chilly. A sweetly bitter autumnal odour came from the neighbouring vineyards where the grapes were waiting to be harvested. Lonely and sad came the sound of the bell from Salmannsdorf. Johann Strauss had presented it. The thin volume of its receding notes accompanied the people as they returned home . . .'[12]

CHAPTER NINE

VIENNESE ROMANTICISM

German and Austrian Romantics—'To Live in Poetry'—
Austrian Romanticism and Art—Portraits and Genre Paintings

Although they write the same language and are on the whole inspired by the same feelings, there are profound differences between German and Austrian Romantics. The latter have none of the tragic, anguished element, the Aeschylean conception of Fate, the radical revolt of the *Sturm und Drang* movement, nor the magical quality, the visionary vehemence which are displayed in the same fashion, although in different media, in the poetry of Hölderlin, the music of Schumann and the painting of Caspar David Friedrich.

German and Austrian Romantics

German romanticism is founded on a painful sense of dissatisfaction, unrest, and the anguish that springs from the disharmony between the individual and the universe. The romantic is, generally speaking, a man whose aspirations are in conflict with the laws of society and the constraint imposed upon him by his human condition.

The problem of the Divine is a source of anxiety; it is as hard for the individual to achieve harmony with God as to find his own right place in nature. The means of expression at the artist's disposal, be he painter, poet or musician, to render what he sees and feels, are bounded by the limits inherent in any sort of language; and, confronted with the inexpressible, suffering through not being able to utter what is unutterable, the artist who is also a seer is smitten with despair at being able to transmit, in his work, only what is communicable and, to him, inessential.

As a last resort, the German romantics often escaped into suicide or madness, as though seeking silent self-obliteration.

Nothing of the sort is to be seen in Austrian romanticism; the nature of their country, their national temperament, their sense of proportion, made the romanticism of Austrian artists superficial, devoid of drama. Vienna knows nothing of those terrible 'ground swells' that sweep so disturbingly through the German romantic movement.

While the German artist is at odds with, or in reaction against society, which sympathizes with him only remotely, if at all, the Austrian on the other hand is, or wants to be, in harmony with society. When we consider an Austrian work of art, the music of Schubert, the novels of Adalbert Stifter, the painting of Moritz von Schwind or Ferdinand Georg Waldmüller – we see that there is no divorce between art and the public. The reader or listener is instinctively able to tune in to the same wave length as the writer or composer, and they for their part are able to give the public, effortlessly, what it wants. The work of art is thus the result of an implicit collaboration between the creative artist and the society for which he creates.

Austrian art during the romantic period – I mean art as a whole, irrespective of the diversity of its means of expression – retains an idyllic character, inspired by the love of things, by a universal tenderness, far less 'demonic' than German Romantic passion; it has the charm, slightly superficial and sentimental but infinitely endearing, of a not-too-serious love affair. And yet one must not take literally the notorious 'lightheartedness' of the Austrians and neglect the depth of feeling, the intensity of passion which it may mask. If Viennese artists do not submit to the terrible, exalting, over-whelming influence of nature as a Panic force, yet they derive an intenser joy, quietly, from the beauty of the natural scene, for they have the gift of making friends with things. Moritz von Schwind has put it charmingly: 'When you look at a pretty little tree with love and joy, you express your love and joy as you draw it, and then the little tree looks quite different from the magnificent daub some ass might have made of it.'

German romanticism cherished Vienna for its charm as an old city, medieval, baroque and rococo. As Karl Kobald has written[1]: 'Vienna, wearing the reflected glory of Haydn, Mozart and Beethoven, appeared to the young poets of the German romantic movement as the Mecca of their dreams. A throng of pilgrims came to the Imperial city: Clemens Brentano, Friedrich Schlegel, Zacharias Werner, Bettina von Arnim, Eichendorff.' They came, but they did not take root there, and Vienna never became one of the centres of the Romantic movement; it cannot be compared to such hotbeds of Romanticism as Berlin, Jena, Heidelberg, Düsseldorf. The drawing-rooms of Vienna included none of the *salons* where Romantic theories were worked out, such as those of the Varnhagens or the Schlegels. In this respect, Vienna plays the part of a provincial town in the history of literature and even in painting. Its supreme and incomparable excellence lies in the sphere of music, although it did not recognize Schumann, the greatest and most significant of Romantic musicians.

The 'great names' of Austrian romantic literature are soon told: the greatest of them, the peer of the German romantic poets, Nicolas Lenau, was not a Viennese; Niembsch von Strehlenau (his real name) was a Hungarian. Having lost his father when he was very young, he came to Vienna with his mother, a frivolous, careless woman who paid little heed to him. His real temperament remains, even in his writings, that of a man from the *puszta*, for which he longed nostalgically throughout his life and sought, later on, in the American pampas to which his adventures took him. His choice of heroes for his books, Savonarola, Don Juan, the Albigenses, Faust, reveals his restless, questing character. Lenau never lost his fondness for the nomadic race of gipsies, dispossessed and homeless, rootless like himself and ill at ease in a world where they have no place. By nationality, Lenau belongs to Austrian romanticism, but he had none of its characteristics, and his vagrant restlessness made him feel as little at home in Vienna as in any other town. If we mention him, it is chiefly to stress the contrast with that essentially Viennese writer, Adalbert Stifter.

Stifter embodies the Austrian spirit at its most generous and exquisite. He was not a provincial novelist, although he clung to the ways and language and tastes of his province; more of a countryman than a city dweller, he adored Vienna, but went back periodically to the mountains, not the hills of the Wienerwald but the mountains of Bohemia where his lyric gifts blossomed freely, with all their power and delicate intimacy. Even if he had not written the books that made him famous, novels that portray society and poems inspired by forest scenes, he would have deserved to be famous for his paintings; these reveal, like his literary works, a keen and subtle sensibility, in close harmony with nature, an intimate understanding of humble everyday reality which would almost have made a 'naturalist' novelist of him had he not been chiefly inspired by that epic greatness which underlies all reality. Stifter is a master of the short story, to which he gives the substance and amplitude of a novel, and which through its symbolic value rises far above the mere 'slice of life' of the realist school.

The main characteristics of Viennese literature, indeed, as of the painting of Peter Fendi, Michael Neder or Carl Schindler, is a lyrical interpretation of everyday reality, of things which would be commonplace if they were not illuminated by sympathy and love. This love, which Moritz von Schwind described, transfigures the most humble objects precisely because it knows how to discover and bring out the intimate and profound poetry in them. 'In Vienna, one always lives half in poetry,' Grillparzer wrote, 'and one is a poet even if one has never written a line.'[2]

It would be wrong to think that the bourgeois prosiness of the Biedermeier period dried up the springs of poetry. The Viennese bourgeois caricatured as Biedermeier had none of the pontifical stupidity of Monnier's 'Monsieur Prud-homme', nor that pretentiousness, that meanness of mind and heart which are so alien to Vienna. Biedermeier was a poet in spite of himself, and without knowing it; he liked solid, comfortable furniture, befitting his portly, well-fed frame. The people of that day practised a simple, homely art of living, virtuous without affectation; they knew how to maintain a wholesome harmony between gaiety and propriety, grace and seriousness, opulence and simplicity, the reasonable thrift of the paterfamilias and the generosity of the Maecenas, the friend of artists. Biedermeier loved the country, and country outings with his family. He seldom went abroad because he adored his Austria with its infinite variety. He never stirred far afield, nor for long, from Vienna, the exquisite and inexhaustible city; the country, for him, meant the immediate neighbourhood of the town, where nature was so pleasant and the villages were so picturesque, full of gay and lively peasants still wearing their traditional costumes. Those costumes, which nowadays are seen only in the Tyrol, where as often as not they are worn by foreign tourists dressed up as chamois hunters or peasant girls, were then to be seen in every market-place and, in their full motley brilliance, on feast days and holidays, as they are so often pictured by the painters of the time, by Ferdinand Waldmüller for instance, in his *Wedding at Pechtoldsdorf* or *The Bride's Departure*.

'To Live in Poetry'

A poetic way of feeling, an aptitude to 'live in poetry' naturally and spontaneously, were more widespread in Austria than in Germany in the Romantic period, but Austria did not produce such great poets as Germany. It is impossible to consider as great poets, indeed, such writers as Johann Gabriel Seidl, many of whose verses Schubert set to music, or Ernst von Feuchtersleben, or Anastasius Grün; their works are not negligible, but they seem very minor figures by the side of their German contemporaries, Eichendorff, Novalis, Hölderlin, Brentano. Their poetry lacks the magic radiance of the great romantics. Nevertheless they are of interest to the historian because they so exactly reflect the Vienna of their day.

Feuchterleben, for instance, was a physician of genius, almost a precursor of psychoanalysis, which Freud was to create in a later Vienna; he liked to mingle with the writers who frequented the charmingly decorated rooms of the Neuners Silbernen, the fashionable literary café, and he wrote his verses there between professional calls. As for

Anastasius Grün, this was the pseudonym of a great nobleman, Count Anton Alexander Auersperg; the Emperor had
forbidden him to publish his writings, not so much because it
was considered unworthy of an aristocrat of such high rank
to indulge in so plebeian an activity, as because Auersperg
professed somewhat advanced liberal opinions. He criticized
Metternich's policy violently and with savage irony. The
books he published in the guise of Anastasius Grün, particularly *Schutt* (the title, 'Débris', is significant) which is a
cruel satire on the monarchy, may have played an important
part in preparing the revolution of 1848; more innocent and
pleasanter reading, with its charming descriptions of the
capital, is the work entitled *Rambles of a Viennese poet*,[3]
which deserves to stand by the side of Adalbert Stifter's
Pictures of Vienna and the admirable writings of Grillparzer.

With Franz Grillparzer, we touch a poetic level which is
almost that of the great romantics. Grillparzer loved his
Austria with a child's passion, as he himself said, and it is
vain to argue that the Austria to which he pledged such
devotion existed only in his dreams. His picture of Vienna
is a true one, even if he has idealized it; he has exactly defined
the characteristics of this lovable race of people, so easy-going
and so easy to govern. It is chiefly in his intimate journal
and in his Autobiography, which unfortunately stops short
at his forty-fifth year (he lived to eighty), that we find the
Grillparzer who interests us today, namely the observer of
Viennese life at this period. His historical dramas, despite the
great beauties of his *Sappho*, his *Golden Fleece* and his *Ottokar*,
have less value for us than his enchanting short stories, which
describe reality with so moving a blend of tenderness and
mischief: *The Poor Musician* is the finest of them. Here we
see the real face of Vienna in the romantic period, with its
fiddle-scrapers at street corners, reduced to beggary by the
hardness of the times, by their own fecklessness, and often,
too, by their desire to escape from the narrowness of bourgeois life in a happy-go-lucky adventurousness.

Like many Viennese – Schubert for instance – inclined to
prefer the wonders of their dream to the banalities of ordinary
life, and to cling to impossible loves because these are never

disappointing, Grillparzer, too, had his *'ferne geliebte'*, his faraway beloved, Käthi Frohlich, whom he never married, for fear of seeing his dream fade if it were brought down to earth. In his recollections, and above all in the exquisite pages of his *Jugenderrinerungen im Grüner* (Memories of Youth under the Greenwood Tree) we read the account of his passion for this gentle, sweet-faced betrothed, whom he never brought himself to marry. Possibly, too, he was reluctant to give up for her sake the other women he loved.

Some of Grillparzer's love affairs came to a tragic end; pretty Marie von Piquot died of grief at his neglect, and so did Charlotte von Paumgarten. On the other hand he suffered deeply from the indifference shown him by other women, lovely Marie von Smolenitz, gentle Heloise Höchner. He had passing infatuations for singers and actresses which did not affect his devotion to the eternal betrothed. Perhaps Grillparzer was afraid of too much beauty or too intense a passion. He has left a revealing comment on Marie Daffinger – she had been Marie von Smolenitz and had married the painter Moritz Michael Daffinger, who painted fascinating portraits of her: 'That woman is beautiful, beautiful, and let the man who comes near her beware of her!' Marie Daffinger had those enigmatic doe's eyes, those deep seductive glances that create havoc in vulnerable hearts. The poet's cry of alarm proves that he too had ventured dangerously near them, bewitched by their intoxicating mystery.

Amongst the romantic poets of Vienna, contemporaries undoubtedly gave high praise to Betty Glück, who wrote under the name of Betty Paoli. Grillparzer called her the greatest Austrian poetess; Hieronymus Lorm went further, saying: the greatest German poetess. We cannot attempt here to criticize or justify the claim to fame of this authoress, who is now completely forgotten. Betty Paoli suffered from an unhappy love affair; she was lady-in-waiting to Princess Schwarzenberg and had the imprudence to fall in love with her son, handsome Prince Frederick; they exchanged a lengthy correspondence, of which nothing more came.

Except for Lenau, Grillparzer and Stifter, the romantic movement in Austria has left no great literary names.

Austrian Romanticism and Art

Vienna, which throughout its history has been the capital city of music, has not always been of equal importance in the world of letters. What position did Vienna hold during the romantic period in the plastic and graphic arts, in architecture, sculpture and painting?

We have already seen what baroque splendour characterized its buildings under the reigns of Joseph I and Maria Theresa, and what an impetus the reconstruction of the city, after the siege of 1683, received from the encouragement of its rulers, who were great builders as well as enthusiastic musicians. The evolution of Viennese architecture exactly reflects the changes of taste and aesthetics in successive generations. As might be expected, Classicism triumphed after the excesses of the baroque age: a neo-classicism inspired by Greece and Rome. Romanticism in its turn introduced into Austria, as throughout Europe, the love of things medieval and the revival of the Gothic, as early as the last quarter of the eighteenth century. It was the enlightened despot Joseph II, a man directly inspired by the ideas of the eighteenth century, who inaugurated, so to speak, the Gothic revival when he ordered the architect Hetzendorf to strip the church of the Minorities and that of the Augustines of all the accretions which had been arbitrarily added to them since the Middle Ages.

Under Francis I, romanticism created its own, original architectural style, which was no mere pastiche of ancient temples or Gothic cathedrals but a sort of harmonious fusion of medieval and Renaissance elements, freely combined, treated as a fresh stock of forms through which the spirit of the age could express itself. Romanticism refuses to imitate or reproduce something already existing; it creates freely, and the best of its creations are the Johanneskirche in the Pratergasse, built by Rosner in 1846, which modified the old building without destroying its spirit, the parish church of Meidling, built at the same time by the same architect, and, most characteristic of all, the parish church of Altmannsdorf, built in 1838 by Loessl, decorated by Fuhrich, Steinle and Kupelweiser. Fuhrich had taken part in the renaissance of painting led by Cornelis and Overbeck which was to produce the neo-primitivism of the 'Nazarenes'. The Guild of St Luke, which promulgated their aesthetic doctrines, somewhat akin to those of the English Pre-Raphaelites, was founded in Vienna, but emigrated to Rome. The 'companions' of the Guild settled in a monastery at Sant'Isidoro and painted in the style of those who were then known as 'primitives', namely Raphael and his immediate predecessors. There was at that time no appreciation of the real primitives, Giotto, Cimabue, Duccio and Cavallini, and the Middle Ages were scarcely distinguished from the Renaissance.

Fuhrich, then, took part in the 'neo-primitive' decoration of the Villa Massimi; this belonged to a German diplomat, Bartholdy, who invited the 'Nazarenes' to adorn it with paintings of religious subjects. Fuhrich returned to Vienna in 1834, and there painted a great series of romantic scenes on religious themes, taken from the Old and New Testaments and from legend, interpreted freely and freshly and with a somewhat chilly grace and elegance.

Eduard Jacob von Steinle also lived in Rome and was in touch with the 'Nazarenes', after completing his studies at the Academy of his native Vienna. He was friendly with many German poets, above all with Clemens Brentano, who encouraged him to study and illustrate old legends, fairy tales and popular poems. Once he had shaken off Nazarene neo-primitivism, Steinle developed an authentically romantic lyricism: his works, which show students on their travels crossing enchanted forests, castles romantically perched on mountain cliffs, and old cities with Gothic spires, have a charm that blends nostalgia for the Middle Ages with an extremely modern feeling. He had been the pupil of Kupelweiser, by whose side he worked in decorating the church of Altmannsdorf – that same Kupelweiser who was the friend of Schubert, of whom he has left several portraits, and who has described those touching and joyful 'Schubertiads', those revels devoted to art and friendship of which the composer was the centre.

It was not only in religious painting that Viennese romanticism found expression; its peculiar characteristics and its most original inspiration are revealed in portraits and *genre* pictures. And if we make no mention of Austrian romantic sculpture it is because this is almost entirely lacking, or has left nothing of importance.

Two names dominate Austrian landscape painting during the Romantic period; that of Joseph Anton Koch (1768–1839) who belongs to the first Romantic generation, and that of Ferdinand Georg Waldmüller, who represents the second, since he was born in 1793 and died in 1865. Koch is a curious figure, a Tyrolean from Elgiblenalp, who went off to die in Rome because he was so fascinated by Italian landscapes that he wanted to end his life among them. He painted religious scenes in the manner of the Nazarenes and tried to vie with Ghirlandaio and Perugino. He illustrated Dante and Shakespeare, and shared the enthusiasm of all Romantics for Ossian – the pseudo-Ossian of the Scotsman Macpherson. Napoleon himself was so passionately devoted to the adventures of the legendary Celtic heroes that Ingres painted for the ceiling of the room the Emperor was to occupy in the Quirinal a highly romantic *Ossian's Dream*. It is not because he imitated old Italian painters that Koch deserves to be remembered but rather because he was the first to create Romantic landscape, particularly in his pictures of Switzerland and the Tyrol, since during his Roman period he was less original, more closely attached to the tradition of Claude Lorraine and the Italian *vedutisti*.

Koch was the first to understand and represent mountain scenery with its waterfalls and glaciers, all the aspects of a wild, powerful, majestic Nature which the men of the eighteenth century had not yet learnt to see, which they merely considered 'frightful' – the word '*affreuse*' recurs constantly in their writings – when they happened to look at it. Perhaps because they were always city-dwellers, men accustomed to calm, orderly landscapes, untamed Nature had no attraction for them, and indeed they knew it chiefly from hearsay, the fashion for mountain excursions being as yet unknown. Travellers gazed at the cloud-capped snowy peaks from the windows of their carriages as they drove past, and never felt a longing to climb them nor even to venture to the foothills.

Koch was able to see mountains and to depict them, when none of his contemporaries were interested in them, probably because such scenery was familiar to him, and he loved it passionately until the exclusive cult of Italy made him forget his native land, almost literally, since between 1795 and 1839 he only left Rome to spend three years in Vienna, from 1812 to 1815. But it was during this visit that he stimulated the inspiration of such young landscape painters as Rottmann and the brothers Olivier and Fohr, to whom he showed the way while respecting their individuality.

Ferdinand Georg Waldmüller was an authentic Viennese, and during his difficult early years it was from the common people of Vienna, particularly from the petty bourgeois of the suburbs, that he got support and encouragement. Son of an ale-house proprietor, he had known extreme poverty; his parents disapproved of his embarking on an unprofitable career, and for a long time he had to paint shop-signs for a living. The portraits he first painted were those of the humble folk amongst whom he lived; these portraits, done with such sure and brilliant mastery to earn a meagre livelihood, won him fame in London and Paris as well as in the imperial city. Vienna took him up, after having disdained him; he soon became an immensely successful painter, for whom fashionable beauties and noblemen sat.

His portraits have the quiet dignity, the easy distinction, the sober grace of these gentlefolk and wealthy bourgeois, leaders of 'biedermeier' society. His family groups are almost *genre* pictures, for he sets his figures against their home background, among their furniture of dark red mahogany or light lemon-wood, their heavy curtains, their elegant knick-knacks. One has only to look at Waldmüller's paintings to understand the way of life of this society, what these people thought and how they felt.

It was as a portrait painter that he won fame and fortune. But his interest for us lies rather in his interpretation of the Viennese countryside. He does not seek out Swiss glaciers and Tyrolean waterfalls, like Koch; he is content with the immediate neighbourhood of the city, the fine fields and woods just beyond its outskirts. These green horizons, these gentle undulations exactly proportioned to man's scale, this genuine, unassuming nature, so inviting to the rambler, like a continuation of the gardens within the city, the link between the Volksgarten, the Augarten, the Prater and the free dense growth of the forest, where one could forget the town's din without going more than an hour's journey from home – this was Waldmüller's world; he depicts it in scenes of such touching beauty and he has so delicately rendered the freshness of morning on the lawns of the Prater, the majesty of sunset on the wooded heights of the Kahlenberg, that the Viennese landscape itself – if we are to believe Oscar Wilde's paradox, that nature imitates art – seems to emulate the paintings of Waldmüller, so profoundly interconnected are the artist's sensibility and the world he portrays.

A number of other romantic landscape painters deserve to be mentioned in Waldmüller's company: Anton Hasch, who specializes in high mountain scenery; Franz Steinfeld, whose torrents have a musical freshness; Friedrich Loos, who loves the broad sweep of the Danube plain; Erasmus Engert, long neglected and recently rediscovered as an exquisite interpreter of peaceful, smiling scenes in old Vienna; Johannes M. Thoma, painter of those charming rustic dwellings built during the romantic period half way between the suburbs and the Wienerwald . . .

Portraits and Genre Paintings

Portraits were just as popular as landscapes, if not more so, among art-lovers in Vienna. And not merely among wealthy connoisseurs but among the lower middle class and the common people. If we remember that Josef Kriehuber painted more than three thousand portraits, and that he was only one of the artists who excelled in this sphere, we may wonder how a town such as Vienna was in 1830 could provide enough customers for so large a number of painters. This fondness for portraits sprang, in the first place, from that love of real life which formed the basis of Austrian artistic taste. For the Viennese, art was not a means of escaping from the world, but on the contrary a means of enjoying it more intensely; for they loved the world they lived in and were happy to be in it; they had no need of the fantastic or the supernatural; the poetry of real life delighted and satisfied them.

We must not forget an economic factor which encouraged this profusion of portraits; they were presumably very cheap. Although we do not know the fees asked by painters – which varied according to their talent and popularity, of course – they must have been fairly low, since we find so many portraits of humble folk; and presumably, since a picture cost no more than a photograph does today, one would have to be very poor indeed to forgo the pleasure of adorning one's home and perpetuating one's image at so small a cost.

The beauty of the women, the distinction of the men, the grace of the contemporary fashions gives these portraits a singular charm. Curls framing the face, shawls slipping from rounded shoulders, low-cut dresses with tight high waists and billowing folds of cloudy muslin, hats picturesquely adorned with feathers and ribbons, all add a piquant grace to the aspect of these princesses and city ladies portrayed in their modest comeliness or aristocratic splendour by Friedrich Amerling, Waldmüller, Josef Danhauser, Peter Fendi or Moritz Daffinger. Famous paintings such as Amerling's *Lute Player*, Schrotzberg's portrait of Käthy Mayrhofer, Daffinger's miniature of Käthi Fröhlich (Grillparzer's 'eternal beloved') and his painting of Marie Smolenitz, whom he married and whom Grillparzer, who had adored her too, thought so dangerously beautiful; the magnificent Tyrolese girls painted by Franz Eybl, and Kriehuber's pencil drawing of Princess Schwarzenberg – these suggest, better than any description, the atmosphere created in Vienna by these lovely women of the romantic age.

These portraits were no longer the formal likenesses of the Baroque era, stiffly posed in the Spanish-style ceremoniousness of a court petrified by etiquette; bodies and minds had grown more flexible and had at the same time gained more freedom, more fantasy and genuine grace. The sitter has not posed for the painter; the artist has striven to make his portrait as natural as possible. He has tried to achieve not merely a physical likeness, a formal exactness, but rather the psychological truth, the personal singularities which make one individual so utterly unlike any other. Viennese artists attained perfection in the art of bringing out individual character, originality of feature and temperament, and one need only glance at the picture of Marie Smolenitz to agree with Grillparzer, and imagine the fathomless joys and sufferings awaiting those who came under the spell of that doe-eyed beauty.

This widespread love of poetic realism naturally favoured the production not only of portraits and of landscapes, but of *genre* pictures. These are stories in painting, akin to those we find in the novels of Stifter and Grillparzer, the plays of Nestroy and Raimund, even in the Eipeldauer's humorous letters; they are not so far removed, perhaps, from Schubert's *Lieder*, where familiar subjects and themes are treated with such moving musical beauty. A Schubert *lied* is in its way a *genre* painting, a picture of the feelings, joyful or heart-broken, whether we consider the *Schöne Müllerin* or the *Winterreise*.

The subjects of these genre paintings are, as can be imagined, infinitely varied, according to the painter's whim and the patron's choice; the popular merrymakings depicted by Leander Russ, the episodes from bourgeois life satirized by Johann Ranftl, Johann Reiter's intimate scenes, Friedrich Treml's village ceremonies, all show different aspects of that narrative art, so witty and amiable, without vulgarity or spite, whose chief characteristics are lightness, grace, good-nature and innocent mischief. The *genre* painting displays all the good humour of the Biedermeier age, enamoured of realism, combined with a delicate, intense, yet discreet romantic feeling, diffidently reluctant to be taken seriously. Among the most remarkable and celebrated of these *genre* painters, we might also include Waldmüller, Daffinger, Danhauser, Amerling and Eybl, for they did not confine themselves to painting landscapes and portraits. Those who distinguished themselves more particularly in painting these homely scenes were Carl Schindler, Michael Neder, Peter Fendi, typical representatives of that everyday Vienna which they interpreted with tenderness, amusement and zest.

Some of these artists were the more adept at describing scenes of popular life in that they themselves came from the common people; Michael Neder, for instance, was a working cobbler in the suburb of Döbling. There is nothing clumsily prosaic about Neder's art; here, too, we see the most ordinary moments of everyday life transfigured by the power of sympathy and love. Closely akin, sometimes, to his contemporary Carl Spitzweg the Bavarian painter, he surveys the men and things around him with mingled irony and affection. A humble artist, neglected by wealthy collectors, working for the poor people of his village and for his fellow artisans, Michael Neder lived in poverty and died in the public hospital, but no other painter conveyed with such truth and vividness the quiet, cheerful life of humble suburbs.

Peter Fendi, on the other hand, is the painter of the well-to-do middle-class, of family life, with a touch of sentiment which could easily turn to sentimentality but for his fine painterly technique and the constant control of feeling, so typically Viennese, that stops him at the point where emotion threatens to become theatrical. The warm, comfortable interiors of Biedermeier homes form the setting for his intimate scenes with their soft lights, their muted tones, their discreet poetry. Looking at Fendi's portraits and groups, where handsome children, petulant and affectionate, play the leading part, one thinks of Schumann's *Kinderscenen*. Carl Schindler, on the other hand, chooses somewhat theatrical anecdotes, in the style of Greuze's paintings and the *drame larmoyant* in France. He came of an old Viennese family; his father taught drawing at the school of St Anne, and he died at the age of twenty-one at Laab-im-Walder, close to Vienna. During his brief career he specialized in the picturesque episodes of military life, showing not battles, but the sorrows of a conscript being torn from his family, or of heartbroken parents learning that their son has been killed in the wars. His favourite technique was watercolour, in which he acquired a virtuosity that made him famous.

Austrian painting during the first half of the nineteenth century produced little that can be set beside the great romantic art of Germany at the same period: the art of

Caspar David Friedrich, Philip Otto Runge, Carl Gustav
Carus, Carl Blechen, Ludwig Richter, Ernst Ferdinand
Ohme, to name only the most 'romantic'. Such romanticism
was beyond the reach of Austrian painters: only certain
scenes suggested in Schubert's *Lieder* deserve to be compared with the visionary landscapes of the Germans. On
the other hand, another aspect of Romantic art, belonging
rather to illustration than to painting properly so called, the
art that relates legends and fables, where the thing told is as
important as the manner of telling – programme painting, if
you will – found a master in Moritz von Schwind, and to a
lesser degree, though he is also remarkable, in Schnorr von
Carolsfeld: the first a Viennese born and bred, the second a
pupil of the Vienna Academy, where he spent part of his
career.

Schnorr von Carolsfeld lived in Rome, in the 'Nazarenes'
set; he painted religious pictures in the style of the Italian
pre-Raphaelites; he was also a fine painter of Austrian landscapes, and a vigorous interpreter of medieval epics, which
were then being rediscovered, in the manner of Carstens,
Koch and Runge. He had a strong feeling for the Gothic
revival which was growing up amongst the Romantics, under
the influence of the conversion to Catholicism of a number of
Protestant artists and perhaps also under that of the Holy
Alliance and the Congress of Vienna.

Like Peter Cornelius, Overbech, Franz Pfohr and Ferdinand von Olivier, he failed to distinguish between German
Medieval Gothic and the early Italian Renaissance. Schnorr
is an eclectic, who owes a good deal to the atmosphere of
German Romanticism, but whose Austrian character remains
none the less strongly marked.

The art of Moritz von Schwind can scarcely be placed in
the category of 'historical painting'; he would be more
exactly described as a painter of legend. The world in which
he moves with incomparable grace, his familiar world, was
that of bewitched princesses, spellbound knights, magic
forests, 'horns of Elfland faintly blowing', gnomes and pixies
and water-fairies. This artist's universe is the scene of continual metamorphoses, of surprising transfigurations; he

roams through this fantastic world as familiarly as other painters in the unenchanted paths of the Viennese forest. For Moritz von Schwind, the miracle of a supernatural presence is always imminent. These enchanted forests were alive and rustling in his imagination. This joyous and fantastic friend of Schubert's recreated a world of wonders without leaving Vienna, which he loved so dearly that he almost refused to stir from it even to go to Munich; as for Rome, he only passed through it; neither Italy nor the German painters living there could hold him. Reality, for him, was the world of his imagination rather than the world of dream; when he depicts the supernatural he does so in terms of visible nature, of familiar forms.

While Romanticism was rediscovering the Middle Ages, while Herder studied its traditional literatures and Brentano and Arnim traced back through the centuries the long uninterrupted continuity of song, fable and proverb, Moritz von Schwind was inspired by, and illustrated, the loveliest tales of all: those tales which reveal, not only the inventive genius of past societies and ages, but an initiatory truth and a magical power; those tales which Novalis considered to be symbols of the greatest and deepest reality.

The paintings of Moritz von Schwind are steeped in the shimmering light of fairy tale: the stories which enchanted Romantic writers, from Goethe to Hoffmann – Fair Melusine, the Seven Swans, Snow White, Puss in Boots, Cinderella – are inexhaustible sources of delight to him. He is, together with Richter, the Romantic illustrator *par excellence*, because the poem or the story sets his inventive imagination working and, far from clinging to the text, he embroiders freely on it, with that lively and refined originality which gives such rare elegance and irresistible suggestive power to all his paintings. Those who care only for pure painting, who believe only in plastic values, in painterly technique, may profess to despise him for laying too much stress on 'the story', but who ever told a story with such brilliant ease, such a blend of humour and genuine feeling, such intimate poetry, never verging on sentimentality?

Amongst the painter-poets who are the embodiment of

German romanticism, Moritz von Schwind is not only one of the most characteristic and delightful, but the one who 'represents', in the strongest sense of the word, the Austrian contribution: the spirit of Austria transposed into the world of fantasy, without that element of parody that we find in Raimund's fairy plays, because Raimund did not believe in fairies, whereas Moritz von Schwind's sense of wonder surely sprang from finding in the world of legend the fabulous figures that already existed in his own mind.

CHAPTER TEN

THE REIGN OF BIEDERMEIER

*The Advent of the Bourgeoisie—Birth of the Industrial Era—
The Jews of Vienna—Relics of Absolutism—Social Unrest*

The biedermeier period, the biedermeier style, these words recur constantly when we are speaking of the way Viennese people lived, thought and felt, the fashion of their homes and furniture, during that period of the nineteenth century between the Congress of Vienna and the Revolution of 1848. The name was used as a term of contempt by men of 'advanced' ideas, by *avant-garde* artists. For a time, the biedermeier style seemed as ridiculous as that of Louis-Philippe in France, its contemporary. Today we judge more fairly and more broadmindedly, particularly in matters of taste, and since remoteness confers grace and beauty on things which were thought ugly and ungraceful when one was close to them, we can appreciate the old-fashioned but endearing charm of the biedermeier style and even grant it certain indisputable aesthetic merits. Herr Biedermeier, the man who gave his name to a style and a period, was stigmatized in his own day as a Philistine, a reactionary, in short a 'bourgeois'; and in fact, the reign of Biedermeier means simply the reign of the bourgeoisie.

If he was really so important as to leave his mark on a whole period, one may suppose Herr Biedermeier to have been a man of strong and original personality, worthy of being remembered with the other great creators of styles, such as Louis XIV and Louis XV. Who was this man? It is somewhat embarrassing to have to admit that there never was such a person as Biedermeier, or that if there really was an individual of that name he was somebody quite obscure, quite incapable of making the impression on thought, sensibility and taste that has been attributed to him. Herr Biedermeier existed only in the fancy of a writer, Ludwig Pfau, who invented the character and in order to give him more reality and substance, published under this borrowed name the poems of a poor village schoolmaster, who had more sincerity than talent, and whose naïve moralizings, somewhat solemn, and somewhat foolish, too, at times, seemed to correspond perfectly to the character of the fictitious Biedermeier.

This dominie was called Samuel Friedrich Sauter; he was born in 1766 at Flehingen, and he fulfilled his worthy duties with a conscientiousness, an uprightness, a simple and profound goodness that should have earned him a better fate than to have his modest writings signed by the mendacious name of Biedermeier. He brought up eight children and spent a long life of poverty, borne with courage and dignity, teaching the alphabet to village urchins. Actually he never witnessed the publication of his writings, for this took place a few years after his death, when two satirists, Adolf Kussmaul and Rudolf Rod, printed these somewhat ridiculous verses in the newspaper *Fliegende Blätter*, under the title of 'Selected Works of Weiland Gottlieb Biedermeier'.

Thus was born an almost entirely fictitious character who was to make his way in the world, and whose name is mentioned with respect by all historians of art. But it sometimes happens that imaginary figures are more vividly representative of their period than are its artists or statesmen, and although this name was made up by a facetious pamphleteer, it is indispensable today, since we have grown used to talking about biedermeier furniture and knick-knacks, and it has become as familiar an adjective as Gothic, Baroque or Romantic.

Having thus settled the question of Herr Biedermeier's identity, and considering that in the mind of his inventor he is identical with the typical bourgeois and stands for everything belonging to the bourgeoisie, we may note that except in a few artistic or proletarian circles – if at all – the whole of Vienna lay meekly under Herr Biedermeier's sway for some thirty years: years which witnessed the growth of wealth and prosperity, the accession to power of a class which hitherto had humbly vegetated mid-way between the common people and the aristocracy, yet far closer to the former than to the latter.

The Advent of the Bourgeoisie

The enormous expenses which the need to keep up appearances at the Congress imposed on an aristocracy already impoverished by war, the vicissitudes of a fluctuating currency, inflation and the excessive multiplication of banknotes, severely affected a class which was already in debt to financial adventurers, namely the bourgeoisie. The golden age of bankers had already begun under the reign of Joseph II, who, paradoxically enough, while advocating the levelling of fortunes, encouraged the rise of a category of men who were soon to lay hands on a considerable section of Austria's national income. 'A hundred florins shared out amongst a hundred purses,' he had written, 'are worth more than a thousand florins in a single purse.' And yet he allowed Austrian or foreign financiers, particularly Swiss ones, to monopolize in some sort the country's fortune.

This was cunningly calculated. Joseph disliked the aristocracy; the great nobles of the Empire frightened and irritated him. The idea of depending on a class which should owe its prosperity to him, and making common cause with it against the feudal lords, those Hungarian, Austrian or Polish gentlefolk who ruled over thousands of 'subjects' and many of whom prided themselves on being of nobler birth than the Emperor himself, this idea led the enlightened despot to create a buffer class which he hoped would be devoted to him and second his reforms. The absolutism of which he dreamed, for all his revolutionary theories, was unrealizable so long as the nobility formed an obstacle to it, unless some party or caste which he had made as strong as, or stronger than, the nobility, should help him to overthrow this obstacle. Against the advice of Kaunitz himself, whose wisdom, shrewdness and experience had been acquired through so many years of government, he built up the financiers' 'bloc'.

'At this period, the bank of Vienna was to a great extent in the hands of foreign financiers. Joseph II, to win the support of these powerful figures, handed out to them a certain number of baronial titles. Thus he conferred nobility on the Fuchs family, on Paul Casati of Prague, Jacob Gontard of Frankfurt, and the Jew Arnstein, while, to the great scandal of the Austro-Hungarian aristocracy, the Protestant banker Fries received the title of Count. Joseph II, who frequently visited the Arnsteins, liked to discuss music and literature with the banker's beautiful wife, Fanny Itzig.'[1]

This sudden rise of the middle class towards a position traditionally reserved for the aristocracy did not take place without opposition from the latter, but once the impulse had been given, the movement could not be checked. The Napoleonic wars, which put kings in debt to financiers, the Congress of Vienna during which the latter controlled the fortunes of the princes who foregathered to settle the fate of Europe, consolidated the financial position of the bourgeoisie and helped them onward towards prosperity and honour. This occasionally happened so fast that these newly enriched bourgeois seemed upstarts, proud of the wealth that had raised them so high.

There never existed in Vienna, however, that passionate, exclusive and almost morbid cult of money which characterized the Restoration period in France, and of which countless aspects are shown in the works of Balzac. Cupidity and avarice were never part of the Austrian character; a man like Old Grandet is unthinkable in Vienna, where everyone spent his income freely and even frequently lived above his means, to the greater gain of money-lenders great and small – of those who advanced hundreds of thousands of florins to hard-up aristocrats, as well as the humble pawnbrokers who enabled some poor clerk or unemployed artisan to last out to the end of the month without starving.

This bourgeoisie, which comprised bankers, industrialists, wholesale traders and State suppliers, and which acquired increased prestige, self-confidence and pride as it grew wealthier – this bourgeoisie imposed its way of life and its tastes at a time when the twilight of the monarchy throughout

Europe foretold an era of democratization, with or without the consent of the ruling class.

The advent of the bourgeoisie which took place in Austria at the same time as it did in France, if not for the same reasons at least as part of a general social evolution, is one of the essential features of life in Vienna in the first third of the nineteenth century. Highly complex economic and political conditions were favourable to the reign of the bourgeoisie, which coincides with the advent of the industrial era and is dependent on it.

The success of the bourgeoisie sprang from the fact that the whole economic life of the country lay in its hands. It grew rich while the nobility grew poor, for the estates owned by the great landed proprietors, which were often as large as provinces, yielded little wealth. Until the beginning of the nineteenth century, Austria had been essentially an agricultural country. The development of industry meant the development of finance; the aristocracy, progressively stripped of part of its fortune by wars, by monetary devaluation and by the impossibility of keeping its income up to the level of its expenses, became more and more dependent on the financiers.

Impecunious gentlefolk, whom neither their national character nor their class tradition inclined to take life seriously, despised the money which they needed. They borrowed carelessly from the funds laid at their disposal by the bankers, without thinking that some day they would have to repay these loans, swollen with heavy interest. As their fortunes melted away, their influence and authority diminished; prestige and power being always on the side of money, from the moment they ceased to have control – or sole control, at any rate – of money, they lost everything else. And so one can say that the leading figures of the biedermeier period were bourgeois personalities who displayed originality and even, sometimes, a certain brilliance.

The outward aspect of society and the whole character of Vienna were profoundly transformed by this social evolution, which gathered considerable strength between the end of the eighteenth century and the Revolution of 1848, at which date we witness not the decline of the bourgeoisie, which still kept control, but the appearance of a new power: the proletariat. Indeed the proletariat is the inevitable consequence of industrial progress, and it was in order to avoid the growth of a poor, dissatisfied class, which might become subversive at the first opportunity, that the government had tried for so long to protect Vienna and its immediate neighbourhood from the invasion and proliferation of factories.

The progress of industry was one of the primary aims of the encyclopedist philosophers and of the enlightened despots who considered themselves their disciples and rivals. Joseph II had certainly not forgotten that Peter the Great, his model, had worked with his own hands in order to learn crafts and techniques, and that the industrialization of Russia had been one of the most efficient ways of modernizing that country. The progress they dreamed of was to make human happiness more accessible and more immediate by entrusting part of man's work to the machine.

This leading idea of the late eighteenth century was too attractive for any obstacle to be put in the way of its realization. The promotion of the city worker to a degree of civilization and happiness superior to that of the peasant was part of the creed underlying the dreams of the age of enlightenment. Thinkers and technicians, who looked forward to mechanical progress, did not imagine it could have other than beneficial results. The radical changes to be introduced into the balance of the social order by the growth of an industrial proletariat at the expense of agriculture, that basic source of wealth for all countries and particularly for Austria, the accumulation of wealth in the hands of manufacturers, merchants and financiers, the wretched pay granted to the army and the civil service, and finally the whole shift-over of money which involved moral and psychological, as well as social, consequences, the gravity of which could not be foreseen: all this prepared the way for an eventual revolution, half a century before it broke out.

The political situation of Austria was, as we have seen, too different from that of France for the revolutionary movement of 1789 to affect her. Sixty years later, the industrialized empire was roughly in the same position as the France of Louis-Philippe, and if the Austrian revolution did not lead to a change of régime as in France, it was because it was put down by repressive reprisals of which France was incapable, because the majority of the people still remained attached to the monarchy, and because the basically easy-going character of the Viennese prevented them from becoming a really revolutionary people.

Birth of the Industrial Era

The birth of the industrial era can be traced, in Vienna, round about 1780; it had been preceded, however, by increasing activity in certain fields, the manufacture of paper and silk, the weaving of linen and woollen cloth, and brewing. The first Viennese paper factories appeared at Rannersdorf in 1732, but they were on a modest scale; far more important were those built by Tratthern and Pachter at Ebergassing in 1767, and at Klein-Nausiedl in 1793. Their number did not greatly increase, for in 1811 there were still only eight paper factories in the whole of lower Austria. The silk industry, on the other hand, which had always been favoured as a luxury industry, had made enormous progress in the same period of time. The number of factories making silk and ribbons, of which there was a great consumption, grew in a few years from fifty to over a hundred. At the same time some of those factories were set up which always cause anxiety to town planners and governments concerned for the people's health; factories making chemical products, ammonia, mercury and paint, oil refineries and so on, had the impudence to find their way into the suburbs, which the Government had not taken the precaution of protecting from them. There were five thousand looms for weaving wool, silk and cotton, often set up in workers' homes. Fifteen years later factories had already displaced private looms and there were six hundred of them for silk alone.

The progress from which philosophers expected so many benefits frequently had disastrous consequences. By December 1810 two thirds of the ten thousand looms in Vienna had stopped work. Impoverished tradesmen, panic-stricken, appealed for help to the State, which, in order to rescue them from the arbitrary power of finance, organized a governmental bank offering loans without interest, or at very moderate interest; this charitable measure almost upset the balance of the empire's finance, so great was the number of needy or insolvent industrialists who applied for help.

All was not for the best in the best of all worlds, even in happy-go-lucky Austria; these economic transformations in the structure of society profoundly modified class relationships and gradually destroyed the sort of homogeneity which, in spite of differences of wealth, still existed in the eighteenth century.

The Jews of Vienna

Without practising definite anti-Semitism, the government of Maria Theresa openly admitted its intention of keeping the Jews under control by preventing them from taking too important a place in the country's economic life. The consequences of this ill-advised policy were quite contrary to its intention. For instance, the Jews had been forbidden to engage in the retail provision trade, which in any case was unremunerative and therefore unattractive. They were thus thrown back on money-dealing, at which they excelled, and which was highly profitable.

The pawnbroker, in particular, even when he charged extortionate rates, appeared as a benefactor to all these feckless, frivolous, pleasure-loving Viennese, who would pledge the necessaries of life in order to keep St Bridget's Day or St Anne's in style, with good fare and new clothes. Among the pawnbroker's most faithful customers were army officers, who incurred heavy expenses for purposes of prestige or pleasure; their pay was inadequate for the upkeep of splendid uniforms and a couple of horses. Even if they did not carouse freely and spend all night at the gaming tables, if they had no private means but only 'expectations' from some rich relative they were forced to borrow money.

Civil servants were as poorly paid as soldiers; their salary was inadequate and irregular, and visits to the money-lender became, under the circumstances, a painful necessity. As the

Viennese were not given to worrying about tomorrow provided they could enjoy today, they readily signed whatever
they were asked. It was said that for a loan of forty florins
the moneylenders Koref and Khuh, from Prague, demanded
from a civil servant whose annual salary was five hundred
florins an I.O.U. for six hundred.[2]

Interest at 20 per cent was commonly asked and almost
normal; a poor clerk, for instance, driven by sickness to
resort to money-lenders, was irretrievably lost. Aware of
this painful state of affairs, Joseph II had promised to
institute a State bank, destined to assist subordinate employees in distress; higher officials were supposed not to
have financial difficulties. Unfortunately the plan came to
nothing. As the monetary situation grew more critical,
because of devaluation and the inflation of paper money
which was printed in ever greater quantities without the
security of real money, and was so casually engraved that
forgers found it easy to imitate, and as a result too of the
ever-increasing cost of living, petty officials did not know how
to make ends meet. The money-lender who got them out of
their difficulties for the time being might pass for a benefactor.

Let us hasten to say that not all the money-lenders in
Vienna were Jews, and that provision-merchants, Gentile
though they were by police regulation, did not act in a
particularly philanthropic manner. The reputation of the
Jews in this ultra-Catholic community was bad enough,
however, to have made them subject in 1670 to a general
decree of banishment from the city precincts. In the reign
of Joseph II this severe decree was modified to allow privileged
treatment to any Jew who had rendered service to the State
or lent it money. Those who devoted themselves to manufacture, and built factories, were likewise tolerated. At the
beginning of the nineteenth century there were several
hundred Jews resident in the capital city and several thousand
staying there temporarily on business.

These individual exceptions must have become very
numerous, since in 1808 the Emperor ordered the revision
of all acts of toleration. At this period, however, Jews formed

only an infinitesimal proportion of the Viennese population; in ten years only a hundred and thirty families had benefited by the 'toleration', but these families were accompanied by so large a staff of servants and employees of every sort that they aroused the anxiety of the Austrians, always apt to consider them as dangerous rivals. A residential tax was therefore imposed on them, originally thirty kreutzers per head for two weeks, which in eight months brought in almost five thousand florins. This tax was continually increased.

Although they were debarred from trading in foodstuffs, the Jews were given permission to sell wheat, in 1816, when a poor harvest alarmed the Viennese, great eaters of bread and cakes. Lazar Biedermann was thanked by the Emperor for his activities in importing cereals. Herz was the first Jew to become purveyor to the army.

Because they were still forbidden to buy buildings, for fear they should speculate on the housing shortage, the Jewish business men of the first decades of the nineteenth century, Moses Lakenbacher, Markus Leidendorf and Salomon Herz, used borrowed names. Owing to the financial difficulties in which the empire was involved as a result of war, wealthy financiers were called upon to save the coffers of the State. Eminent statesmen such as Metternich suggested that these generous donors or lenders should be rewarded with titles.

Thus it happened that rich bankers, the Rothschilds, the Arnsteins, Eskeles, Liebmann and Herz were made knights and barons. This point having been won, it became more and more difficult to keep them out of the administration. The first victory was in the department of Excise duties on tobacco, which brought in a considerable income to the State (the importation of foreign tobacco was forbidden and the consumption of Austrian tobacco was made compulsory in Italy, for instance – which aroused much fury at the time of the Risorgimento). Aaron Höng von Hönigsberg, nominated Imperial and Royal Councillor, presided over the destinies of smokers.

Leopold II allowed Jews the entry into the legal and medical professions; in the latter field, they soon became so numerous that, in order to avoid a surplus of doctors and surgeons, the

Government retaliated by banning Poles; this, one can well imagine, increased the incessant state of tension between the Empire and its Polish provinces, which proved so turbulent during the Congress and displayed with almost insolent enthusiasm their admiration for Napoleon and their sympathy for imperial France.

Only a handful of diehards were surprised or shocked to see people of the highest rank, including the sovereigns themselves, frequent the salons of the great Jewish families during the Congress. Actually, nothing distinguished the receptions given by these Jews from those of the Christians, except that their intellectual interests were probably livelier and more modern in spirit. There was also a greater display of wealth, for the financiers grew richer in proportion as the State and the aristocracy grew poorer, since it was they who lent the money which was promptly swallowed up in the bottomless pit of sumptuary expenses. The resources of the nobles did not increase, for the cost of living grew ever heavier, while in order to keep up their rank in this dazzling round of festivities where their womenfolk had constantly to display new dresses and new jewels, the landed gentry beheld the income from their farms melt away like snow in the sun.

They could not raise their farmers' rents, for the rise in the cost of living brought little or no profit to the producers; despite the prudent regulations laid down by the Emperor, it was, as always, the middlemen who grew rich in the commerce of food products. The immutable economic law by which the price of products rises as demand increases, so long as production remains stationary, was felt to the full during the Congress, where the large number of consumers, who were particularly demanding because accustomed to sumptuous living, made all supplies scarce and therefore dear.

If the social situation began to deteriorate as the gulf between the way of life of rich and poor widened, it was largely on account of the blatant inequality displayed during this period of excessive luxury and extravagance on the occasion of the Congress. The constant growth of the industrial proletariat in an overcrowded city where foreigners, inevitably imitated by the Austrian aristocracy, squandered their wealth without any direct benefit to the people, was largely responsible for that discontent, that sense of frustration and envy that led up to the troubles which broke out thirty years later; the starting point of the revolution of 1848 was the illusory prosperity with which the Congress dazzled Vienna.

One of the basic traits of the common people of Vienna was their good-natured ability to watch others enjoying pleasures beyond their own reach, to consider the display of great folks' wealth as a delightful pageant – *totus mundus agit theatrum*, ran the motto of Shakespeare's Globe. Eminently docile, ready to see the good side of everything and concentrate on that – to look at a friend side-face if he was one-eyed, according to Joubert's wise maxim – which certainly made life easier, since things did not always go smoothly under the Hapsburg sway, these Viennese citizens, so undemanding provided they had their *panem et circenses*, were none the less subjected to a harassing administration, a meddlesome bureaucracy which was a heritage from Maria Theresa's autocratic régime.

*   *   *   *

If the spirit of revolt was not natural to the people of Vienna, if it took, to drive them to insurrection, a large measure of injustice and suffering, the gloomy picture of which was brought home to them and no doubt exaggerated by foreign agitators, nevertheless they had plenty of cause for discontent, and the restrictions laid on the enjoyment of the most elementary liberties would soon have provoked to revolt a population less easy-going and resigned than the Viennese.

Relics of Absolutism

It took a very long time – and even the reforms of Joseph II were not sufficient – to do away with or even to attenuate the rigidly autocratic régime of Maria Theresa, who had an almost medieval conception of absolutism and was deliberately inaccessible to modern ideas. The ban on building new houses and factories within the precincts of the town can be explained and justified by a legitimate concern with public health amenities, but that people should be forbidden to marry without the permission of the authorities is less understandable, and must be considered purely arbitrary.

Thinkers and sociologists like Eger and Zinzendorf protested with violence against this iniquitous measure, which was still in force at the beginning of the nineteenth century, and which presumably affected only the poorer citizens and the proletariat. In 1816 only aristocrats, civil servants, lawyers, tax-payers, house-owners and landowners, masters of guilds and manufacturers had the right to marry freely. It is difficult to believe in the existence of such a crying injustice, but the documents are there to bear witness to the fact, and proof can be found in the State archives.[3]

This restriction on one of man's most sacred liberties dated back to a time when Vienna had begun to be overcrowded, when it had been invaded by a throng of people without means of subsistence who, with their families, constituted a burden on the community. The Government was disturbed at seeing the streets full of uncared-for children running wild. Joseph II, however, being a philosophical king, considered such a measure contrary to natural law, and he altered the iniquitous regulation which deprived the poor of their only available source of happiness, family life. He did away with the ban on marriage, but made it dependent on permission granted by the authorities. Only claimants who had lived a certain time in Vienna and owned sufficient means to provide for their children would receive this permission. Was it granted more frequently than not? It is impossible to establish statistical evidence, but the mere fact that this law, subjecting the marriage of working-class people to the consent of officials, was still in existence almost on the eve of the Revolution, shows that the Viennese, easy-going as they were, had some reason to be dissatisfied with the condition in which birth or unfortunate circumstances had placed them.

The restrictions on the stay of foreigners were more normal, and can be explained by the fact that in the old days Austria, despite its cosmopolitanism, unique in Europe, had to some extent the close-knit character of a family. In time of war, naturally, the expulsion of aliens was a legitimate precautionary measure. It applied even to the French émigrés who had found employment in Viennese families as tutors and governesses. In 1793, it was considered unwise to entrust the education of wholesome German youngsters to Frenchmen who were suspected of entertaining subversive ideas, even if they themselves were victims of the Revolution. French tutors and governesses were therefore expelled from Vienna and relegated to Bohemia, where it was thought their teaching might be less harmful; they were not allowed to return to the capital until 1797, and then only with police permission.

Without being xenophobes in the least, the Viennese liked to keep themselves to themselves, and though they were generously hospitable towards foreigners, they kept the latter firmly in their place. The Emperor Francis, no doubt considering that idleness is the mother of all evils, dreaded idlers above all, and particularly idle strangers who might be capable of evolving and spreading all sorts of pernicious ideas. In the early days of the third coalition, hostility towards tourists and temporary residents was so great that all non-Austrians were forced to leave the capital within a week.

The housing shortage and the consequent rise in rents played a considerable part in these laws against aliens' residence and working-class marriages. And yet it seemed almost a paradox that at the same period, when living accommodation was so hard to find, the building of new houses was prohibited. In that part of the city within 'the line', the houses were so closely packed together at the end of the eighteenth and the beginning of the nineteenth centuries, that new building would have increased congestion to a dangerous extent. In spite of the replanning of the city which had been undertaken after the Turkish siege, and after the plague, large parts of Vienna were, as we have said, still quite medieval.

Beyond 'the line' there were still some empty spaces, but the surface available was constantly dwindling, for the poorer classes, driven out of the interior of the town, invaded the suburbs, where their 'rabbit-hutches' of homes, overcrowded with wretched families, were huddled tightly together in a chaos that shocked the authorities. These sporadic constructions soon grew into villages, then into small towns, and encroached on the portion of land lying between the fortifications and the 'line' which the Government hop.d to keep as a 'green belt', for the sake of public health as well as for less disinterested considerations of political security.

In 1802, the Emperor issued a decree by which any new building within a radius of a mile beyond 'the line' was subject to his personal approval. In 1803 he extended this safety zone to two miles. It was chiefly feared that new buildings might become an object of speculation for greedy and unscrupulous financiers, but it is questionable whether, as Zinzendorf thought, the ban on 'rabbit-hutches' did not rather, willingly or not, play into the hands of these speculators. The Archduke Charles, encouraged by Kollowrath, the minister, maintained that house-building in the suburbs and outskirts was an excellent investment for people who did not know what to do with their money.[4]

There seems to be some irresistible natural element in the development and growth of a town which laughs at laws and regulations. Statistics show that despite all obstacles, all restrictions, the number of houses rose between 1790 and 1820 from 6,159 to 7,540. Attempts were made to get round prohibitions by making underground dwellings, the unhealthy character of which ran directly counter to the Emperor's concern for public health. In 1811 there was not an inch of ground left unbuilt-on in the suburbs. Such paradoxical measures as the exemption from taxation and military service of *all those who were not building houses*, were necessary to curb the building mania that possessed Vienna during this period. Encouragement was given, too, to those institutions that left the interior of the city to settle outside, and the Emperor sent special congratulations and thanks for their good example to the heads of a girls' school which had moved out to Hernals.

Similar efforts were made to check the increase of factories, which were held to constitute a threat from the economic and political point of view as well as a danger to the health and beauty of the city. From the beginning of the nineteenth century, the industrial era, as the older citizens foresaw, was to transform the appearance and character of the town. Here, too, it was impossible to oppose an inevitable development, but in order to limit and localize the damage, State Councillor Lorenz proposed to institute a six-mile zone beyond 'the line' where factories might not be built. The prohibition was accepted in theory, but the zone itself was restricted to four miles, which at first seemed adequate. Experience soon showed how right Lorenz had been and how mistaken the authorities were not to follow his advice.[5]

The Government's chief fear was that a 'zone' of hovels, harbouring undesirable elements of the population, might arise on the outskirts of Vienna. The industrial era had brought destitution to many, while it enriched a few. In 1810, there were twenty-seven thousand workers in the factories; they lived precariously, entirely dependent on the success of the particular enterprise that had engaged them. Wages went up or down according to the profits of the factory, and if the owner saw his turnover diminishing he immediately dismissed a number of his workers.

Social Unrest

The workers thus lived from hand to mouth; the conditions of child labour, for which rules had been made in 1816, following those laid down by Joseph II, were fairly onerous, even if they did not rival the iniquitous cruelty of English factories. Vocational schools were therefore set up, in which children were taught a trade while at the same time acquiring some general education. Wages were low; even when a worker was fully employed his family had difficulty in making ends meet. Food was the main item in the budget. The Viennese, as we have seen, were large eaters; they consumed a considerable quantity of foodstuffs, particularly meat, which was exceptional in the working classes of that time. Statistics set down in 1808 (and there is no considerable fluctuation before and after that date),[6] give the following figures: the population of Vienna being reckoned at roughly 250,000, the average annual consumption of each inhabitant (excluding the garrison) was 105 kilos of meat, 260 kilos of flour, 174 litres of wine and 148 of beer.

This does not mean that everybody could eat his fill. Whole classes were permanently impoverished: the 'diurnists', or daily workers for instance. The name was applied to those employed by the administration who did not enjoy a regular official's salary, supernumeraries taken on by the day and dismissed as soon as the piecework for which they had been engaged was completed. The destitution of these poor wretches is mentioned repeatedly in the writings of the time. The provisional wage they received could only be a sheet-anchor to save them from ruin, and they had to practise the strictest economy, living on scraps and getting their clothes from old-clothes dealers. Among them were many penniless retired officers, reduced to this wretched occupation in order to subsist.

Changes in customs and fashions, moreover, had serious repercussions on certain categories of workers; when the use of sedan chairs disappeared, many honest fellows who could not find employment elsewhere were promptly thrown out into the streets. The war, which paralyzed certain industries for lack of raw materials, condemned thousands of workers to unemployment, and bad harvests filled the city with an influx of peasants, unable to get a living from the soil and attracted by the mirage of easy money and constant pleasure. In 1816, when economic difficulties and famine forced most of the factories to close their gates, tens of thousands of men were practically dying of hunger, and respectable working-class families were driven to resort to shameful expedients simply in order to subsist.

Mendicancy increased, owing to unemployment, inflation, and the large number of cripples produced by the war; beggars became so numerous and so inevitably importunate to passers-by that the Government ordered the police to arrest them. A limited number of beggars was tolerated in certain public places: the Hofburg itself had its quota, who must have been greatly envied by the rest. When police round-ups took place the churches were invaded by hordes of poor people, seeking refuge where the officers had not the right to pursue them, and where they caused a good deal of disturbance.

A few workhouses were set up for the unemployed, a few institutions providing voluntary or compulsory work: measures of relief were taken by public charity and by the State, but these were only palliatives against the spread of pauperism. In 1819 the evergrowing number of suicides aroused general anxiety, and the Emperor was distressed to see his happy-natured, carefree subjects driven to this horrible extremity by their misery.[7]

The army was still a possible resource for the workless. Even after compulsory service had been instituted, owing to the shortage of men resulting from the Napoleonic wars, there were still numerous categories of people exempt by reason of their profession: scholars, noblemen, civil servants, merchants, doctors, houseowners and others whose lives were presumably considered too precious to be risked in battle. At first the attraction of a fine uniform, with regular if modest pay, and the prestige inseparable from a military career, induced many young men to join of their own accord. The heavy losses sustained by the Austrians as well as by their adversaries during the Napoleonic campaigns quickly cooled the volunteers' enthusiasm, and patriotism had to be forcibly stimulated by pressing into service the workless and beggars picked up in the streets, as well as malcontents arrested during public demonstrations. The paternalist Hapsburg government was driven to take these rigorous measures by the disastrous economic situation, caused principally by the wars and by the over-rapid and uncontrolled growth of industry. Great public works projects had been started to occupy the unemployed; protective walls were built along the Danube and the canals, streets were repaired in the suburbs, but even these measures were inadequate.

Public unrest, in the face of the rise in the cost of commodities and the decrease in the value of money, broke out in local revolts, caused by hunger and discontent. Thus in 1805 the bakeries were plundered because the flour supply was inadequate for the people's needs. The butchers were similarly attacked in 1808. These outbreaks of popular anger were by no means revolutionary, but some of them went rather far, for in 1809 when wood was very dear during a hard winter, the people went and cut down the fine trees in the Prater for firewood.

Physical punishment was still in use under the Hapsburgs; offenders were flogged, sent into the army or shut up in gaol, but the problems that underlay the disturbances were not solved by such means. Fearing lest drunkenness might be one cause of the change of mood of this formerly docile population, the Government closed down a number of wine and beer shops and suppressed the old tradition of 'Blue Monday', that prolongation of Sunday's leisure to which the workers were so much attached.

The cobblers' revolt, in 1811, was to be remembered by Governments as one of those riots that are liable to turn into revolution. Fifteen hundred workmen whose salaries had been reduced joined battle with the troops that had been sent to assist the police, and it took the cavalry to get the better of the insurgents. The leaders of the revolt were punished with flogging, chains and the pillory; they were exposed on the Hohen Markt with placards round their necks enumerating their misdeeds and the faults that had earned them this punishment.

The biedermeier period corrected a number of social inequalities, it put an end to unwelcome measures that savoured too much of Spanish despotism, but it is questionable whether the common people were not irritated rather than satisfied at seeing an 'inferior' class rise to the level of the aristocracy, share its privileges and live on the same footing, without the justification of centuries of tradition. The bourgeoisie whose virtues were, on the whole, popular virtues, were more unpopular than the nobility, because the working-class Viennese considered them as upstarts. Their cult of respectability was made fun of as a sign of hypocrisy; their luxury, their carriages and fine country houses were looked at with envy, whereas aristocratic splendour had never aroused envy, so great had been, hitherto, the belief in a sort of 'divine right' enjoyed by the nobility almost as much as by the Imperial family.

Except for a few extremists, the question of an eventual change of régime, of the introduction of a republic into Austria, never arose, any more than a desire to dispossess and destroy the aristocracy. The progress of the bourgeoisie, the injustices and abuses of the industrial era – employers came to consider their workmen as so much 'human material' – the perfecting of machines, one of the first consequences of which was to make a less costly, more easily replaceable machine out of the wage-earner, created an ever deeper division between classes, despite the traditional and immortal good-nature of the Viennese. 'Herr Biedermeier' mingled less readily with the workers – with people who were 'not of his class' – than princes and counts had done in the old days. The series of public disturbances aroused in him a feeling which was unknown in the days of Maria Theresa and Joseph II: fear.

CHAPTER ELEVEN

THE END OF A GOLDEN AGE

March 1848: a Fateful Date—Portents of Revolution—The First Troubles—Barricades—Liberty Let Loose—Vienna Reconquered

The economic transformations that caused such upheaval in the life of the Viennese during the first decades of the nineteenth century would not have sufficed, however, to explain or justify the revolutionary disorders of 1848; many factors were involved, some of them connected with the country's political evolution, others resulting from events in other European countries. The people of Vienna were traditionalist, and even to a large extent reactionary, by nature. Social ideologies scarcely disturbed their peace of mind and their readiness to conform; they felt no need to change their institutions and if they resented something in the State they took their revenge with a witticism.

It may be said that the revolution did not spring from the Viennese people themselves, but from foreign elements; namely from natives of other provinces of the Austrian empire, who had left their native lands, attracted by the mirage of industrial prosperity, to try and make their fortunes in the factories of the capital. Amongst these foreign elements were certainly some Hungarians and Italians who, though they had emigrated to Vienna, still felt united with their compatriots, whose liberal ideas they shared. The problem of Austria's position in the Germanic confederation and the nationalist ambitions resulting therefrom played their part too. And moreover, however static Vienna was by nature, Austria could not entirely stand aside from the great movement of ideas that was stirring France, Italy and Germany.

Kralik analyzed the position correctly when he wrote: 'at the basis of this revolution lie social, political and national problems, but underlying all these other questions is the specifically Austrian problem.' 'Once again,' he writes, 'history raised the question whether Austria had a real and legitimate existence, if Vienna could consider itself the real Imperial city. The Viennese revolution was not a local movement; it was an earthquake which shook the whole monarchy and threatened to dislocate it; in Italy, in Hungary, in Bohemia disturbances arose, some of which had an even more tragic outcome. All these upheavals had their centre in Vienna. Very old questions of public law were settled out of hand in the most drastic fashion, as well as local questions about the relations of the Imperial power and the rights of cities and States. These questions had been urgent issues in Vienna ever since the days of the House of Babenberg, Frederick the Warlike, the burgomasters Vorlauf, Holzer and Siebenburger, Frederick II, Frederick II and Ferdinand I. As in 1522, so in 1848 we see the city and the States on one side, the Imperial government on the other.'[1]

March 1848 : A Fateful Date

This revolution destroyed the rosy dreams of peace in which the biedermeier bourgeoisie lived; it forced that bourgeoisie to realize that its calm was illusory, its tranquillity artificial, its indifference dangerous. The bourgeois found himself involved, by virtue of his citizenship of Vienna, in disorders and atrocities which horrified him, the more so because there was no parallel to them in the city's history; no one could have imagined the unprecedented spectacle of Vienna being stormed and reconquered by the Imperial armies from the rioters who had seized it. That sort of thing happened in Paris, which had known repeated insurrections and where, only a month before, in February 1848, barricades were being raised again; but not in Vienna! And so this tragic date of March 1848 remained a fateful one in the history of the capital and of the whole of Austria, and the terms 'before March' and 'after March' are used to define the events leading up to, and following, those catastrophic weeks when Biedermeier, like the French themselves, lived under a reign of terror.

The atmosphere of uncertainty and then of alarm that replaced the delightful calm of an uneventful existence clearly endangered the idyllic peace of old-time Vienna. Confronted with new ideas, with brutal facts that made it imperative to take sides, the Viennese could no longer remain unaware that an insurrection is enough to overturn the whole prudent edifice of tranquillity, security and well-being with which a far-seeing monarch surrounds his subjects, for his own peace and for theirs. Were the 'ides of March', in the words of the revolutionary poets, going to involve the ruin and destruction of the Viennese?

It nearly happened. If Kossuth's Hungarians, who were coming to the aid of the revolutionary troops, had entered Vienna before the troops of Windischgrätz which were hurrying to crush them, no doubt the course of events might have been very different. A republican government might have replaced the Empire, and who knows but that the dictatorship of the proletariat might have overturned the city's institutions and the fate of its inhabitants. The Viennese were clearly aware of this, and the warning was a grave one. Although the revolution was unplanned, it took advantage of the Government's indecision, its blunders, its timidity, its half-measures; for the first time in their history the bourgeois of Vienna no longer felt themselves protected by a paternal Empire; they lost confidence in the omnipotence and vigilance of the Emperor, whom they had been so ready to obey in exchange for the security he promised them. Unwilling to follow the revolutionary trend, except, of course, for a few intellectuals, bourgeois or even aristocrats who had accepted modern ideas, the bourgeoisie experienced a disappointment and a discouragement which profoundly shook that harmonious union with their rulers which was the solid foundation of their political life. They felt themselves isolated, threatened by the common people and deserted by their own leaders. Their benefits and privileges were challenged, and unlike the Parisian middle class which was the real gainer by the revolutions of 1830 and 1848, they had nothing to gain and everything to lose, for they cared little for such trifles as the freedom of the press, for which the battle was ostensibly being fought.

When Viennese blood, which gave its name to one of Strauss's finest and most brilliant waltzes, was shed on the pavements during the fratricidal conflict, it became clear that these eventful days, from March to November '48, marked the end of a world, and that Vienna would never again be what she used to be. Indeed, wars, financial disasters, sporadic disturbances maintained henceforward an atmosphere of disquiet against which the Viennese struggled valiantly. They tried to enjoy themselves as of old, and they succeeded, since the Viennese character was the strongest factor after all, but that sort of childish innocence that had existed 'before March' was never to revive.

With its four hundred thousand inhabitants (not to mention those of the suburbs, outside the *Linienwall*) Vienna was still rigidly bound by almost medieval institutions, under the direction of its burgomaster Czapka, who had been in office since 1838. Out of these half-million inhabitants only thirty thousand were taxpayers. The bourgeoisie were responsible, together with the aristocracy, for supplying the needs of public finance, but they were not represented in Councils of State, and the city itself had no autonomy. Popular representation was non-existent in Imperial Austria at this time; certain nations had their own councils, their own parliaments, but Austria, as such, had none.

Portents of Revolution

Consequently, the first demands set forth in 1845 by certain intellectuals who addressed a petition to the Minister of the Interior in order to gain some alleviation of the censorship, which had remained very strict despite the liberalism of Joseph II and his successors, related to the condition of the Press, the representation of the bourgeoisie in the government, and the publication of the public budget. Newspapers abounded, for the Viennese had always been great consumers of daily, weekly or monthly journals – waiters would bring their customers great piles of them, along with cups of coffee. The *Wiener Zeitung*, founded in 1805, was 'controlled', if not always inspired, by the Hofpolizeistelle, the Ministry of Police; so its harmlessness could be relied on.

245

The *Humoriste*, founded by Saphir in 1837, was malicious but not subversive. The papers owned by Friedrich von Gentz, *Osterreichische Beobachter* and *Wiener Jahrbucher*, were equally inoffensive; the same may be said of *Wiener Zeitschrift für Kunst, Literatur, Theater und Mode*, of Frankl's *Sonntagsblätter für heimatliche Interessen*, Seidl's *Aurora*, and others, which had given proof of their docility and were thus safe from the severities of the censorship.

This, however, remained sufficiently harassing for the greatest Austrian writers, feeling themselves insulted and wounded by excessive watchfulness, to sign their names enthusiastically to the petition of March 1845. Franz Grill-parzer, Eduard von Bauernfeld, Adalbert Stifter, Anastasius Grün, Friecrich Halm, Baron von Zedlitz, Baron von Feuchtersleben, Friedrich Castelli, Baron von Hammer-Purgstall, Moritz Gottlob Saphir, Franz Stelshamer, Baron von Rokitansky and Ladislas Pyrker are among the best known of the signatories; these were not subversive minds, destroyers of the established order, fanatics or dreamers, but men of good sense and sound judgment, supporters of the régime – the question does not even arise – belonging to the aristocracy or the solid bourgeoisie. The anxiety of the age had affected them too. Castelli, who ran a journal 'of instruction and entertainment', *Der Sammler* (The Collector), was disturbed at the state of things. 'Our age is sick,' he wrote, 'and incurably so; the golden calf has been set up on our altars, the arts sadly count their wounds, and alas, poetry falls asleep, moaning.'

In 1846 revolution broke out in Cracovia, and the peas-antry rose in Galatia. In 1847 even peaceful Switzerland was rent by a civil war called the Sonderbundskrieg. In 1848 there appeared for the first time in London a work destined to become very famous, the *Manifesto of the Communist Party* by Karl Marx and Friedrich Engels; it is strange to find it being published in a country where liberals had the greatest difficulty in getting the working day for children under ten reduced to ten hours, and where this measure, when at last introduced, seemed highly generous, modern and philanthropic!

Troubles arose in Bavaria, famine raged in Silesia. In Vienna itself, there were distressing signs of unrest; resentful of the municipal slaughterhouses built at St Marx and Gunpendorf by Burgomaster Czapka, which constituted a threat to their privileges and interests, the butchers of Vienna demonstrated in the streets. At Neulenfeld, fifteen hundred weaving workers were discharged as a result of the rise in price of raw cotton; as no immediate measure was taken to feed them, these starving unemployed workers plundered a few bakeries. As a crowning disaster, the harvests had been very bad during the past three years and the price of flour rose from three florins to ten between 1845 and 1847. It was with an accurate presentiment of things to come that Eduard von Bauernfeld wrote in his journal on January 1, 1848: 'Important political changes will take place this year, of that we are all convinced.'

Attempts were made to assist the poor by setting up popular soup kitchens at the beginning of January; the first were opened at Schottenfeld and Mariahilfe, on plans laid down by the American Rumford, and the first steam bakery was also opened. During this same month of January Metternich warned the Emperor against 'the wind of insurrection which is driving subversive parties to overthrow established and legitimate institutions, and because Austria is considered the essential representative of these, it has become the main target at which they aim.'

To the Austrian people, Metternich was so completely the embodiment of absolutism in all its inflexible rigour, incapable of compromise or progress, that his dismissal was loudly clamoured for. The censorship sought to protect itself against public opinion by banning the production of *The Fiescho Conspiracy* and *William Tell* by Schiller, and by forbidding the papers to mention Milan, where there had been a few outbreaks of violence, directed notably against the Austrian excise; some harmless individuals, unaware of the patriotic watchword laid down by smokers of *toscani*, had been attacked for smoking Austrian cigars. Demands were made for the public administration of justice, the autonomous organization of the free towns, the creation of chambers of commerce

R

and agriculture, and with increasing urgency, for the freedom of the Press.

Meanwhile small seditious journals arose here and there, ever more numerous and ever more violent. Tactless and ridiculous Governmental measures exasperated malcontents. The latter, in Milan, took to wearing large broad-brimmed hats, which under the name of 'Calabrese', 'Puritan', or 'Hernani' became a badge of revolution and were soon to be seen on many a Viennese head: a symbol of the struggle against Herr Biedermeier, in his chimney-pot hat.

The First Troubles

The first disturbances made the bourgeois uneasy, and their first reaction was to exchange their paper money, in which they never had great faith, against good ringing coin; pusillanimous hoarders hid their gold and silver and rushed to the counters of the National Bank brandishing their remaining notes, of which they were determined to be rid. Once again the economic maxim that 'bad money drives away good' was confirmed; florins and even kreutzers disappeared from circulation, and panic grew, reaching its height when a lawyer from Budapest, called Lajos Kossuth, uttered in the Landtag that famous speech which has been described as the baptism of the Austrian revolution, demanding among other things the establishment of a constitutional government.

On March 12, a great meeting of students was held in the University; they demanded the liberty of the Press, of teaching, and of belief; in order to show that their teachers were on their side, they begged two of these, Professors Endlicher and Hye, to take to the Hofburg the petition they had drawn up, and which had been preceded, twenty-four hours before, by one from the bourgeois of Vienna assembled under the auspices of Baron von Bach, less radical in tone and concerned chiefly with the organization of industry, commerce and agriculture.

The Imperial Council examined these demands, satisfied some of them and set aside the rest for further examination. Meanwhile the Emperor had decided to call a general meeting of all the States in the Empire and Marshal Montecucoli was instructed to summon the deputies. Next day the representatives of Lower Austria met in session, began their work, read petitions and received delegations. It seemed as though the era of reforms had begun, and these would be carried out in peaceful and orderly fashion, but March 13 was the fateful day that was to usher in the revolution. Henceforward events moved too swiftly and too powerfully for men's will. The tragic machine was set in motion by the very fact that the bourgeois militia had been armed, as a precautionary measure, to keep order in the streets and had assembled on the glacis.

A crowd of onlookers, excited by the sight of people hurrying to and from the palace where the 'States' were in session, by the deputations filing past, and by the hysteria of a few agitators, watched this opening scene of the revolution as though they were at the theatre. But for the 'States' to do their work in peace, the streets had to be cleared. It was one o'clock in the afternoon. To maintain order, the bourgeois militia had been fetched from the glacis and the Imperial regiments from their barracks. Agitators, standing on improvized platforms, harangued the people in the court of the palace; two doctors won attention and applause, Josef Goldmark and Adolf Fischhof, but their speeches were so violent that they stirred up their audience to invade the hall where the deputies were in session. Workmen had deserted their factories; crowds flowed from the suburbs towards the centre of the city.

Seldnitzky, Minister of Police, afraid of being overwhelmed and of acting too late, ordered the Palace of the States to be cleared and sent Italian troops to do so. These latter had never been very popular, and had no love themselves for the Viennese. What happened is not quite clear, but the bourgeois militia and the Italians met; by some fatal error, each thinking the other was an enemy, they began to shoot at one another, and stray bullets hit harmless passers-by.

While these dramatic events were taking place within the city, workmen were setting fire to the factories and the owners' houses. In order to avoid bloodshed, Burgomaster Czapka, whose conduct seemed too democratic to some and too reactionary to others, asked the Archduke Albert, who was in command of the troops, to withdraw his regiments; he asserted that the bourgeois militia would be quite capable of restoring order when the plumes of the Italian soldiers had disappeared. As might have been foreseen, the militia was powerless to control the infuriated crowd, further excited by a taste of plunder; it looked as if the town would become a prey to the rioters, when Jenull, Rector of the University, went to Archduke Louis and suggested that arms be distributed to the students. These having for the most part a good liberal reputation and being popular with the working class and the bourgeoisie, their intervention would surely prevent the situation from worsening. The Archduke accepted; they were taken to the arsenal and given guns, after which they set off in pursuit of plunderers and incendiaries, in the company of the bourgeois militia.

The Hofburg was taken aback by the outbreak of rioting. The Archduke decided to make a first concession to the people by asking Metternich to retire, which that great statesman did immediately, with considerable dignity. 'My feelings, my views, my decisions,' he wrote to the Emperor, 'have always been the same throughout my whole life, they are unalterable forces which nothing will ever extinguish in me. I have summed them up in a sentence which I bequeath to my successors so that they can remember it and take it as their motto : strength lies in right.'

That same evening Metternich left for London, with his wife; the Minister of Police, Seldnitzky, also left the capital for his estates, where he felt safer. That night Vienna was like an armed camp, contemporary observers tell us. Militia and students patrolled the streets putting out fires, to the great relief of the bourgeois who lavished on them applause, encouragement and handshakes. As befitted an intellectual centre like Vienna, the university had saved the situation. Next day the Hofburg announced, amid great enthusiasm, that the censorship was suppressed and the freedom of the press guaranteed. Shops and houses flew flags; a permanent national guard was set up, of which militia and students formed the core; order was restored, and the bourgeois breathed again.

The necessary reforms, it seemed, would be carried out in legal and orderly fashion. The constitution having been granted on March 15, the town was illuminated, and the Emperor was greeted with cheers as he passed through the streets in his carriage, with his nephew and future successor Francis Joseph by his side. With their customary optimism the Viennese decided that it had been a false alarm and that everything was going to be all right; but men better informed politically noted with some anxiety the arrival of the Hungarian delegation at the States Assembly; this delegation was led by the forty-six-year-old lawyer from Budapest, Kossuth.

Liberals and extremists welcomed the Hungarians and their leader, whose energy and revolutionary sentiments were well known. Despite this alarming portent, the bourgeoisie felt radiantly serene. They had done their duty by the victims of March 13, since a funeral service had been held in their honour. A responsible Ministry had been appointed, a municipal council was about to take office in the City Hall, martial law threatened the rioters who might indulge in plunder and arson under cover of the disturbances, newspapers were pouring from the printing presses and everybody wanted to read them, even those that made the most extravagant demands. Grillparzer expressed the opinion of all Vienna when he acclaimed his country's 'rebirth': 'I greet thee, O my Austria, stepping forward today on untrodden paths. My heart beats with thee today, as always.'

Patriotic poems in profusion were also published, for it seemed as if every Viennese loved his city and his country the more for having emerged intact from this brief crisis; the composer Suppé set several of these poems to music, transforming them for the occasion into hymns in honour of the students (*Who advances today with so bold a step*, by Frankl) and the National Guard; Castelli's verses on the latter theme have the interest of being the first poem published without a visa from the censorship. Castelli also printed a hundred thousand copies of another poem entitled: *What has happened in Vienna?* which was distributed throughout the country; this pamphlet earned him such unexpected popularity among the peasants that he was visited every day by dozens of *Eipeldauers* coming to ask his advice on the most varied and embarrassing questions. By a curious paradox Austria felt so proud of having escaped a revolution that there was an extraordinary recrudescence of the most chauvinistic nationalism.

It might be noticed however – and the symptom would have disturbed any other set of people than the Viennese – that there were in the streets an increasing number of Calabrese hats worn on long-haired, bearded heads: the uniform of the enemies of the *toupet*. Johann Nepomuck Vogl, the satirical song-writer, celebrated in burlesque verses the death of the *toupet*, which for Austrian liberals was the detested emblem of the class that must be destroyed. On this theme, a German author wrote a comedy, *The Toupet and the Sword*, which scored a huge success at the Theater an der Wien; writers were quick to make use of topical themes, and the theatre, which in Vienna even more than elsewhere has always reflected social life, delighted spectators with witty references to the political vicissitudes of the rulers of the Empire. Amongst the more weighty and earnest poetic writings, more disturbing too for the régime, if it had known how to read them, there appeared the republican manifesto of Georg Herwegh, whom his friend Heine called the 'Iron Skylark'.

All this was still taking place in an atmosphere of concord and good humour. Even when the Prince-Archbishop Midle was serenaded with a rowdy *Katzenmusik* this demonstration reflected the people's high spirits rather than their antagonism. Demonstrations seemed as entertaining as a play, while the theatre for its part reflected the scenes in the street.

Writing to Roderich Benedix, the Saxon writer, author of the play *Das bemooste Haput*, or *The Long Israel*, which was put on at the Theater an der Wien and was the first play exempt from the censor's certificate, an employee of the Scottish Foundation vividly describes the performance, and nothing could more clearly display the mentality of the Viennese in the early days of April.

'It was not a stage performance, but a festival of rejoicing in honour of the students! We were not listening to a comedy, we were watching an amazing display of friendly and joyful emotion. The actors would speak to the students in the pit, and the students answered the actors back. The young spectators waved their hats, the actors waved their headgear, the students' song was sung on the stage* and the whole audience took up the chorus. My eyes were full of tears. When the hero of the play cried out: "Long live liberty!" and the actor Karl Treumann added: ". . . and the man who has given us liberty!" the whole house were on their feet, cheering; the students in the pit shouted: "Vivat Ferdinandus!" '

The Emperor, obviously, still played a paternal rôle in this family drama.

To wear the uniform of the national guard was an honour, not a tedious duty for the citizen of Vienna, and Herr Biedermeier proudly buckled on his army belt. Hermann Meyner published a new paper called *The National Guard*, which the bourgeois read as a relaxation from the patrol duties and sentry-go, and which set forth the latest reasons for believing that the dreaded revolution was definitely crushed and that the 'golden age' would come back, with its junketings and patronal festivals.

What had happened in Vienna? as Castelli's poetic pamphlet asked. Everything and nothing, one might reply. The government had forbidden the export of money abroad, in order to keep its 'good money' at home. The Monastery of the Redemptorists at Maria Stiegen and their estate at Wahring were pillaged because they were said to exercise a reactionary influence on the court. Noisy scenes took place outside the Nuncio's residence. Somebody proposed that the celibacy of the clergy be abolished, to which Metzger retorted ironically that 'liberty was not for the priests'.[2] A certain anti-clericalism became marked, because once more the 'curés' were suspected of being hand in glove with bourgeois reactionaries. The Jews, on the other hand, complained that they had not been adequately represented in public assemblies, as if there still lingered in this new, enlightened Vienna something of the old Austrian anti-Semitism.

While Ministers came, and went, and came back, the Emperor's fifty-fifth birthday was celebrated in state with the collaboration of Liberal poets. On April 25, at last, the

* Frankl's poem had been incorporated in the play.

promised Constitution was promulgated amidst great enthusiasm, although it brought bitter disappointment to many by its highly undemocratic, not to say anti-democratic character. But only the liberals complained; for the bulk of the Viennese, the important thing was that the old order of things should be maintained with as little alteration as possible. Far more interesting than the details of the Constitution was the admirable parade provided as free entertainment for the good people of the Royal and Imperial capital by the actors of the theatre director Carl. He had formed a military company out of the members of his troupe, the 'Actors of the National Guard', and had equipped them with the wardrobe and arsenal of the theatre. It is easy to imagine the crowds that flocked along the Jaegerzeile when the favourite actors of the Viennese public, including Scholz and Nestroy, paraded armed with muskets borrowed from Wallenstein's troops, with Roman swords and Turkish scimitars.

Barricades

It was not enough, however, to applaud an anti-Jesuit play at the Josephstadt theatre, or to make rowdy scenes under the windows of Minister Ficquelmont. The students, in agreement with the workers, had declared on May 2 that they were not satisfied with the Constitution. Although the concession had been won that the right of suffrage was no longer limited to tax-payers, yet the working class and domestic servants were still deprived of it. After two months' respite, two ominous facts disturbed the population: the Emperor left Schönbrunn with his family on May 17, and next day the money-market was closed, with a consequent drop in the value of paper money. On May 18 two extremist leaders, Leopold Hafner, who ran the journal *Constitution*, and Joseph Tuvora, founder of *The Freethinker*, held a great meeting among the workers at Mariahilfe, during which they foretold the imminent establishment of a provisional government, shortly to be followed by the proclamation of the Republic. These agitators were beaten up by some of their hearers and subsequently arrested by the police, but the dreaded word *republic* had been uttered.

Eduard von Bauernfeld, returning home after a journey on May 16, was struck by the change of atmosphere. The soldiers, the National Guard and the Academic Legion (consisting of students) were patrolling the streets and fraternizing as before, but the newcomer noticed their 'grave, almost anxious faces'. There were no disturbances, however. 'The proletariat, that continual nightmare of the Viennese, seemed to have vanished. It looks as if people almost wished for the return of Metternich, in order to be reassured.' And Adalbert Stifter wrote these disillusioned words to his publisher Heckenast: 'I am one who loves moderation and liberty; both these are unfortunately in jeopardy today, and many people think they can establish liberty by repudiating the old system; but then they end by creating something quite different from liberty.' This became evident when the second revolutionary wave broke, on May 25, in consequence of the Government's ill-advised order to close the University and disband the Academic Legion; on May 26 barricades were set up in the streets.

'To the barricades! To the barricades! Vienna has never yet known such things; these are the first to rise, threatening, on the sacred soil, as undeniable proof of the wrath of the people's conscience...' Thus spoke the poet Ludwig Bowitsch, in a transport of zeal, in one of the countless little journals that abounded at that time, some of which lasted a week while others did not live beyond their first number. The rioters did not confine themselves to uttering invectives, even in rhyme; they sacked the palace of Minister Pillersdorf, they took Count Hoyos prisoner, set free the 'republicans' Hafner and Tuvora, and put up fences and wire entanglements round the town to prevent Imperial regiments from reinforcing those already engaged against the supporters of the revolution. The national guard was replaced by 'security militias' consisting of armed students and twenty thousand workers from the suburbs. One significant fact: the paper *Wiener Zeitung* appeared for the first time without the Imperial eagle beside its headlines.

Amongst the decrees hastily passed in order to calm popular fury, if possible, was that granting the right of suffrage to the workers. On June 1 the *Allgemeine Osterreichische Zeitung* published a fiery poem, sent from Dresden, where storms were brewing, and entitled *Saxony Salutes the Insurgent Viennese*. The last of the fourteen verses of this inflammatory epistle closes with a cry of admiration for the Austrian rebels. 'You have confirmed your theory by your actions, faithful heroes of Vienna, and we promise you that if someone dares say to us "Be slaves once more!" we shall answer with this threat: "We will do as the Viennese have done." ' This poem, which displays more enthusiasm than genius, was signed Richard Wagner.

While the Emperor, at Innsbruck, anxiously read the messages sent him by Archduke John, who was acting for him at the Hofburg, disorder increased in the city, where the extremists were growing more and more violent and powerful. There were daily skirmishes between armed forces, the Academic Legion assisting the workers against the National Guard when it attacked them, but joining forces with the guard occasionally when the revolutionaries got out of hand. The latter took their orders from the editorial board of *The Radical*, which consisted of Becher, Tuvora, Messenhauser, Hebbel, Tausenau and Nordmann.

'Paving-stones are being torn up in the streets and so are the foundations of the State and society,' wrote Friedrich Hebbel, the German dramatist, visiting Vienna where he was writing his play *Libussa* while the disorder in the streets grew wilder. 'There comes a moment when a nation, like an individual, has to pass judgment on itself. Then it will have the chance to repair the past and expiate bygone sins. But at this moment Nemesis is on the left, and woe to the nation if it does not seek the proper path.' In the extreme confusion that rent Vienna, the way seemed obvious to Herr Biedermeier, who was always on the side of order, because order meant the safety of the streets, the quiet ownership of justly – or unjustly – earned wealth, and the supremacy of masters over servants and manufacturers over their workmen.

Archduke John, who had the onerous responsibility of administering the State and in particular of watching over

Vienna during the absence of Ferdinand, was luckily very popular; he was considered a 'democrat' because instead of choosing an aristocratic wife he had married, for her charm and beauty, a postmaster's daughter, Anna Brandhof. The Hofburg had looked askance at this union, but the misalliance, so severely criticized at the time, now served the Imperial cause magnificently. On July 24, at Mariahilfe, Anna Brandhof presided over the ceremonial presentation of the flag to the National Guard, of which she was sponsor. On St Anne's day a great festival was held at Schönbrunn in honour of her patroness and herself. Students made torchlight processions past her windows. And it was perhaps her beauty and her glamour that brought about what no statesman's skill could have achieved; the fraternizing of the Imperial regiments, the Academic Legion and the National Guard, at a fête in the Augarten.

The University, which had been at the head of the liberal movement four months earlier, was now disturbed at the anarchic turn events were taking; like the bourgeois of the National Guard, the intellectuals were alarmed at the preponderance of subversive elements among the workers. Suspicious foreigners, come from nobody knew where, were leading the insurgents; these folk were not Viennese, their interests were not those of Vienna, and the worst might be expected from the domination of these professional agitators who were, in some sort, travellers in insurrection and social subversion. The new masters of Viennese public opinion were Czechs, Hungarians, Germans, adventurers sprung from the ghetto and the slum; that was enough to make them suspect in the eyes of Herr Biedermeier.

As for the students, these were patriots and not partisans, ideologists and not rioters. Having set the machine going, they became alarmed at being unable to stop or control it; and they themselves seemed suspect to the new leaders of the revolution which they had imprudently instigated. Concern was also felt about the unrest growing amongst the peasantry, for whom the youngest deputy in the Reichstag, Hans Kudlich, with youthful ardour, was demanding equality of rights and duties.

257

Liberty Let Loose

Marshal Radetzky's victories in Italy stirred up great excitement. On the occasion of his entry into Milan on Sunday August 6, Strauss had composed his famous *Radetzky March*, which was played for the first time on August 7 at a great military fête held on the glacis, for the benefit of the families of soldiers killed in the Italian campaign: this provided the opportunity for a fresh demonstration of concord and friendship between the Imperial regiments, the students and the bourgeois militia. The sporadic excesses committed by the workers, the threat to her very life that Austria read into the words 'republican', 'radical' and 'communist', impelled all moderate parties to form a common front against the insurgents, who held sway in the suburbs of the city. There was such general loyalty to the Emperor that when Ferdinand returned to his capital on August 12, the National Guard, to welcome him, lined the streets from Schönbrunn to the Hofburg. The Government considered it had solved the social problem by providing useless tasks to occupy the unemployed.

Unfortunately these charitable enterprises were heavy on the budget, for the workless were very numerous, and an ill-advised attempt was made to decrease their allowance by five kreutzers, on the suggestion of the Minister of Labour, Ernst von Schwarzer, who argued that they were already being overpaid for their unprofitable labours of digging in the Prater. This reduction gave agitators a further pretext to renew their attacks on the Government. The workers in the Prater decided to go to the Emperor himself to ask for their five kreutzers, and on August 23 they set off towards the city centre. When they came up against a barrier set up by the National Guard, shots were exchanged and there were casualties on both sides, but chiefly among the workers. Once again class war had broken out.

The Government thought it had achieved a master-stroke by sending ten thousand navvies out of Vienna, but the men refused to leave the city. Divided once more between their liberal aspirations, their love of justice and their fear of falling once again into the power of blind absolutism, the students did not know whether to make common cause with the proletariat or the bourgeoisie. They had paid close attention to the lectures being given to working class groups by a young German economist from Trier, Karl Marx; these opened up new perspectives to them. Karl Marx told them among other things, as we know from the summary of one of his speeches made by the paper *Radikale*, that it made no difference what Minister they had, since in Vienna as in Paris the struggle was between the bourgeoisie and the proletariat. The liberals did not know which way to turn. Honest, well-intentioned men sounded their consciences anxiously, and many muttered despondently, like Grillparzer: 'In the days of the persecution I was called a liberal; now that liberty is let loose I am said to be servile; looked at askance by both sides, I almost consider myself reasonable.'

The time for reason had gone by; the time had come for the display of mass will and force. The extremists gave a solemn funeral to the victims of the August shootings, hoping thus to provoke fresh disturbances, which inevitably happened. Imitating the men of '89, the revolutionaries demanded the suppression of courtesy titles. The agrarian leader Kudlich brought to Vienna crowds of peasants, excited by his eloquence: 'Be vigilant,' he told them. 'If the lion of the court, the University, should slumber in spite of imminent danger, light the beacon from hill-top to hill-top. You must assemble here in a mass gathering and prevent the students from being crushed and our new-born liberty destroyed.' Each side wanted the support of the students, because of their intellectual prestige and the 'guarantee' thus conferred on the party with which they collaborated.

Amongst the partisans of the revolution themselves, some deplored the fact that the original generous and idealistic impulse had been succeeded by a systematic application of the methods of the Terror. Many of them admired a poem by Ludwig Goglar, expressing his grief at not having died during the 'Ides of March', now that he saw petty tyrants and demagogues replacing the great tyrants of yesterday: he meant Metternich. What would become of the Empire if the radicals won? They wished to detach from Austria all the non-Austrian States and vindicate the claims of all nationalist groups. The most popular figure among the proletariat of Vienna at that time was Kossuth, who with his Hungarians was engaged against the Austrian troops of Ban Jellacic, and who in the eyes of the liberals stood for the heroic fight for freedom.

On September 28 Count Lamberg, whom the Emperor had named Palatine of Hungary in place of Archduke Stephen, was assassinated in Budapest. Several Viennese regiments were therefore ordered into Hungary, but the radicals, hoping for Kossuth's victory, incited the soldiers to disobedience and insurrection. General Breda was killed during the affray, and the Imperial regiments were forced to draw back under the assault of the masses of the people, who poured into the centre of the city. They advanced, crushing every obstacle, as far as the Ministry of War, seized the Minister, Count Latour, unpopular because he advocated relentless war against the Hungarian insurgents, and killed him in a particularly horrible fashion. He was first hanged from a window shutter, but the rope broke; the body was then hoisted on to a street lamp, and the enraged crowd fell upon it and tore it to pieces.

The 'March revolution' was now reaching its phase of acute terrorism. The bourgeoisie were so well aware of this that twenty thousand of them in one day left the city in terror, imitating the example of the Emperor, who had gone to Olmütz. During this time the populace besieged arsenals and barracks, killed the soldiers and seized their weapons. The bells rang uninterruptedly to incite the insurgents to action, but actually there was more noise than damage, and the general massacre dreaded by the bourgeoisie never took place. We can trust the evidence of the writer Eduard von Bauernfeld, a true liberal in the noblest sense of the word, who concluded that all the disturbances were systematically fomented by paid foreign agitators. The 'holy war' waged by the Hungarians, inviting the proletariat of Austria to second their efforts, idealized the figure of Kossuth who, in fact, had become the true leader of this third act of the revolution: the October days.

'This October revolution,' Kralik writes,[3] 'the third revolution of the year 1848, had quite a different character from those that had preceded it in March and May. It had quite other promoters. Viennese society properly so called, which had played so considerable a part in the Spring revolutions, hardly intervened in the October conflicts. It was a struggle to occupy Vienna, which represented a strong position in the general war, but in Vienna the leading part was not played by the Viennese but by people from outside.'

Two Poles, principally: Smolka, who was the president of the Parliament, and Bem, the military leader of the revolution. By their side, two Germans from Frankfurt: Julius Froebel and Robert Blum. Under their orders were the twenty-five thousand men of the National Guard, commanded by Wenzel Caesar Messenhauser, who got his orders from Bem, and the ten thousand workers of the mobile guard. Opposite them were the imperial regiments commanded by Auerspeg, who had retreated to the Laaerberg; the insurgents were practically masters of the city, and were awaiting the arrival of Kossuth with his Hungarians to complete the organization of victory. The revolutionary leaders, in fact, were quarrelling about questions of prestige and precedence. Carelessness and disobedience were rife; the masses intended to take advantage of their liberty to disregard any orders, even from their own leaders.

Vienna Reconquered

This internal weakness of the revolutionary elements, who had no real leader and who were impatiently waiting for Kossuth, probably the only man capable of filling that rôle, encouraged the Emperor to attempt the recapture of Vienna. He gave Marshal Windischgrätz the order to march on the city and reach it before the Hungarians. The Marshal therefore left Prague and advanced by forced marches. Who was going to win the race? The Imperial troops, or the Hungarians who counted on joining forces with the peasants roused by Kudlich, and who were roaming the countryside summoning workers on the land to support their brothers the city workers?

Messenhauser had declared a state of siege, the people's Parliament had denounced Windischgrätz's action as illegal, and his troops were stigmatized in *The Freethinker* as being like those hordes of Turks who, two centuries before, had besieged Vienna. 'Why do we not choose the simple and only reasonable form of government, the republic?' boldly demanded the *Students' Courier*. The reason was that Jellacic was at Schönbrunn with his regiments, and the following day, October 23, the relieving forces reached Hetzendorf. The day after, they were camping in the Brigittenau. The Hungarians were still a long way off, the agrarian revolutionaries too dispersed to achieve any concerted movement: victory seemed certain.

Windischgrätz methodically tightened the iron ring with which he had encircled the town. He made sure of the Northern railway station, the Nussdorf line, and the waterworks, while Ban Jellacic took possession of certain strategic points, such as the Leopoldstadt district, which was a very active revolutionary centre. Fierce battles took place, during which the Actors' Legion, fighting with its stage weapons against the adversaries' cannon, suffered heavy losses: the comedian Strampfer was among the victims and all the Viennese lamented his death, whatever their political opinions, for he had been one of their favourite actors. The workers had flown the red flag from public buildings, but they could not withstand the severe bombardment which set fire to some churches and a good many houses; the city had suffered less from the French guns in 1809. Disasters were reported on every side; the Court Library, it was said, was in flames.

The journalists led by Becher and Jelinek fought to the last. Windischgrätz having demanded unconditional surrender, the provisional government accepted, but when the insurgents learned that the Hungarians were on their way, they forced Messenhauser to take up arms again and the battle was renewed. For a short time only, however: on November 1 the white flag flew from the towers of St Stephen's Cathedral, whence the red flag had been torn down, and the next day the Imperial colours were seen flying there.

A military commission was set up, before which the leaders of the revolution, Blum, Froebel, Jelinek and Jelowiky, were arraigned. General Bem had managed to escape; he had reached Wallachia, where he was to live until his death in 1850 as a convert to Islam under the name of Murad Pasha.

The victorious general was welcomed as a liberator; Prince Eugene had not been acclaimed more enthusiastically when he freed the city from the Turks. Herr Biedermeier came home to stay, and so did the twenty thousand bourgeois who had fled the country. Resentment was keener against the students than against the workers; a regular man-hunt broke loose against all those who still wore long hair and beards and broad-brimmed hats. 'People were afraid of them,' Robert Hamerling reports, 'as if they had been so many Samsons whose invincible force lay in their hair.'

Repression was proportionate to the fear that had been experienced. Seditious journals disappeared, and the censorship was reinforced. The most deeply implicated of the republican leaders were shot in the city moats; fellow-travellers were spared. Some of the ultra-radicals, as Friedrich Hebbel calls them, had been able to escape; by way of revenge, Messenhauser, Blum, Brogini, Jelowiky, Becher and Jelinek were executed. Peace having been restored, the debris was cleared away, the theatres and cafés reopened and life began again as if nothing had happened. Every evening audiences applauded a new play which had just opened at the Burgtheater, greeting with enthusiasm a passage in praise of 'the good old days'. *Lichtsinn aus Liebe*, Lightness through Love, was the name of this play: the Viennese might have taken these words as their motto.

Commenting on these events, however, Friedrich Hebbel declared: 'It doesn't seem possible to go back along the same rails . . . Let well-wishers of the monarchy and the people understand this lesson; what was good in the old days, what is reasonable in these new times, must be combined.' Such was a poet's opinion; the bulk of the Viennese only wanted to go back to the old state of things, even if it had become impossible.

Outwardly, nothing had changed. Vienna, in November, seemed no different from what it had been 'before March'. On November 26, Hebbel notes in his diary: 'The city has resumed its usual appearance. Elegant folk walk along the pavements, carriages drive along the streets. At the windows behind which the Ciceros of our Parliament, the commanders of the Academic Legion, a dozen Magyars and some of the last pilots of the State were wont to show themselves, sure of immortality, one now sees Windischgrätz, Jellacic and Radetzky.' But the truth was that a deep rift had divided the population. The bourgeoisie mistrusted the students, whom they had once so readily welcomed in their drawing-rooms; they shuddered when they passed a workman in the street, suspecting him of having been, and of becoming once more if conditions allowed it, a rioter and an incendiary. They forgot that the liberators' guns had done more damage, perhaps, than the torches of the demonstrators.

After having granted his people a constitution which was not as liberal as might have been desired, Emperor Ferdinand abdicated in favour of his nephew Francis Joseph, who was only eighteen, and retired to Prague. With a new sovereign, a new era was to begin, in which festivities, pageants and processions were to take place with the same brilliance as in former days; but the new ideas had been launched, they would take their course, and it seemed clear that Herr Biedermeier's golden day was over. Other fashions, other tastes, other favourite actors, other popular writers would take the place of their predecessors. The outward aspect of a city changes, even when its innermost heart remains unalterable.

NOTES

CHAPTER ONE:

VIENNA, THE FORTUNATE CITY

1. Wilhelm Hausenstein, *Europäische Haupstädte* (Prestel Verlag, Munich 1954).
2. See Egon Komorzymski, *Der Vater der Zauberflöte* (Vienna 1948).
3. Kralik, *History of Vienna* (French translation, Paris 1932), pp. 267–268.
4. Quoted by Kralik, *op. cit.* p. 266.
5. Quoted by Kralik, *op. cit.* pp. 272–273.
6. Sainte-Aulaire, *Mémoires*, ed. Thiébaut (Calmann-Lévy, Paris 1927).
7. Sainte-Aulaire, *op. cit.*

CHAPTER TWO:

THE VIENNESE

1. Adalbert Stifter, *Wien und die Wiener*.
2. Walter Zinzenbach, *Joseph Richter, bekannt als Eipeldauer* (Stiasny Verlag, Vienna) contains selected extracts from the *Eipeldauerbriefe*, some poems, and the picturesque *Dictionary*.
3. Reichsl, *Wien zur Biedermeierzeit* (Vienna 1921).
4. Heinrich Laube, *Reise durch das Biedermeier*, edited by Ludwig Speidel from the original *Reisenovellen* published by Laube between 1833 and 1837. The name Biedermeier had not then been invented. (Wilhelm Andermann Verlag, Vienna 1946.)
5. Quoted in Reichsl, *op. cit.*
6. Collected by Wilhelm Borner, published by Anzengruber Verlag.
7. *Wiener Umgebungen auf zwanzig Stunden im Umkreise*, 1835.
8. *Beschreibung einer Reise durch Deutschland*, 1785.
9. Quoted in Kobald, *Alt-Wiener Musikstätten*, (Amalthen Verlag, Vienna 1923).

NOTES

CHAPTER THREE:

THE CAPITAL OF MUSIC

1. Karl Kobald, *Alt-Wiener Musikstätten* (Vienna 1923).
2. Jean Chantavoine and Jean Gaudefroy-Demombynes, *Le Romantisme dans la Musique européenne* (Paris, Albin Michel 1955).
3. Robert Pitrou, *Schubert, Vie Intime* (Paris, Emile-Paul, 1949).
4. Annette Kolb, *Schubert* (Paris, Albin Michel, 1952).

CHAPTER FOUR:

THE THEATRE

1. Egon Komorzynski, *Der Vater der Zauberflöte* (Paul Neff Verlag, Vienna 1948).
2. See Marcel Brion, *Mozart* (Paris, Amiot-Dumont, 1956) for an account of the composition and production of *The Magic Flute*.
3. See Joseph Gregor, *Weltgeschichte des Theaters* (Phaidon Verlag, Vienna 1933) with regard to Prehauser and Kurz.
4. For the history of the Burgtheater, see J. Gregor, *op. cit.* chap. xvi.
5. See Marcel Brion, *Goethe* (Paris, Albin Michel, 1948).
6. Joseph Prechtl, *Vaterländische Blätter für den österreichischen Kaiserstadt* (Vienna, 1800).
7. Pezzl-Ziska, *Beschreibung von Wien*, 1826.
8. Published by Fritz Bruckner and Otto Rommel, Vienna 1923.
9. Otto Forst de Battaglia, *Johann Nestroy, Abschätzer der Menschen, Magier des Wortes* (Leipzig, 1933).

CHAPTER FIVE:

SHOWS AND ENTERTAINMENTS

1. Schönholz, *Traditionen zur Charakteristik Osterreichs, seines Staats und Volksleben unter Franz I*, Vol. I.
2. Realis, in *Das kaiserliche Lustschloss Belvedere*, Vienna, 1840.
3. Reichsl, *op. cit.* p. 88.
4. Reichsl, *op. cit.* p. 101.
5. Gaheis, *Wanderungen und Spazierfahrten*, Vienna, 1808.
6. Particularly Otto Nierstein, *Luftfahrten im alten Wien*, and Gugitz, *Die ersten Versuche des Aeronautik in Wien*.
7. Reichsl, *op. cit.* p. 109.

CHAPTER SIX:

VIENNA AT WAR

1. Kralik, *History of Vienna*, French translation, p. 281.
2. Kralik, *op. cit.* p. 288.
3. Kralik, *op. cit.* p. 332.
4. Kralik, *op. cit.* p. 305.
5. Kralik, *op. cit.* p. 307.
6. Kralik, *op. cit.* p. 311. See also Karl Weiss, *Geschichte der Stadt Wien*, Vienna, 1883.
7. Kralik, *op. cit.* p. 314.

CHAPTER SEVEN:

CONGRESS DANCES . . .

1. M. H. Weil, *Les Dessous du Congrès de Vienne* (Paris, 1917), Vol. I, p. 11, note 14, July 1, 1814.
2. Weil, *op. cit.* vol. I, p. 11, note 15.
3. Weil, *op. cit.* vol. I, p. 10, note 13, July 2, 1814.
4. Weil, *op. cit.* vol. I, p. 124, note 153, September 27, 1814.
5. Weil, *op. cit.* vol. I, p. 255, note 323.
6. Weil, *op. cit.* paras. 327 and 440.
7. Weil, *op. cit.* p. 211, note 257.
8. Weil, *op. cit.* p. 110, note 130.
9. Weil, *op. cit.* p. 366, note 498.
10. Harold Nicolson, *The Congress of Vienna* (Constable, 1946), pp. 126–7.
11. Harold Nicolson, *op. cit.* p. 291.
12. Weil, *op. cit.* vol. II, p. 555, note 2368.
13. Weil, *op. cit.* p. 674, report 1050.
14. *Journals and Correspondence of Miss Berry* (London 1865).
15. *The Croker Papers* (John Murray, 1884), vol. I, p. 65.
16. Nicolson, *op. cit.* p. 9.
17. Weil, *op. cit.* vol. I, note 881, November 23, 1814.
18. Nicolson, *op. cit.*

CHAPTER EIGHT:

IN THE LAND OF THE WALTZ

1. H. E. Jacob, *Johann Strauss und das neunzehnte Jahrhundert* (Amsterdam 1937) English translation by Marguerite Wolff, *Johann Strauss: A Century of Light Music* (Hutchinson, 1940) from which all passages quoted have been taken.
2. Jacob, *op. cit.*
3. Jacob, *op. cit.*
4. Heinrich Laube has described in his *Reisenovellen* the wonders he saw in Vienna between 1833 and 1837. He naturally visited Sperl's on one of its gala nights. See his description in Ludwig Speidel's selection from the *Reisenovellen*, *Reise durch das Biedermeier* (Vienna 1946).
5. Jacob, *op. cit.*
6. Ann Tizia Leitich, *Damals in Wien* (Forum Verlag, Vienna, 1956).
7. Jacob, *op. cit.* See also Freidrich Reichsl, *Wien zur Biedermeierzeit, op. cit.*
8. Groner, *Wien wie es war.*
9. Laube, *Reisenovellen.* Quoted in Jacob, *op. cit.*
10. Jacob, *op. cit.*
11. Jacob, *op. cit.*
12. Jacob, *op. cit.*

CHAPTER NINE:

VIENNESE ROMANTICISM

1. Kobald, *Kunst in Volk* (Vienna 1952), p. 270.
2. Grillparzer, *Abschied von Wien.*
3. Anastasius Grün, *Spaziergänge eines Wiener Poeten*, 1831.

CHAPTER TEN:

THE REIGN OF BIEDERMEIER

1. François Fejtö, *Un Habsbourg révolutionnaire*, Joseph II (Paris, Plon, 1953).
2. Mayer, *Wien im Zeitalter Napoleons* (Vienna 1940), p. 112.
3. *Hofkanzlei* 93 vii 14 StR 2720. Note Kollowrat 92 x 22 3644. Prot 94 xi 23 4072. *Hofkomm. in Gesetzessachen* 97 vii 10 2015. Police notes 02 ix 20 3678. Circular 97 ii 7 15 III 16. Patent. K. Pribram, l. c. 587–591. J. Richter, I, 44. J. Slokarl, 30. In general, Mayer, *op. cit.*, p. 87.
4. F. Malcher, *Erzherzog Karl von Osterreich. 'Ausgewahlte Schriften'* (Vienna 1894). V. 504.
5. Kollowrat, note 03 II ii StR 602. *Hofkanzlei*, 02 iii 1069.
6. Fleischke 03 xii 9 4646. *Konsumextrakt* 1809. *Zinzendorf Handschr.* 166, p. 493. Mayer, *op. cit.* p. 134.
7. C. Wolfsgrüber, *Hohenwart* (Graz, 1912), p. 294.

CHAPTER ELEVEN:

THE END OF A GOLDEN AGE

1. Kralik, *History of Vienna* (French translation), *op. cit.* p. 342.
2. Maria Theresa Wanderer, *Revolutions-Stürme Achtunvierzig* (Vienna 1948).
3. Kralik, *op. cit.* p. 350.

INDEX